PRAISE FOR

STRIKE HARD AND EXPECT NO MERCY

"CPT Galen Peterson, USA, Retired, provides a true account of one main's journey through the crucible of combat. I firmly believe that what Galen has written in this short but powerful book is a primer for every junior military officer who is blessed to lead others in and out of combat. If you're looking to learn about the complexities of small-unit leadership, this book is well worth your time."

—Brigadier General Kevin Admiral, 52nd Commandant of the US Army Armor School

"Galen Peterson, one of my top junior leaders, captures the life of a tank platoon leader preparing for and conducting counterinsurgency and combat operations in Iraq. He immerses the reader in the emotion and intensity of combat while leading his platoon at the tip of the spear against the Jayesh al Mahdi in Sadr City. During the months of tough urban combat, he lived up to the battalion motto: Fight Like Hell!! If you want to understand small-unit leadership, then this is a must-read for you."

—Michael F. Pappal, US Army, Colonel (Retired), Former Commander, 1-68th Armor Battalion

"What an education is to be had from Mr. Peterson's great story. Having fought my war on the ground in Vietnam, I never even saw a tank. Understanding what a valuable tool and the expertise of the 'tank people' I am in awe. Great read."

—Harry Rubin, *Traitor's Revenge*

"*Stike Hard and Expect No Mercy* is a powerful story of dedication and courage; an ode to the nobility of American soldiers on the cutting edge of the War in Iraq. 'Right-seat ride' with Galen Peterson as he leads his platoon of Abrams tanks on combat operations through the city of Baghdad. With tank killer IEDs and insurgents at every turn, you are the biggest target on the urban battlefield."

—William Craun, *Working the Kill Zone: An American Mercenary in Iraq*

"To gain a real appreciation for what our men and women in uniform go through to preserve our freedoms and way of life, Galen Peterson's *Strike Hard and Expect No Mercy* is a must-read for those who have never served our country in battle."

—Samuel G. Tooma, Environmental Scientist, The SOOF

"A captivating and vivid firsthand perspective from a young officer who lived the hardships of the modern battlefield with a firsthand point of view of the tanker on the battlefields of the Iraq war. There are many books written at the more senior level or from the perspective of the infantryman on the street, but none provide the raw and unvarnished perspective of the fighting in the streets of Iraq from that of an Armor leader like this book. Galen, a trusted friend, proven leader, and gifted storyteller, brings the fog of the war, the bonds of brotherhood, and the reality of the modern battlefield to life like no other. A must-read!"

—Colonel Scott Taylor, Former Commander, 1-68th Armor Battalion

"Ranks up there with With the Old Breed, We Were Soldiers Once and Young, and Chesty."

—Nathan Yancer, Iraq War Veteran Tanker

"Riveting and insightful! Everyone who has served can identify with this gripping story."

—Lieutenant General (Retired) Buster Hagenbeck, 57th Superintendent, United States Military Academy at West Point

"Every American should read "Every American should read this book to understand what our young military leaders have done in the Middle East: the courage, the strength, the sacrifice, the strategic thinking, and ultimately, the resilience they exhibited for America and its people!"

—Lieutenant General (Retired) Bill Lennox, 56th Superintendent, United States Military Academy at West Point

"Beyond just a tale of two deployments, this is a book about leadership. It is also a testament to the dedication of those who served in the 1/68 Armor at the time, and the brotherly love that held that pointy end of the spear together. In the aftermath of two wars that leave an incredibly bitter taste in the mouth of the veteran, the epilogue is powerful."

—Danger Five Two

FOR A DEEPER DIVE INTO THE EXPERIENCE FOLLOW FOR RESOURCES, MORE PHOTOS, AND MORE INSIGHTS.

Strike Hard and Expect No Mercy
by Galen D. Peterson

© Copyright 2021 Galen D. Peterson

ISBN 978-1-64663-436-1

All rights reserved. No part of this publication may be reproduced, stored in a retrieval system, or transmitted in any form or by any means—electronic, mechanical, photocopy, recording, or any other—except for brief quotations in printed reviews, without the prior written permission of the author.

Published by

köehlerbooks™

3705 Shore Drive
Virginia Beach, VA 23455
800-435-4811
www.koehlerbooks.com

STRIKE HARD

AND EXPECT

NO MERCY

A TANK PLATOON LEADER IN IRAQ

GALEN D. PETERSON

VIRGINIA BEACH
CAPE CHARLES

I really thought that time would lessen the pain. I was wrong.

More than ten years have passed, and the anniversaries of particular brutal days have only become harder each year. Perhaps sharing what is buried in my chest will lift the load from the shoulders.

This is our story as seen from my eyes. While time has not eased many memories, many names and stories have eluded me as I write. Without copies of my sworn statements and daily journal, this narrative would not be possible. Even still, I have had to rely on others to help piece things together. It is my shame that I cannot honor everyone by name that deserves it. I was truly in the company of lions, men who were my brothers and my heroes.

I would like to thank General Fred Franks (Ret.) for mentoring me as a young officer and encouraging me to share my story through publishing. Thank you to Tony Farina for encouraging me to write in the first place. Thank you to John Koehler and the team for making this happen. Thank you to Hannah Woodlan and Kellie Emery for carefully polishing the story of my heroes into a worthy form. Thank you to my family for patiently tolerating me spending endless hours writing, editing, and at times brooding.

In loving memory of Mike Elledge and Chris Simpson:
two great men who gave everything during my watch.

For my loving Sarah, Brynn, and Abby.
You are my happy ending.

TABLE OF CONTENTS

Prologue 1

PART I: BAQUBAH

Firing the Forge 15
In-Country 25
Iron Triangle 34
Blood and Darts 62
Intermission 81
Final Blessings 105

PART II: SADR

Half-Baked Plans 125
Change of Mission 139
Ambush 153
Awakening the Dragon 170
The Dragon Emerges 205
Dragon's Fire 219
The Dragon on the March 237
Tipping the Scales 268
Epilogue 281

PROLOGUE

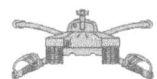

"KNIGHT SIX, SABER ONE; OVER." The crisp radio call of the scouts followed a beep in my tanker's helmet earphones.

"Knight Six." My senses perked up as I keyed the microphone.

"Four tanks, four PC moving west into positions on Objective Hammer. Four PC moving into positions north of TRP one. Over." The battalion's scout platoon had spent the night getting into position to watch our first objective, a ridge that dominated the entire valley. Now they had spotted four enemy battle tanks and a total of eight infantry armored fighting vehicles (personnel carriers, or PC) moving into defensive positions. The scouts had already reported that an anti-tank ditch and extensive wire-and-mine obstacles blocked the northern approach to the objective. Enemy engineers had placed a halfhearted wire-and-mine obstacle to the west. That one would not slow us down at all.

"Acknowledged. Out." The scouts had successfully accomplished their mission already. Now it was our turn to perform.

"Guidons, guidons, Knight Six. Scouts report no change to enemy defensive positions. Execute SBF one." With that simple order, the company team's M1A2 Abrams tanks and M2A3 Bradley infantry fighting vehicles rolled out of attack positions a ridgeline away and nearly 4,000 meters—two and a half miles—away from Objective Hammer.

This attack was not going to be easy. The company was depleted. Only Second (White) Platoon had all four tanks, and the platoon leader now had to also serve as my acting company executive officer. Third (Blue) Platoon could only muster three tanks. Casualties had dropped many of the crews from four down to three per tank. The leaders had been hit the hardest, and Blue Platoon was now led by a junior staff sergeant. First (Red) Platoon was attached to one of our sister infantry companies to lend them some firepower. Three attached infantry platoons—Gold, Green, and Black Platoons—added another nine Bradleys to the company. In total, we had eight tanks, nine Bradleys, and three infantry squads. The infantry were also depleted in soldiers. A murderous artillery barrage on our assembly area a few days ago had nearly wiped out two-thirds of the squad members, forcing the platoons to consolidate. While it was a lot of moving pieces for one commander to manage at once, it was far short of what the book said was required to attack a prepared defensive position.

During the previous twenty-four hours, the scouts had identified a large enemy force—a heavily reinforced mechanized company—on the objectives. Objective Hammer was defended by ten PCs and four tanks. An additional engineer platoon was sighted. They added another four PCs that were just as likely to fight. Just north of Objective Hammer, scouts found six full squads of enemy infantry defending the pass. I named their position Objective Crunchie. Another 2,000 meters east of Objective Hammer was Objective Anvil. The enemy headquarters and support vehicles were located there.

Somewhere on the valley walls would be the enemy scouts in a combat security outpost. We knew they had two PCs and enough anti-tank missiles to cause a lot of problems. The enemy's reinforced company team was fresh, and they outnumbered us. The book called for us to outnumber the defenders by three to one when attacking. It would be a bitter fight, but we had no choice. Our battalion was desperate. If I could kick in the enemy right flank on the stagnant front, they would have to react to us instead of continuing to mass forces for an attack farther south.

Battalion, now led by a major who had been the executive officer, was still trying to organize a defensive position with its back to the wall. Heavy enemy attacks had pushed us to within a mere three miles from the last good highway connecting us to the rest of the brigade and our lines of communication. We had battered an enemy division to a standstill, but at great cost. While enemy artillery could now savage our rear areas, they seemed content to dig in and await reinforcements before the final push to take the city and its vital road hub.

While fresh enemy units were streaming towards us, no American units would be due in theater for at least another week or two. We desperately needed breathing space and time. A successful attack kicking the enemy back would do just that and give the illusion of American strength gathering. As the last remaining experienced company commander in the battalion, I drew the task.

The sun was still not quite up, its early-morning glow illuminating the horizon to the east and bathing the landscape in a grayish light. It was too bright for night vision, too dark for naked eye. Last night's rainstorms had left the ground damp but not muddy. The cool, stable air forced the humidity into a thick haze that blanketed the ground. It was perfect.

We were attacking from the northwest. A tall, steep ridge ran from the main road nearly due east. The ridge formed the northern valley wall. A small trail ran through a narrow valley north of the ridge and crossed a small pass onto the north edge of Objective Hammer. This narrow valley was extreme flank of the battlefield. There was not another pass through the forbidding terrain north for another twenty miles. A wooded spur ran due south from the west end of the ridge where the pass out of the narrow valley cut through the northern valley wall. The trees were sparse enough to maneuver through quickly.

About halfway between the base of the spur and the ridge of Objective Hammer, was a small rise. The rise had some larger boulders on it, and while it did not show up on a map, it extended south for a mile. Just west of this rise, a deep wadi or ravine created a natural obstacle to any vehicle and paralleled the rise all the way to the southern wall of the valley, which was as steep and forbidding as the northern wall. Unlike the northern wall, it was scarred by scores of small draws. The ridge of Objective Hammer cut the valley in half. West of it, the valley was very wide, some two miles wide. Behind it, the valley narrowed like a funnel to Objective Anvil. The valley floor was nearly devoid of trees or buildings, but many small rises offered cover and concealment to the skilled tanker who could find and exploit them.

"Knight Six, White One; LD." John McHugh called out on the radio that White Platoon had crossed the line of departure and was now committed to the northern approach. Behind him, three Bradleys from Black Platoon followed, bringing some infantrymen to help root the enemy squads out of the trees. John had the tough job of creating a diversion. We could not afford to have the six enemy squads come south over the pass and counterattack into our flank while we were attacking Objective Hammer, so I needed someone to keep them pinned on Objective Crunchie. John had to find the balance of keeping them engaged without getting mauled in the process.

My tank was following Blue Platoon, so they did not need to radio their progress to me, but they would for the sake of the rest of company team. The tracks kicked up dust as we rumbled south around the west end of the ridge. The humidity kept the dust within a few feet of the ground, preventing it from rising up and giving away our presence to the enemy.

About 500 meters north and behind me, the Bradleys slowly rolled south, giving my tanks a chance to set the conditions for their attack. Support-by-Fire (SBF) One was on the top of the spur running along the road. Blue Platoon and my tank would establish positions to engage the enemy on Objective Hammer from long range. Once we had achieved some effects on the enemy, a platoon of Bradleys would attack east to the rocky rise in front of Objective Hammer. I had designated the rise SBF Two.

"Blue Four, contact tanks east. Out." Sergeant Young's quick report announced he had found and was shooting at the enemy tanks on Objective Hammer. As my tank joined the platoon on the top of the spur, I saw the glowing outlines of tank turrets in my thermal viewer. *Fools.* The enemy turrets were very warm, indicating the crews had run their heaters during the night, so now the tanks were easy to spot against the cold ground. Blue Platoon had all of my company master gunners, and their skill quickly achieved effects on the enemy 2,000 meters away. After each shot, each tank would back into the protection of the lee side and slide farther south for a new firing position.

I looked at my watch. Five minutes had passed. It was time to get the show moving before artillery rained down on us.

"Gold One, Knight Six; execute SBF Two." The Bradleys of Gold Platoon had slowly crept south in anticipation. When I gave the command, they were less than a hundred meters north of us, tucked on the lee side of the spur, protected from enemy fire. The loud growl of diesel engines accompanied the Bradleys' dust as they sped down the face of the spur just north of us towards the valley floor. An armored vehicle moving at thirty miles an hour is an awe-inspiring sight. Miraculously, all three Bradleys made it to the rocky rise and added their twenty-five-millimeter rapid-fire cannon to the fight. They were only about 800 meters away from the enemy positions on Objective Hammer. The fight was past the point of no return.

A shriek and loud *whomph* announced the beginning of artillery raining down on my position. "Blue One, Knight Six; execute SBF three now! Green, as soon as the barrage ends, push through and join us." We could not wait for Gold to suppress the enemy enough to move out of the artillery impact zone. All plans survive until enemy contact. My plan was unraveling a bit. Support-by-Fire Three was a position about 1,000 meters south of SBF Two. The plan was to bound platoons to support-by-fire positions south until we were around the enemy's left flank. We were not strong enough to merely assault the enemy position. With the enemy firepower forcing us out of positions too quickly, I needed Green Platoon to merge with us, and we would bound by vehicle in a continuous movement south.

The happy whine of my tank's turbine engine vibrated the low ground as we darted around trees like an alpine skier. The tracks flinging dirt clods twenty feet in the air, we rapidly descended the spur and raced towards the small rise. In a small grove of trees, Murphy's Law kicked in. My tank suddenly stopped, suffering a catastrophic mechanical breakdown. At least I was in a spot sheltered from enemy fire.

"Blue Four, Knight Six; my tank's dead. Come here so I can jump tank," I directed Sergeant Young. My crew would stay with my disabled tank, but as the commander, I needed to stay with the fight moving south at about a kilometer every five minutes. In a few minutes, I was in a new tank and back in the fight.

"Missile, missile, missile!" Enemy anti-tank missiles fired from the woods on the north wall and the wooded knoll on Objective Hammer. Instantly, all three tanks began a series of radical turns back and forth to shake the enemy gunners' aim. The sagger drill, as it was called, was as demanding on a machine and crew as any movement could be. My driver rapidly jerked the controls while maxing out the throttle. In the turret, I hung on tight as the high-G turns at thirty miles per hour rocked me violently.

The enemy missiles took a toll. As I reached the relative safety of a clump of trees almost a mile south, I noticed my tank was alone. Green's Bradleys were decimated, but the weight of the attack seemed to have shaken the enemy.

"Knight Six, Gold One; the enemy is displacing off Objective Hammer." At least someone behind me was still in the fight. The enemy was dislodged and likely disorganized. There was an opportunity to exact some revenge. Quickly, like a lion on the savanna, I darted my tank along the lee side of the rise as it rose to connect with the southern valley wall. I wanted to find a spot in the draws where I could ambush the enemy as it displaced southeast from its positions on the ridge. It would be a close race for position.

With John's attack on Objective Crunchie raging on the other side of the pass and Gold still active west of Objective Hammer, the enemy tanks and PCs had their weapons pointed towards the ridge. None of them noticed my tank stalking them from along the south wall. I was a little disappointed at how many of the enemy vehicles were still alive and moving south.

Just as the enemy vehicles reached the southern wall, I sprang my trap. Steadily, we climbed each rise between draws and fired the cannon point-blank into the enemy vehicles. Capitalizing on the confusion, I bounded from one enemy position to the next. The enemy seemed to mistake my cannon for their own, and they continued to scan the ridgeline for the predator that was systematically destroying them. The shock on the faces of enemy crewmen bailing out of their destroyed armored vehicles was ended by machine-gun fire from Sergeant Young and me. Ten minutes later, I was on the west edge of Objective Anvil. The blood was in the water as I scanned the draws cutting through Anvil. *Bingo!* A tall antenna poked out of one of the draws. I had found the enemy command post. A few minutes later, the command post and its collection of "soft vehicles" (trucks) joined the fate of the rest of the enemy company.

Even as my tank ravaged the enemy command post, the company radio net was alive with First Sergeant Waylon Petty already coordinating casualty collection and Sergeant First Class Kime Morgan leading efforts of the mechanics to quickly recover any vehicle worth saving. A squad of Gold's infantry reported they completed clearing the northern wall's woods.

As the sounds of battle died down, loneliness crept over me. The three other crewmen of my tank and I were a long ways from the rest of the company. We had taken the field and destroyed the enemy, but it had been costly.

Fortunately, this was only a training mock battle. The casualties were not permanent. Still, there were some valuable lessons learned. As I surveyed the battlefield, memories overcame me. On another field, on another day, I'd surveyed a vicious battlefield while standing with just three other men.

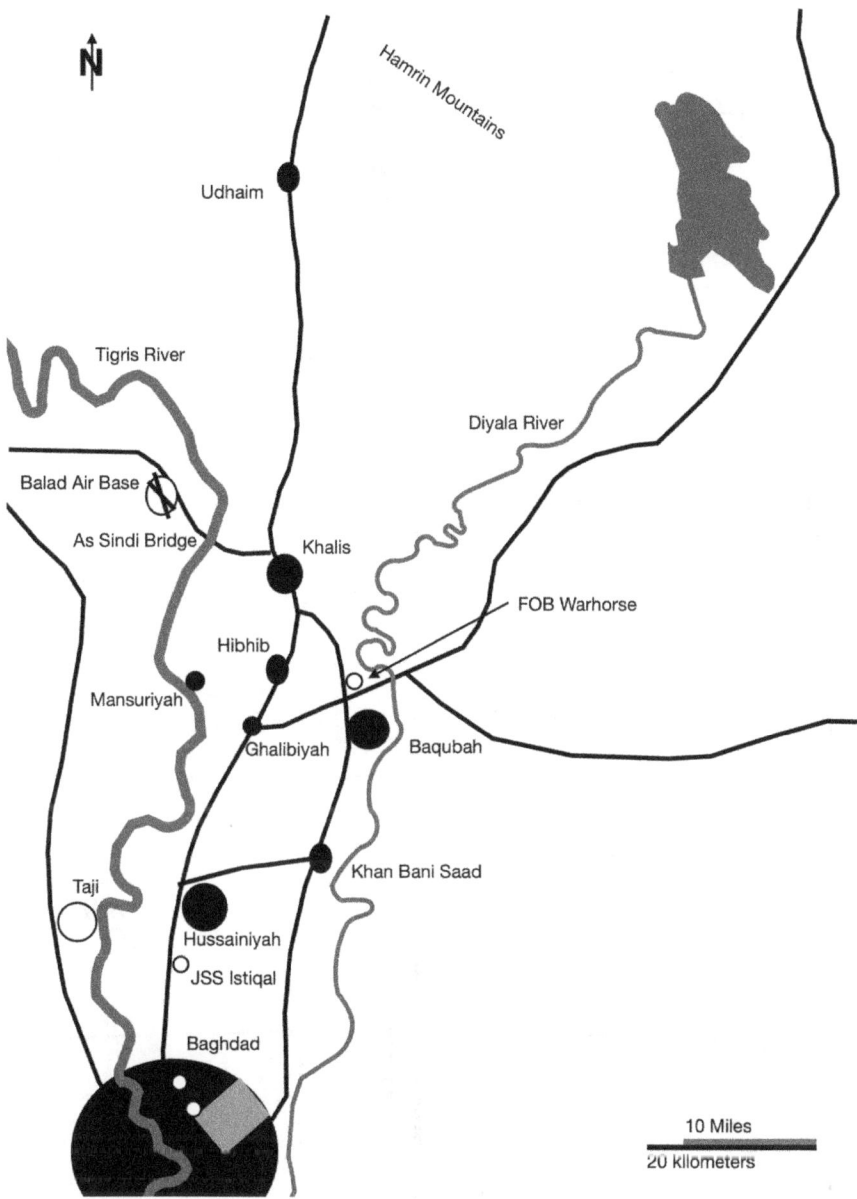

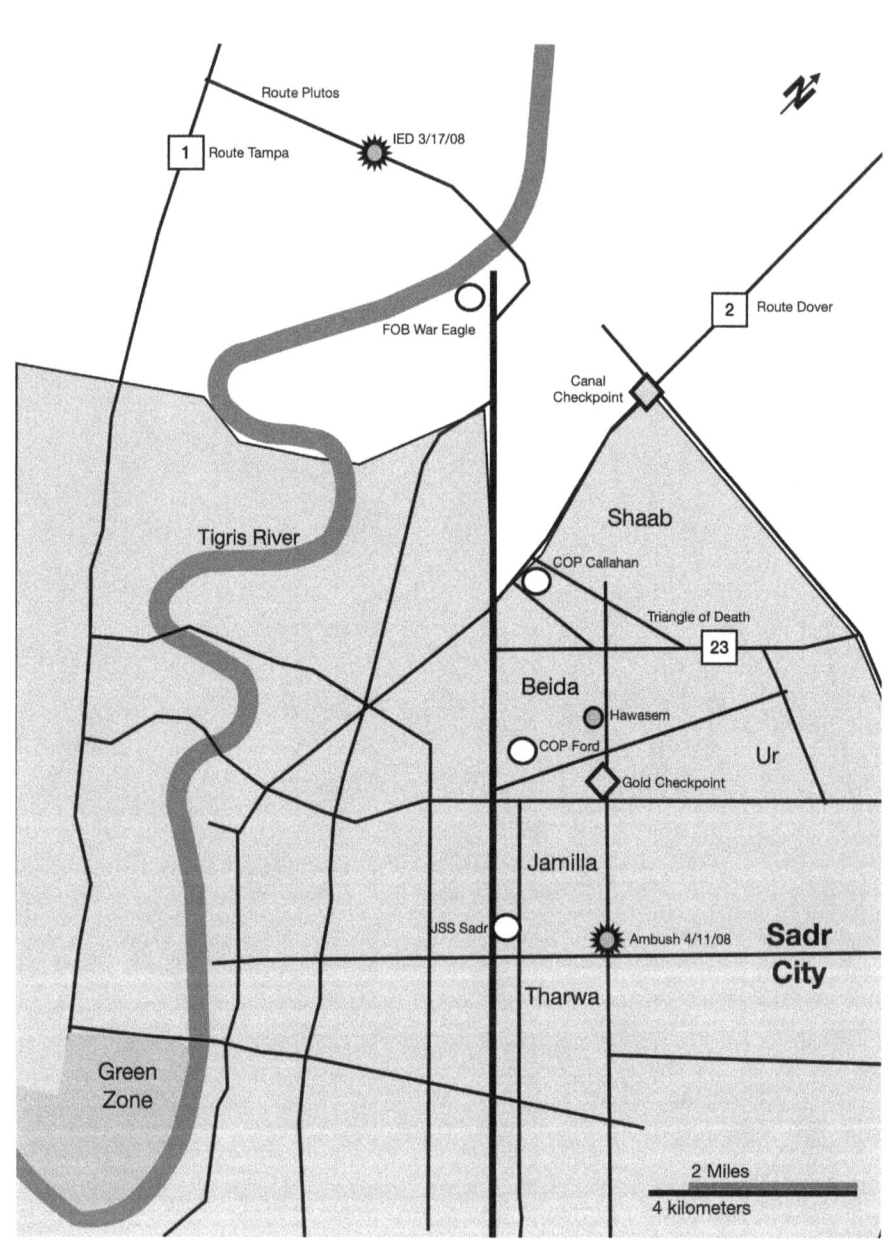

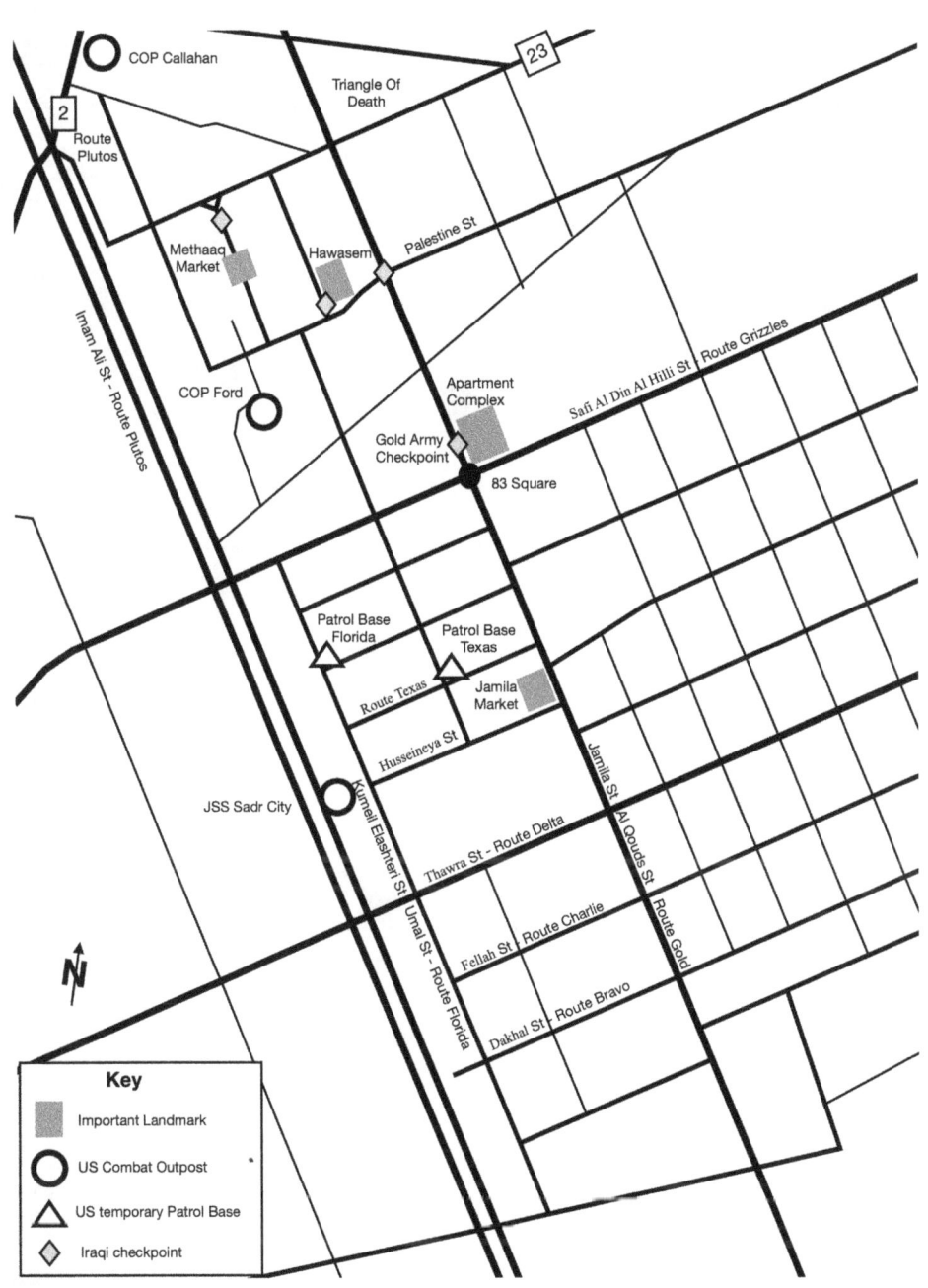

Part 1
BAQUBAH

There's a breathless hush in the Close tonight—
Ten to make and the match to win—
A bumping pitch and a blinding light,
An hour to play and the last man in.
And it's not for the sake of a ribboned coat,
Or the selfish hope of a season's fame,
But his captain's hand on his shoulder smote
"Play up! Play up! And play the game!"

The sand of the desert is sodden red,
Red with the wreck of a square that broke;
The Gatling's jammed and the colonel dead,
And the regiment blind with dust and smoke.
The river of death has brimmed its banks,
And England's far, and Honor a name,
But the voice of a schoolboy rallies the ranks,
"Play up! Play up! And play the game!"

Excerpt, "Vitai Lampada,"
Sir Henry Newbolt 1892

FIRING THE FORGE

THE HOOK OF THE TANK landed me fair and square in 2002. Up until then, I had dreams of being a light-fighting infantryman. I was a cadet at the United States Military Academy's Camp Buckner that summer. Advanced field training introduced us to the different branches of the Army. Each branch made a valiant effort to show us their best side and recruit the best future officers to its fold. The engineers let us play in the dirt and make a pontoon bridge across Stillwell Lake. We blasted different explosive charges, even watching a mine-clearing line charge blow a football field–length hole in an obstacle. The Air Defense Artillery showed us their toys, allowing us to try to shoot down a Styrofoam drone. Aviation gave us a stomach-in-throat UH-60 Black Hawk ride at treetop level while conducting infantry air-assault raids. The Field Artillery let us fire cannons, and we practiced adjusting indirect fire. But it was the M1A1 Abrams tank that won my heart.

At Fort Knox, Kentucky, we spent some seven days tasting the dirt and cordite and feeling the power of mechanized warfare. The highlight was conducting a force-on-force armored battle. I lucked out and got to be a tank commander for the mock battle. After a day in the commander's hatch of a tank on the attack, the hook was set.

From then on, I was a student of mechanized warfare. I read books, sought out mentors, and learned all I could about being a tanker. It was an unusual time to become a tread head. Light infantry was dominating the military scene. Rangers had conducted a parachute attack to seize airfields in Afghanistan, and the mountain and air-assault infantry were critical in the fight for the mountainous country. Nearly all of my classmates were completely focused on the light fight and planning their career path to Aviation or Special Forces.

The following year landed me some rare opportunities. I got to go to Heidelberg, Germany, the headquarters of V Corps, for the beginning of the invasion of Iraq. While the majority of the staff was in Kuwait, the portion in Heidelberg was also tracking the fight. I was awestruck at how far and how fast the mechanized 3rd Infantry Division was moving. What really caught my attention was that the Army airlifted a mechanized company team in to the 173rd Airborne Brigade where it had parachuted into northern Iraq. The need for the mobility, firepower, and shock of the armor justified the massive quantities of fuel that had to be flown in.

The summer of 2003 saw me back at Camp Buckner and Fort Knox. This time I was a cadet squad leader leading the next class of cadets through their advanced field training. While facilitating their training, I got a free lesson in combat leadership, including hands-on practice at keeping up morale while sitting through pouring-rain storms at the bottom of muddy foxholes at night and sweating under the afternoon heat while lugging our heavy kit up and over mountains on patrols. At Fort Knox, this time I got to lead a platoon of tanks in the armored clashes, loving every minute of it.

The next year took my development as a combat leader to the field army. In March 2004, I joined Apache Troop, 1-113 Cavalry, deployed in Kosovo. Technically, cadets shall not deploy to war zones. Since Kosovo was considered a peacekeeping mission and had been quiet, it provided a great opportunity to push the boundaries of experience gathering. Four years had passed since our forces occupied Kosovo as part of the international peacekeeping force to end the ethnic violence between the Serbs and the Albanians. While the initial years were quite tense, things had simmered down significantly, and land mines were the biggest threat. The Serbian Army had been forced out of Kosovo, still a province of Serbia, and the Albanian militias had laid down their arms. Our time in Kosovo was cut short when widespread and extremely violent rioting broke out, resulting in numerous NATO casualties. An entire Greek infantry squad died a horrific fiery death, and many other soldiers of all nations were injured.

While my stay in Kosovo had been brief, the combat lessons I learned were invaluable. Later that summer, I was able to join another platoon out in the "Real Army." This time, I went to Korea, where I learned vital administrative skills. After thirty-two days in Korea, I was even more convinced that mechanized forces were the only sane way to fight a war. I was also convinced to do my absolute best to never, ever, ever get stationed in Korea. Between the headaches associated with soldiers being in garrison but separated from their families for a year at a time, minefields everywhere I really wanted to hike, and the thought of living within artillery range of the most unpredictable dictator in the world's army, Korea was not for me.

As I finished up my time at West Point, I continued pushing myself to learn as much as I could about mechanized warfare and the insurgency in Iraq, and making peace with the prospect of being in combat soon. All too soon, I graduated and commissioned into the Army as a second lieutenant in the Armor Branch. It was time to get into the action.

A light crust of snow covered a chilly Fort Knox when I reported to the Armor Center for Armor Officer Basic Course. My class would be the last of them, as future generations of armor officers would go to a different program called Basic Officer Leaders Course. I was happy to bear the butter bars of a second lieutenant on my fatigues. I was even happier to be surrounded by historical tanks and armored vehicles.

My class was relatively small, probably only thirty-five officers. Two senior captains conducted the lectures to the whole group. The two officers already had combat experience and plenty of the dry, blunt wit that often marks a veteran. In every class, the pair reminded us of the value of armor on the battlefield.

"Remember, if the infantry is the queen of battle, then armor is the bodyguard who keeps her from getting raped." Our instructors joked, but there was a lot of truth behind the witticisms.

We were broken down into small groups of about twelve. Senior sergeants first class were the small-group instructors. They were all experienced platoon sergeants who would help mentor us in the way of the tank. The Army is not always known for selecting the best of the best to train the next crop of leaders, though, and some of the small-group instructors were best categorized as "washed up" or "burned out." My small group went through three instructors in three months. Despite their various issues, they all had valuable experience to draw upon.

The course was a mix of technical and tactical training. Everything was both lecture and hands on. We didn't just learn about the risk of relying on GPS for navigation; we put it into practice, stumbling through thickets and swamps while following the arrow of a GPS without a map. In less than an hour, we were believers in maps. Gunnery training included pairing up into gunner–commander pairs and shooting. Tactical training included lectures, preparing and issuing orders, time in simulators, and actual mud-flinging maneuvers.

The simulators were like the greatest video game on earth. A large warehouse held a bunch of them, all connected to the same scenario. Each simulator was designed to have the same interior setup as a real tank, with numerous screens providing the world around. The terrain was a digital recreation of real land so we could use real maps. Each scenario either pit us against fellow officers in other simulators or against the computer. The computer could be adjusted from what we called "Hellen Keller mode"—where the enemy would not shoot at you—up to the most accurate gunners in the world. While the system was fairly accurate at modeling warfare, it was harder to navigate, communicate, and shoot than real life was. The advantage of this handicap was that if you could succeed in the simulator, real life would be much easier. Still, it was sobering ending a scenario with the small-group leader announcing, "Congrats, sir, you just killed your platoon."

I didn't realize it yet, but the arrogance of the US Army influenced our training. Instructors belittled enemy equipment and capabilities. We were taught the M1 Abrams was the superior battle tank, and we garnered a feeling of invulnerability. Instructors pointed to the domination of the Abrams over the Iraqi T-72s in 1991 and 2003. Very few infantry anti-tank weapons were referenced. Of course, there were very few instances of infantry anti-tank weapons actually being used on the M1 Abrams–series tanks. Some of my friends who were classes ahead of me had shared stories and pictures of what roadside bombs could do to a tank, though.

The one person who influenced me the most at Fort Knox was actually a classmate. Each class had a number of foreign officers. My battle buddy was a Greek officer, Lieutenant Panos Gkatidis. He already had three years of experience as a platoon leader of Leopard tanks before coming to Fort Knox. Generally, European officers were handpicked for their quality when sent to an American school. Panos was no exception. We called him "Panos the Great," and he was a tanker's tanker. When we were in the field, his skill shone like a beacon on a hill. Panos was not afraid to maximize the mobility capabilities of the tank. He would dart the tank from hiding spot to a firing spot; then, as quickly as he appeared, he would disappear and go hunting from a new vantage point.

Panos taught me how to live the saying "Dog soldiers always die." It was a reference to the plains tribes' dog soldiers, who would tie themselves to a stake pounded in the ground on the battlefield. It was extremely brave and honorable. Being tied to the ground, they were completely vulnerable to any standoff weapon like a bow and arrow or rifle. In modern combat, though, nobody "counts coup." It was Panos who taught me how much a tank could move around within the bounds of the mission in order to mitigate enemy efforts to kill you.

The counterinsurgency war in Iraq started to influence how the Army trained. We dedicated several days and a full field exercise to the tactical operations used to fight insurgents. We spent time learning about the culture and how to win the hearts and minds of the populace. Part of that meant learning how to do the infantry's job with a third as many soldiers and none of the specialized weapons they are equipped with.

Our training exercise for this was at Fort Knox's mock-city training site. Not only did the exercise teach lessons about counterinsurgency, but it also taught the sharing of valuable resources—such as the mock-city site. To maximize utilization, we would prep for our mission on the outskirts while somebody else executed theirs within the little city.

While we were prepping for our next mission on the outskirts one day, a collection of Humvees came roaring out of the city and abruptly pulled into the field that served as the staging area.

"NEEDLESS TO SAY WE WON'T EVER DO THAT AGAIN!" All of us stopped what we were doing and turned towards the Humvees as a Navy SEAL dismounted, yelling at the top of his lungs. *How is he so loud? I gotta master that!* The rest of the SEALs gathered around him, and his volume dropped. Intrigued, we tried to listen and learn what "that" was. A few minutes later, they took off again, and shortly the sounds of weapons firing came from the city. We resumed our own preparations, really wishing we could have gained a free lesson from the SEALs. Soon it was our turn, and we entered the city and stormed a four-story building. It was a goat rodeo.

We spent less time working on "sagger drills," a zigzag maneuver to dodge enemy missiles, and more time learning to look for roadside bombs. In counterinsurgency, the tank becomes a hammer for smashing enemy strongpoint buildings. Maneuver is constrained to roads. Gunnery is simplified to short ranges and smaller ammunition selections. Theoretically, an insurgent enemy has nothing that can destroy a tank by direct fire. Only massive bombs can destroy a tank, either by the explosion or by catching it on fire. Insurgent forces are not supposed to be large, and the platoon is capable of defeating the small ambush cells that insurgents use. Not once while training for the counterinsurgency fight did we ever confront an enemy force larger than five fighters. Raids were designed to capture enemy fighters instead of killing them. Operations resembled police work. We studied nebulous insurgent organizations so we would be able to understand and find the enemy hidden amongst the people.

The fundamentals of breaching an obstacle fit perfectly for the hazard created by a roadside bomb. The only difference was that there was one or maybe a few explosives compared to the hundreds in a well-done minefield.

About two weeks before the class was over, I got a phone call. I would report to 1st Battalion, 68th Armor (known as 1-68 Armor), 3rd Brigade, 4th Infantry Division upon completion of my training at Fort Knox. The battalion was currently deployed to Iraq and had just gone through a series of nasty fights. It needed replacements, so I would not get to do any further schools at Fort Knox before reporting. The personnel officer informed me I needed to be prepared to deploy shortly after signing in at Fort Carson, Colorado. I would not get leave, only the minimum travel time authorized to move from Fort Knox to Fort Carson.

Four days after leaving Fort Knox, I signed in to Fort Carson. I was sleeping on my sister's couch on the north side of Colorado Springs. It was an exciting and nerve-wracking time. I was a soldier and would soon be going forth into battle. In-processing at Fort Carson included getting issued my desert camouflage fatigues. We called them "warrior suits" as the uniform was only worn when deployed or just about to deploy.

After three days of in-processing the post, I reported to 1-68 Armor's Rear Detachment. It was the big moment I had waited for and dreamed of while in training. First thing in the morning, with my dress green uniform looking as impeccable as possible, I knocked on the commander's door, marched to the desk, and saluted.

"Sir, Lieutenant Peterson reporting as ordered!" I barked the well-rehearsed and well-worn phrase. The major behind the desk didn't even look up as he returned my salute, continuing to stare at his computer screen.

"Oh... okay. Well, I don't want you hanging around the detachment, lest you become as disillusioned as the rest." Then without so much as a "welcome to the team," he sent me out of his office, the air rushing out of my balloon. As I left, I ran into a first lieutenant who was using a cane, the consolation prize for a leg wound. He was heading to the barracks to inventory the rooms of two soldiers who had just gone AWOL—absent without leave. The lieutenant seemed nice and so I helped him. A sergeant and a specialist joined us with a stack of boxes to pack the items found.

The first room was easy to inventory. It was completely cleaned out. That was one soldier who was not planning on returning from being AWOL. Before we opened the door to the next room, the specialist warned us, "Look out for IEDs. This guy hated officers and knows you are going to be inventorying it." *Okay...*

The room was a pigsty. Worse than a pigsty. The room stank of unwashed clothes, rotting food, and marijuana. We did not find any bombs, but we did find a metric ton of marijuana. It was the most I ever found in a barracks room during my career. He had harvested buds, plants, and seeds for his next crop.

Drugs are one of the few crimes in the Army the chain of command will call the military police for. Nearly everything else is investigated, prosecuted, and adjudicated by the chain of command. While we waited for the MPs, we went out onto the balcony of the barracks to enjoy some fresh air. About fifteen minutes later, the MP Special Response Team, their SWAT team, rolled up to the empty barracks building across from us, and MPs raided a room. Confused, we started yelling, "Wrong team, wrong building!" The drug investigator from the Criminal Investigations Division arrived a few minutes later. In a hilarious coincidence, the SRT had been undergoing a training exercise. After an eventful first day with 1-68 Armor, I was instructed to report tomorrow to the individual replacement company for training.

The next six weeks were full of last-minute training. Two other classmates from West Point joined me for our journey to 1-68 Armor: JB Boland, who was a field artillery officer, and Matthew Vigeant, another armor officer. Craig Brewer, also an armor officer, was heading to the brigade's 2-9 Cavalry.

We needed to be "certified" on a list of tasks before we could deploy. Along with about a hundred other individual replacements, we took Arabic classes, medical training, rifle marksmanship, and a host of other individual skills. The individual replacements were assigned to different battalions within the brigade, and as a result we had a wide variety of job functions and skill sets. The training was frustrating. Those soldiers who were unlikely to ever leave the wire or interact with Iraqis found it hard to be motivated for Arabic classes and tactics. Classes on radios some would never see were a waste of their time, and they visibly showed their annoyance.

Some were plain scary with weapons. One female cook was afraid of getting in trouble for a live round she found in her uniform after we left the rifle range. Knowing we would have a check for live rounds again when we got off the bus, she hid it in the chamber of her rifle. As she got off the bus, she somehow pulled the trigger and *BANG*, she blasted the round at our feet.

The last task was Soldier Readiness Processing. If you ever want to watch a veteran try to crawl into a hole and hide, tell him he has to go to SRP again. Early in the morning we all reported to the building housing this man-made hell of pure boredom. Each of us got a packet that included checkboxes we had to get signed off. After waiting in line for eternity, I would enter the doorway to the station.

"Do you have both sets of glasses and gas mask inserts? Yes? Here you go. Next!"

And just like that, on to the next station and waiting in line. "Is your will done? Yes? Next."

One of the stations involved recreating my lost immunization records the hard way, but this time they also added in smallpox and anthrax vaccines. After my voodoo doll experience, both arms throbbed. Several hours of shuffling in line around the three-story building later, I was done and returned home to pack, repack, inspect, and repack yet again.

We all got a couple days off before our flight. That Sunday morning at Holy Apostles was one of the few services I can remember. All of my family in Colorado Springs gathered for a BBQ. We were a bit more subdued than normal. What do you say when it might just be the last goodbye?

My alarm went off at 2 a.m. I was already awake. I got up, grabbed my gear, and looked around the home. It was time.

IN-COUNTRY

IT WAS A COLD AND drizzly July night as we boarded a charter airplane at Colorado Springs Airport's Jet Center. In the dark of the night, we somberly loaded up and prepared for what would be nearly a straight day on an airplane. I was thoroughly amused, though. Despite the fact that we were soldiers who were sworn to defend our country, TSA regulations applied to us. We had to remove the bolts from our rifles. Of course, in the interest of not losing a critical part, we placed the bolts in our pockets. Despite already carrying a weapon, we were also required to pack our pocket knives in our "checked" duffle bags. Drug-sniffing dogs went down our line of bags and through our formation.

Rain was falling when we landed in Bangor, Maine, a critical layover point before the flight over the Atlantic. The Bangor locals made it a point to greet every single plane of troops, coming and going. They were saints and a great reminder of what we were fighting for. It was pouring rain in Dresden, Germany, when we stopped there for another break. Instead of pulling up to a terminal, we were bused to a little building that was completely isolated from the rest of the airport and surrounded by fencing. This would be the last place we didn't need weapons and ammo.

We landed at Kuwait International Airport at about 9 a.m. The sun was already up and beating down hard. As soon as the plane came to a stop and the doors opened, a stifling, humid heat overwhelmed the plane. The temperature was 100 and climbing steadily. After cold rain everywhere for the last day, the heat was even more of a shock. To add to our misery, our smallpox vaccine sores were all oozing, and most of us had a fever from it or the anthrax.

We boarded buses and began the long convoy out into the empty desert to Ali Al Salem Air Base, the main hub for moving people in and out of Iraq. C-17s and C-130s made constant trips between it and the various air bases inside Iraq. As we traveled, I couldn't help noticing that the convoy was led by a truck sporting a machine gun and we had an armed guard on each bus. We were not in Iraq yet, but we were in the heart of the Middle East. Terrorists lurked.

Ali Al Salem Air Base was a monument to life in a war zone. Unlike bases in America, every hanger was a bomb-resistant bunker, scattered to make it difficult to bomb multiple hangers at the same time. The fences were not just chain link; each also had rows of razor wire, and there was more than one belt of fences. Getting from point A to point B required going through multiple checkpoints.

In a small building, our ID cards were scanned, and we were officially deployed on paper. A series of briefings regarding extra pay for being in a combat zone and the rules of the personnel depot tested our ability to stay awake in a time zone nearly opposite of home. Following the briefing, we filed into a warehouse to draw more supplies. By the time we were done, I had some 150 pounds of crap to carry. Three duffle bags, a rucksack, and a smaller pack were all stuffed to the brim. Of course, I would use less than a third of the stuff during my deployment. *Why couldn't we have been given this stuff at Carson so we could leave the other stuff behind?* Essentially the only difference in the redundant supplies was the camouflage pattern. Then we were off to some small tents to await our flight into Iraq. In classic military fashion, it would be "soon," and we were admonished not to wander off.

True to the word *soon*, a few hours later we rounded up our charges and filed back into the building. Quickly we were manifested onto flights.

The C-130 can hold sixty-four soldiers. The seats are little more than a piece of canvas draped between a pair of bars to create a bench. It is exquisitely uncomfortable. The plane quickly fills with the smell of exhaust, and the noise is nearly unbearable. Earplugs help some, but the engines' droning wears the ears out. At least most of our bags were on pallets at the rear of the plane. With my rifle between my knees and my pack on my lap, wedged as I was between two other soldiers like sardines, I knew this would be the longest flight, despite being a shorter distance than previous legs of the trip. By the time we were airborne, my legs were asleep.

A plane is most vulnerable during landing. Landings are easiest if the plane slowly and steadily loses altitude on a smooth glide path that takes it to the runway barely above stall speed. Of course, that style of flying is easy to shoot out of the sky. In a combat zone, things are done differently. Our C-130 remained at high altitude until nearly directly over Balad Air Base, some thirty miles north of Baghdad. Once over friendly positions, the airplane began a tight and fast spiral down from altitude, leveling out just in the nick of time to land.

Balad Air Base was huge. The only difference between it and Kuwait was the fact that blast walls surrounded many of the buildings and compounds to help protect against indirect fire from mortars and rockets. Buses crisscrossed the base to take people to the dining facility and the post exchange (PX) store. Despite being a war zone, nobody wore body armor or even helmets. Everyone had a rifle or pistol, but they were not loaded, and the magazine was in a pocket or strapped to the stock of the rifle. Of course, the replacements hadn't been issued ammo yet.

Once again, hurry up and wait was the order of the day. We bused to some plywood buildings where we awaited the next leg of the journey. As soldiers lined our bags up in rows, the other leaders and I checked in with the sergeant running the transient barracks.

"You will have the first three buildings." The sergeant pointed at a row behind us. "Accountability formations are at zero eight hundred and eighteen hundred hours. Chow is over that way a couple blocks. Make sure you have your weapons with you, but they need to be green and clear. Cover, eye pro, and a reflective belt are required. Questions?"

With that, we returned to the other replacements and repeated the instructions to them. Finally, I carried my pile of bags into a building and dumped them on a bunk.

Unlike our previous layovers, this one was exciting for me. My brother, Patrick, was stationed at Balad. He was patrolling the area around the air base and even crossing the Tigris River from time to time on missions. My first order of business was to find a computer and email Pat.

I returned to my bunk and pulled out a book. Barely an hour into reading, the door slammed and a familiar giant of a man blocked the overhead light as he stood over me. It was Pat, with his typical grin. Pat looked every bit the bad mamba jamba I knew him to be. His patrol cap was tightly curled and ranger rolled. His face was tanned to the color of his mustache. His Ranger tab was as faded as the rest of his uniform, but the pistol in his drop-leg holster was gleaming clean. I hadn't seen Pat in about seven months, and the fact that we were thousands of miles from home and in a war zone made the meeting even more poignant. It turned out that his company's compound was just a few blocks way.

"Welcome to hell, parson. Let's go get some dinner." Pat smiled. "You need your weapon and a magazine. But don't load it. It has to be in a pocket or strapped on the butt, but never in the well."

"I don't have ammo, Pat."

My reply caused a momentary furrow of Pat's forehead.

"Well, that's stupid. No worries; I will fix you up. Bring some magazines." The no-nonsense logic of a Ranger matched with the protective attitude of a big brother. I dug into my duffle, retrieved three magazines from my kit, and dumped them in my cargo pocket, slinging my rifle on my back.

Shortly, we arrived at his long-range surveillance detachment's compound and went into his platoon's building. It was a nicely built barracks that had been for Iraqi pilots, with nice tile floors and running water. As Pat introduced me to the members of his infantry team, I loaded ammo into my magazines.

"Now you are not a target. You are a soldier who can fight. I'm hungry. Let's go eat."

Together Pat and I went to the large dining facility, a warehouse-like structure. The roof was pretty flimsy and a nice bright white. In the event of a mortar attack, it would be the last place I wanted to be. However, the food was good and all you could eat. I quickly understood why some people who didn't do patrols could get really fat while deployed.

Soldiers like to make up names for things. Every war has its own collection of memorable lingo. The war in Iraq gave birth to the term *fobbit*, a reference to the hobbits in Tolkien's books and the bunkered buildings of forward operating bases, FOBs. A fobbit was someone who never left the wire on patrol. While they contributed to the war effort in their own mostly invaluable ways, they were ridiculed by those soldiers who ventured out into the valley of death daily. The fobbits were the ones who typically gained the most weight, and Balad Air Base was packed with fobbits.

Over dinner, Pat gave me advice and insight that might keep me alive. Some was straightforward; some was amusing.

"The terps are of varying help. Some speak English better than others, but very few have any military training. If you even think something is about to go down, get them somewhere safe so they aren't a liability. And be careful what you let them hold. One day my terp started playing with a pen flare in the back seat of the Humvee while we were overwatching a farm. Next thing I know, he somehow shoots it off. The flare bounced off the roof and into his thick hair and caught his fro on fire. Poor dude bailed out of the Humvee, ran a few meters, and then fainted. The blast from the fire extinguisher woke him up."

Soon our conversation turned to home. I updated him on the folks, the crops, friends from growing up, and the happenings around town. While talking, I completely lost my anxiety over looming combat operations and reporting as an individual replacement. The dinner with Pat was priceless. We said our goodbyes well after the sun went down, unsure of when we would next see each other.

The following morning, our accountability formation was met by a new face. Command Sergeant Major Dave List from our brigade joined us. Dave was, in a nutshell, a great character. He wore the tall, leather cavalry boots that only tankers who had served with the Mounted Riflemen of the 3rd Armored Cavalry Regiment wore. To top it off, Dave also sported a mustache that looked like it had been perfected by Frederick Remington, the great Western artist. Dave was there to take us "home" to FOB Warhorse outside of Baqubah, where we would meet up with the rest of the brigade.

A collection of trucks pulled into the parking lot of the temporary barracks. Each truck had an armored bed with the tops left open and then covered with camo netting to provide some shade. The majority of the replacement soldiers went into the beds of the trucks. *No thank you!* As an officer, I got to ride inside a Humvee so I could see the battlefield that I would soon be leading soldiers on. Our convoy pulled out of Balad Air Base and began the drive east to Baqubah.

This was not the barren desert shown on TV. Lush fields and orchards were everywhere. As we entered the Tigris River's floodplain, elephant grass as tall as the trucks lined the road all the way to the edge of the pavement. My body cringed at the thought of how easy it would be to hide a roadside bomb.

The Tigris River was pretty wide, nearly 1,000 feet across, and the bridge was a pontoon bridge. *Crap.* Crossing pontoon bridges in vehicles is an unnerving experience. Walking on a waterbed is fun when you know you aren't going to die if it breaks. Crossing it in an armored vehicle is not fun. If it breaks or the driver goes off, drowning is a huge likelihood.

We had just entered the area that would be my platoon's area of responsibility, although all I knew was that we had entered 1-68 Armor's area, and I studied the land intently. Soon we left the elephant grass and climbed over canals to enter a patchwork of fields. After driving through a run-down city, we turned south and a few miles later were at FOB Warhorse.

Like Balad Air Base, FOB Warhorse was huge, and blast walls were the order of the day. Many of the blast walls were made of Hesco baskets—large wire-and-fabric baskets filled with dirt. FOB Warhorse had once been the small Baqubah Airport. Only a few real buildings dotted the base. Soldiers were housed in "CHUs," containerized housing units, each a twenty-foot container modified to have a door and a couple windows. Orderly compounds were filled with them, each CHU being further bunkered in by smaller Hesco baskets and sandbags.

The FOB was about a mile in length. On the north end were 1-68 Armor's company command posts in small plywood buildings, beyond which lay only an artillery battery's firing positions and some tank firing positions on the berm. On the south end of the FOB was the motor pool. This open area was where we parked the tanks and other armored vehicles. The battalion headquarters was positioned just north of the motor pool. It too was a plywood building. Just a few weeks before I arrived, it had taken a direct hit from a mortar round. The tall radio antennas that accompanied command posts make great targets for enemy mortar teams. About halfway between the command posts stood the CHUs for the company I would join.

I was excited to report in to the battalion even though I knew I would not likely get a platoon. After some initial paperwork with the personnel office and dropping our gear in a CHU, JB Boland, Matt Vigeant, and I arrived at the battalion TOC to report to our battalion commander, Lieutenant Colonel Fisher. I had been warned ahead of time that he was quite the character, so I was prepared for the welcome speech he gave us.

Patiently we waited in a corner of the TOC until Colonel Fisher strode into the building in full combat kit. He waved us to follow him as he turned into his office next to the TOC.

"Grab a chair and sit down." Colonel Fisher stripped off his body armor and laid it on a cross-shaped hanger tree in the corner as we set up folding chairs, sat down, and pulled out notebooks.

"Welcome to the Silver Lions. We are in this COIN fight, and we are going to do our piece before we go home. Right now, I don't have platoons for both of you." Colonel Fisher wagged his finger at Matt and me. "But I don't need another junior officer on staff. I need warriors. I would rather you go out there and gain some invaluable experience so when I do put you in a platoon, you are seasoned. You will make better decisions and fight harder. So one of you will go to a platoon in Destroyer, and the other will go to Steel and learn. Don't worry; they will put you to good use also.

"It is important that all three of you remember the Iraqis think we are amazing. It is on you to ensure we stay magical to the Iraqis. They are blown away by our willingness to come and fight for them, and our technology further awes them. Stay magical.

"Above all, you will fight like hell. We dominate in battle. We are aggressive and we win every fight decisively. This is because we deliberately intend to dominate the battlefield each and every time. Here in Diyala, your patrols are scattered out on a wide area. You will get into a fight and you must hold your own. But I can promise that if you hold your own for fifteen minutes, I will have every resource available, and even some that aren't, fighting by your side. That also means if you hear troops in contact on the radio, you haul ass there and fight.

"Last but not least, we are in this for the long haul. Take care of yourselves. Every day, you need to make someone smile. We will be back in Iraq again after this deployment. I can promise you that. Wars don't end when the victors declare success; they end when the vanquished accept defeat. Remember this. Now go forth and fight like hell."

As one, we rose and saluted Colonel Fisher before filing out of his office. As Matt was senior to me and graduated from Ranger School, he got the open platoon. I went to C Company, known as Team Steel, where I would be the assistant platoon leader for White Platoon. Of course, a tank platoon does not need an assistant platoon leader, but the newly created position would allow me to learn and find ways to make myself useful.

Lieutenant AJ Boyes was the platoon leader and Sergeant First Class Sean Rinder the platoon sergeant. The platoon was a product of the "life cycle" personnel manning system the Army was trying. Soldiers were assigned to units at the beginning of a three-year cycle and supposed to remain in place for the entire cycle, with new soldiers only arriving to replace losses. This created a unit with stagnant positions. As soldiers were promoted, they did not have positions appropriate for their rank available. As such, the platoons were already leader heavy. Other members of the platoon were Staff Sergeants Arleth and Persinger, Sergeants Roberson, Beasley, Daniels, and Bryant, Specialists Arca, Cole, Hanson, Henderson, Miller, Newell, Tomelloso, and Yancer, and medic Heinreich. There were no privates.

The rest of Team Steel consisted of another tank platoon, called Red Platoon, the battalion mortar platoon, a headquarters section, and a maintenance section. Captain Todd Looney was the company commander, and First Sergeant Conrad Gonzales was his right-hand man.

IRON TRIANGLE

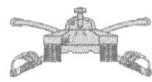

THE ENEMY WE FOUGHT WAS wary of going toe to toe with us. There were few firefights as the enemy had lost all of them pretty dramatically. Instead, the enemy focused on roadside bombs and indirect fire attacks on the FOB. Roadside IED bomb strikes on a patrol occurred several times a day. The majority of them occurred on a series of roads that made a large triangle—the Iron Triangle. This area was in the heart of C Company's area of responsibility, which went from the outskirts of the city of Baqubah in the south all the way to the edge of the Hamrin Mountains in the north. The Diyala River formed the eastern boundary, and the Tigris River the western.

The huge area encompassed the large city of Khalis, home to some 250,000 people. White Platoon was responsible for the area just west of FOB Warhorse. This included all of the Iron Triangle and then from the pontoon bridge south along the Tigris nearly to the city of Hussainiyah. On the western leg of the Iron Triangle was a city called Hibhib where Zarqoui, the leader of Al Qaeda in Iraq, was killed in June. Red Platoon patrolled the area northwest of the Diyala River and northeast of the Iron Triangle. The mortar platoon, "Thunder," patrolled the area north of Khalis up to the Hamrin Mountains.

The area was part of the so-called Sunni Triangle. The Sunni-sect

Arabs mainly lived in a triangular area starting just south of Baghdad and then following the Tigris northwest. The area was also home to a sizable Shia population. The two sects did not get along, with a history of distrust and hatred stretching back over a thousand years. Some towns were an even mix. Some were nearly homogenous. As a result, we faced many different insurgent groups, including Al Qaeda in Iraq, Badr Corps (or Badr Brigade, depending on who described them), and Jaish Al Mahdi.

For patrolling this vast area, the platoon could choose either Humvees or tanks. The Humvees were the M1114 up-armored version with the latest armor add-on package called "Frag-5." While the extra armor offered more protection, the added slabs on the doors extended below the level of the frame. When an IED went off, it often flattened the tires. Once the tires were flattened, the seven-ton vehicle ended up resting on those armor slabs, and nobody could open the doors. The only way out was through the gunner's hatch. If the Humvee was on fire, escape was unlikely. Additionally, if the back door was open, you could not open the front door.

Riding in a Humvee is not nearly as fun and cool as most people imagine. It is a military tactical vehicle, after all, and any comfort in design is accidental. The transmission is wide and forces the commander's legs to the right, which does wonders for your lower back, and there is little leg room; fortunately, I'm not a big guy. Since the seats were designed two decades before our bulky body armor, we barely fit. My side plates were firmly wedged between the door and the electronics on my left. The radio stack forced the computer screen out over my left leg. This of course made visibility less than ideal.

If the front seats were cramped, the ones in back were just cruel. A support strut ran behind the front seats, forcing the shins against an unforgiving metal bar. Every bump left a mark. The gunner sat on a hammock-like sling in the middle of the four seats. Depending on which direction he was supposed to be facing, his butt or his knees were against my shoulder.

Every Humvee was equipped with an electronic IED countermeasure called "Warlocks," which came in different versions. At the time, we had both "ICE" and "Red-Green Combo" Warlocks. They worked by jamming the frequencies the insurgents used to send detonation signals to the IEDs. Each Warlock created a bubble of signal dead-zone around the Humvee. The bubble was not very big, so we had to travel close enough to each other to create a continuous bubble while we passed the IED. Of course, if the IED's signal was not jammed or it used a hardwired connection, the bomb still exploded.

One of the downsides to the Warlocks is they further increase the electrical demand upon the batteries and alternator. The Humvee's battery box is located under the commander's seat, the seat a civilian would call the passenger seat. The electrical capability of the Humvee has been unchanged since the 1980s. Now we were asking the system to handle its normal automotive and radio demands, plus a ruggedized computer system, a GPS, and now a powerful electrical jammer. It was too much. Naturally, Murphy's Law dictated the point of weakness that burst into flames would be the battery connections four inches under the commander's butt. I suspect this led to Specialist Keith Hanson's wag of a warning on his sun visor: *Abandon all hope.*

Our tanks were exactly like the tanks we trained on, with one minor exception.

The loader's M240 machine-gun mount had a shield added for protection. Since the extra armor protection package was designed for the M1A1, the commander's machine gun did not have a shield. The M1A1's fifty caliber could be operated from inside the tank and did not need additional protection. Of course, after you fired all 100 rounds in the ammo can, you had to expose yourself to lug a new fifty-pound ammo can into place.

These M1A2s did not have the same setup. When they added new electronics for the commander, they had to take out the system that allowed the machine gun to be fired from inside. The machine-gun mount was now hand aimed. Unfortunately, the design was not well done. Instead of using the tried and true spade grip the fifty caliber had used since 1918, the tank had a bicycle handle bar–looking grip. To put a fifty caliber in it, a backplate without the spade grips was needed.

Since the Humvees needed the spade grip, we had to change backplates constantly. It was stupid and annoying. The bicycle grips were useless. Still, the fifty caliber was an awesome weapon you did not want to leave at home. It was extremely reliable, never jamming, and fired half-inch-diameter slugs that had some serious heft, capable of penetrating walls, metal plates, and doing amazing things to soft tissue.

Despite being a bigger vehicle, the tanks did not have a Warlock like the Humvees did. One of the company's missions was to counter roadside-bomb placement on the Iron Triangle. Twice a day, we would send a section of two tanks along the routes to try and soak up some of the bombs. In addition, White Platoon set up positions to ambush enemy teams placing explosives in the "IED hot spots" where bombs were more frequent than others. We also conducted patrols to partner with the local populations and security forces.

The counter-IED patrols were fun. The tank-section patrols were my favorite. As a tanker, being in a tank was my calling. Also, both AJ Boyes and Sean Rinder were happy to let me lead their sections on patrol so they could do other things. Since there was no doctrinal call sign for the non-doctrinal position of assistant tank platoon leader, we adapted and I became "White Five."

We would load up two tanks and head out the east gate of FOB Warhorse. Tank tracks could rapidly damage the weak asphalt at the main gate, so instead we were banished to the moondust lane wrapped around the FOB. From there we had two choices: either go north first, or south first. Going north, we would patrol the highway to Khalis. From there we headed down the divided highway south through Hibhib. At Ghalibiyah was a large overpass interchange with another divided highway that went east to Baqubah. From there we would head back to FOB Warhorse. If we went south first, we did the route in the opposite order.

In the tank, I stood on the floor of the turret so that my eyes were barely above the hatch. In training at Fort Knox, we learned to stay at name tape defilade, exposing the top half of the chest and head to get maximum awareness of our surroundings but still be mostly protected by armor. With the primary threat being shrapnel from roadside bombs, name tape defilade seemed too exposed. Nobody in the company ever gave me advice or direction regarding the best level. I placed an ammo can on the floor and folded the seat up so I could stand with my whole body tucked in but would be able to climb up the seat if needed.

At the time, the typical roadside bomb was made from a single 120 mm mortar or 122 mm artillery round. Some larger 152 mm or 155 mm artillery rounds were used. These bombs were often detonated on command by a triggerman using a wire or cell phone. When one went off next to a tank, damage to the road wheels was expected, but little more than that. If detonated on a Humvee, the shrapnel could penetrate the crew compartment and injure or kill someone. Tires would be flattened and sometimes the engine removed or the frame bent by the force of the blast.

My arrival to the company landed in the middle of the "Happy Times." Our local insurgents were not able to read the Russian markings that labeled a vast majority of their munitions. High-explosive was the most common round available, but our locals had procured a large collection of illumination rounds we called "flash-bang bombs." When the illumination round detonated next to your vehicle, the worst injury caused was a sunburn and seeing stars and floaters. It sure beat shrapnel.

To further hamper the insurgents' efforts, they managed to disrupt their own IED communications. Cell phones were their primary trigger method. Since the tanks didn't have Warlocks, it worked for them quite well. However, during the Happy Times, the local insurgents decided to attack the local phone infrastructure to make the government look bad and weak. In the middle of the night, a team of sappers blew up the electrical box for the large cell phone tower just off the Ghalibiyah interchange. Cell phone signal decreased, and the phones most affected were those buried under an inch or two of dirt.

On the divided highways, one tank would drive in the center of each side. To allow the Iraqi motorist a chance to get out of the way, the right side would lead the tank going against traffic by 100 meters or so. We were not too worried about a head-on collision in daytime because a tank is like a house rolling down the road. We were already three full years into the war, and the Iraqis fully understood the rules of interacting with American forces. When we came down the road, they pulled over out of the way. When following us, they stayed back a good distance. Motorists that failed to do so either had a death wish or were likely suicide bombers.

At night, we drove with lights on for the safety of other motorists. To ensure they got out of the way, we had a huge laser that combined four beams to produce a massive one visible at great distances. We only used that laser with the tanks. We would open the breach of the cannon and shine it down the barrel. The gunner would aim the gun to the side of the highway and have the loader turn the laser on. Then the gunner would slowly traverse the gun towards the cars on the highway, careful to never actually allow the laser to hit a car. We did not want the Iraqis to know that it was harmless, and we also did not want to blind anyone while they were behind the wheel. As a result, the Iraqis thought we could shoot a laser out of a tank cannon and would all but crash their car trying to avoid the Death Star's beam.

Diyala Province in 2006 was car bomb central. We had intelligence on a prolific car bomb factory in Khalis, though we couldn't figure out where exactly. As the summer grew hotter, we gained information that a semi-truck was being turned into a car bomb. Such a bomb would cause an extreme amount of damage and even be able to completely destroy a tank. This nasty threat was always in the back of my mind when outside the wire.

The divided highway through Hibhib was usually fairly crowded, so when we headed north from Ghalibiyah one afternoon and there was no traffic, I got worried. My wingman was in the northbound lanes on my right and in front of me. My tank was staggered back and to his left in the southbound lanes. The enemy had something planned for us. Cringing against the coming blast, I scanned the road north of me.

Just south of Hibhib's outskirts, I saw a fuel semi-truck heading south towards us. At about half a mile away, it pulled over on the side of the road as if the driver had seen us and was obeying the rules of the road. At about a quarter mile away, the truck suddenly lurched back into motion, gaining speed and heading straight at my wingman in the opposite lane. *Uh-oh, car bomb!* Instinctively I reached for my rifle that I kept positioned next to my hatch. As the truck neared my wingman, it suddenly veered towards him, and appeared to be fully laden.

Shooting at the cab or engine with a machine gun would be bad. The rounds would likely hit high and penetrate into the fuel and could cause it to explode without the enemy trying. Rapidly, I rose high enough in the hatch to shoulder my rifle and began to fire shots at the passenger-side tires. I didn't dare shoot at anything higher on the truck. In a few shots I blew enough tires to cause the truck to pull heavily to the right, away from my wingman. As the truck settled on a course in the median, we dodged to the left, out into the field, giving the truck a wide berth.

"White Three, White Five; what was that all about?" I asked Sergeant Persinger.

"No clue, but I am not asking him either!"

"No kidding. Let's pop smoke and charlie mike." With that, I reached down with my right hand and switched to the company radio. "Steel X-Ray, White Five; checkpoint two-two-four, charlie mike, over." We got out of Dodge as fast as we could, leaving the disabled fuel truck in the median. *How in the world do I report this? I can't report just speculation, and I don't know if it was a car bomb or a suicidal driver, or who knows what.* In the end, I decided I really did not have anything of military value to report.

My introduction to the unmanned aerial vehicle (UAV) war came that night when I went to dinner and ran into the brigade commander,

Colonel Jones. After I saluted him but before I could get past him, he asked, "Have a rough day on Dover, Lieutenant?" Apparently, he had watched the event live from the UAV feed. Fortunately, I knew that the UAV picture would not have picked up on the shots fired.

In all the counter-IED patrols, I only spotted one IED without it blowing up first. Sometimes luck was on our side. One afternoon, I led a section south from Warhorse. At the traffic circle, we turned west, traveling the thoroughly blasted divided highway to Ghalibiyah. The highway had seen so many bombs that it resembled the surface of the moon. Almost halfway to Ghalibiyah, luck smiled on me. Not 100 meters in front of the tank, there was a small poof of dust, and an object rolled out into the roadway. *IED!*

"Driver, stop tank!!!" I yelled loud enough he could have heard me without the intercom system. The tank nosedived as it skidded to a halt. Instinctively, I ducked down completely inside the turret and looked around. The IED had been buried on the right side of the westbound lane. The trigger man had to be somewhere north of it. While I looked for secondary devices, my gunner scanned for the triggerman.

"Steel X-Ray, White Five; contact IED, mike-charlie-six-zero-seven-one-three-six-seven-seven. It's a dud now sitting in the middle of Route Scunnion. Over." Belatedly, I remembered to call in the find. *Oops, rookie mistake. Correct that with a solid nine-line report.* I looked at my nine-line unexploded-ordnance-report format taped to the turret wall, and a minute later, I had my completed report ready and called it in.

The IED had been made from a 122 mm artillery round. Now that artillery round sat square in the middle of the westbound lane, and there was no way around it. Sometimes you could shoot machine-gun bullets into an IED and cause it to explode, but that practice was severely frowned upon by higher headquarters. Their reasoning was that if it did not work, the explosive was even more unstable for the bomb squad to deal with.

We would have to babysit the bomb until the bomb squad came. The "real" route-clearance patrols of engineers were the ones that were supposed to find and dispose of the roadside bombs, so they had all the tools they needed, including their own bomb squad. Sitting on the Ghalibiyah highway, I now had to wait for them to come from wherever they happened to be currently patrolling. At least we were in tanks and the enemy was very unlikely to attack us in the open fields.

Forty-five minutes is a very long time to wait in the hot Iraqi sun. As time slowly ticked by, my focus on my surroundings became fuzzy, and my forehead poured sweat, burning my eyes. I periodically pulled a package of baby wipes from my pocket and wiped my forehead and face.

Finally, from the east, the route-clearance patrol arrived. One of their specialized armored cars pulled up to my tank and surveyed the site. Then, without so much as a word, the bomb squad drove up to the artillery round. A soldier got out, kicked it over with his foot, and then picked it up and placed it in his vehicle. Again without a word, they drove off. The artillery round must have not been primed to detonate anymore, and now the road was safe for everyone.

In addition to the tank patrols, we tried to monitor the IED hot spots where the roadside bombs were most frequent. We would establish an observation post to watch for the placement teams. Sneaking anywhere in a countryside full of people is difficult. Our vehicles looked nothing like the ubiquitous blue or white Bongo trucks that every farmer seemed to have, nor did they resemble the more common Opel sedans. Instead, our large armored vehicles were distinct in size, shape, and sound. Additionally, we traveled in groups of multiple vehicles. Even when we drove in the dark without lights, the simplest of people could figure out an American patrol was passing. Diyala Province was full of people who quickly reported our passing to the local insurgents.

Further challenging our efforts to travel the area unnoticed was the presence of a few major irrigation canals. These canals were more than thirty feet wide and fifteen feet deep. One in particular traveled north to south in the middle of our battle space. It was concrete lined, and only a few bridges crossed it, mainly the highway bridges. A few smaller bridges could be crossed by people and small vehicles, but a Humvee would quickly collapse them, with the likely result of killing the crew in the water.

The canals were lined by thick dikes on both sides that served a dual purpose as road or path through the farms and orchards. The roads were dirt, bumpy, and often prone to collapsing under the weight of armored vehicles. When driving down them, it was important to stay away from the edge on the water side. The risk of a rollover accident was high, so we all wore our seat belts and proceeded carefully.

The art of sneaking a small team in to observe a hot spot was not easy. Walking from the FOB was out of the question. Our body armor alone weighed more than thirty pounds. My fighting load, armor, ammo, radio, smoke grenades, fragmentation grenades, star cluster pyrotechnics, and water took that weight to over seventy pounds. Movement was a major physical exertion and demanded even more water. Iraq in summer saw the mercury rise over 120 degrees, and humidity lingered around 90 percent. A more complex method was needed to shorten the distance we had to walk.

One method was taking a patrol out in the Humvees. We would wander around the battlefield, stopping often and getting out for some foot patrols near the Humvees. At some point, not everyone would come back to the Humvees, and a four-man team would stay hidden. The rest of the platoon would drive off and attract attention away from the observation team. The observation team would then work their way to a preselected place to observe the IED hot spot. In the meantime, the Humvees would keep moving in the area, careful to not come too close to the observed hot spot. It was a delicate balance of being close enough to respond for a fight but far enough to give a false sense of safety to the IED-placement teams.

Establishing an observation post came with the thrill of the hunt. After spending 90 percent of our time being the targets, a chance to ambush the enemy was a welcome change. We were hunting the most deadly of game. Our quarry was a vicious one, capable of turning the tables on us, and assisted by a network of allies. Every member of the observation post had to be fully alert and ready. We could never assume that we were completely unnoticed and had to be ready for a counter ambush.

Nearly all of our observation posts were in the area of Hibhib. The city seemed to have the highest concentration of IEDs and the highest concentration of people who did not care for us. Route Dover, known to the Iraqis as Highway 2, ran from the Shaab neighborhood in Baghdad to Khalis. Hibhib had a population of about 22,000 people at the time, though geographically it was barely bigger than a square mile. Part of the city was hidden in the palm groves to the west of the highway. About half of the city, including the government buildings, was east of the highway and protected by a large canal on its eastern border. Only one bridge strong enough for Humvees crossed the canal into town from the east. North of town, the canal wrapped around the city edge and then paralleled the highway just a couple hundred feet from it. Where the highway bisected the city, there were no buildings up against it, allowing insurgents to place roadside bombs right through the heart of the city without damaging buildings of "friendly" locals.

Hibhib's animus towards us went beyond its being the home to Abu Zarqoui, the leader of Al Qaeda in Iraq killed in June. About the time I arrived, our artillery at FOB Warhorse had a big oops. They were conducting a training exercise and forgot to tell the cannon crew the critical phrase "do not load" before giving the fire command. The cannon crew dutifully aimed the cannon at the azimuth and elevation provided to them and then fired. To the horror of the leaders and the fire-direction center, the high-explosive round flew without problem until it smacked into a small group of innocent civilians. At first the people of Hibhib thought Al Qaeda was retaliating for ratting out Zarqoui, but when our brigade commander paid $50,000 in cash to the families, the gig was up, and the town increased its hatred towards us.

Sometimes we would set up our observation in a government building. This was our least favorite place as we did not trust them any more than we did the insurgents themselves. Sometimes we would use an abandoned building. The best spots were small rises in the ground that allowed us to see over the tall elephant grass and reeds growing between the canal and the highway.

As adrenaline pumping as the hunt was, it was principally marked by a whole lot of waiting—followed by even more waiting. We conducted our ambushes exclusively under the cover of darkness. With a national curfew at 10 p.m., kids were less likely to wander into our position. Many an observation post has been compromised by some small child.

Since the beginning of time, criminals and people needing anonymity have relied on darkness to hide their actions, and the insurgents preferred to do their work at night as well. Electricity was not reliable in Iraq. With the curfew preventing a night life, the car lights, streetlights, and lit-up signs were absent. And the nights were as quiet as they were dark. Rural farmland offered the occasional animal calls—the city only a few dog barks. It was so quiet you could almost hear your thoughts.

One sweltering night, AJ led the ambush patrol to an observation post on the north side of Hibhib. It was a glorious spot: a small pile of rubble in the tall grass with gorgeous fields of fire over the highway. While his team watched the hot spot, I led the mounted patrol of our four Humvees. The plan was for me to patrol the farmland in the center of the Iron Triangle. We did not often venture there, and nobody was familiar with the quality of the roads. Satellite imagery showed some were passable, including a paved road that ran from Hibhib's eastern bridge up through the middle of the triangle to the southern tip of Khalis. I would explore the road, trying to stay within about ten minutes of drive time from AJ's position.

"Be back in four hours," AJ told me as his four-man team unloaded from the Humvees in the darkness. We both looked at our watches.

"Sounds good." We stealthily closed the doors on the Humvees. With a wave of a hand, the four men set off towards their ambush site.

"Two, Five; roll." With three simple words, we were back in motion. We had been stopped for maybe thirty seconds. The first couple miles of the patrol went really well as we meandered east through Hibhib, letting the trucks' progress away from the ambush be noted. We crossed a small bridge over the canal on the east side and turned north.

Sergeant Arleth's voice came over the speaker box. "White Five, White Two; we have an obstacle." His truck came to a stop, and we got out to investigate, all executing what we called our five-twenty-five. We carefully checked the area five meters out and then searched twenty-five meters, scanning for any signs of a roadside bomb. *If it was my obstacle, I would add a booby trap too.* Someone had used a loader or dump truck to make a four-foot-high berm across the road. Since the road was on top of the canal dike, there was no bypass. The dirt looked fresh and loose still.

"Sir, we can get over this." One by one, the Humvees bounced their way over. Unfortunately, my driver let off the gas, and we didn't hit it with enough speed and got high centered. A few minutes were wasted pulling it off the berm. With four men in the observation post, we could not afford another incident at a berm. With that in mind, we changed our plan and stuck to roads we knew were completely passable. The patrol ended without further incidents.

The ambush patrols required a significant amount of preparation to successfully execute. AJ, Sean, and I spent time analyzing patterns in IED strikes, intelligence reports, and imagery. We would select what looked to be the best place to set up the observation post. Before we could use it, we needed to see it from the road to make sure it would work. The drop-off and pickup locations needed careful selection. It would not work if someone watched the drop-off from their house. In a country that had no more than a few cell phones three years ago, everyone had one now. The route for the Humvees also required planning to strike that perfect balance of distance and time from the observation post. Finally, all of the equipment had to be in working condition, with backups in place. Redundancy was a key to survival in war.

"Kinetic" patrols, or patrols with the sole purpose of taking the fight to the enemy, were not our primary focus. While every patrol, regardless of purpose, was a combat patrol with an equal chance of running into a fight, the majority had a specific non-kinetic purpose. Iraq was a counterinsurgency fight, and winning the hearts and minds of the people was the only path to victory. It was an uphill battle in Hibhib. My least favorite patrols were the government meetings. Once a week, at the same time on the same day, we would pull into the Hibhib governance building and spend more than an hour talking with the local leaders. It was more agonizing than a PTA meeting. Nothing was ever accomplished. While AJ, Sean, and I sat in uncomfortable chairs and listened to "leaders" talk in circles, the men outside sweltered in the midday heat.

The worst part of the consistent meetings was they set us up for ambush. There were only a handful of ways to get to the governance building. To make things worse, the building was right in the heart of an IED hot spot. I felt like bait in heavily chummed water.

I was not surprised when in late August we received intelligence that an IED was in the parking lot itself. No route change would avoid that, and the Iraqi Police had to know about an IED in their own parking lot. Either they were immensely corrupt, or they were insurgents themselves. The latter was more likely. Corruption in Iraq was a given, but allowing a bomb in the parking lot was a completely different story.

The next meeting was not going to be pleasant. This time, we traded the Humvees for tanks. Our show of force was aimed at the Iraqi Police in Hibhib, and our message was clear: If we get hit in your parking lot, you get the brunt of the firepower response.

We rolled in from the north, hot and heavy in our tanks. A section peeled off the highway at the north edge of town and cut through the dirt field between the houses and the highway. The other section of tanks went to the main street and cut in towards the governance building from the west. The gun tubes aimed at the building could not have gone unnoticed. While AJ went into the meeting to have a pointed discussion with the leaders, I led a foot patrol around the building, checking for anything suspicious. In one particular car in the lot, we found a collection of cell phones. Possessing multiple cell phones was a telltale of an insurgent leader or IED cell member. While we could not find the owner, we knew it was someone tied to the governance building. With the ultimatum delivered but no insurgents rooted out, we loaded back up into the tanks and departed.

That night, we got a call from our informant. He was laughing hysterically. Apparently the IED had been in place before we got there with the tanks. Despite our not having any Warlocks on the tanks, the IED failed to detonate when the triggerman tried to set it off because it had been buried too deep to get signal reception. After we departed, the insurgent Iraqi policemen dug the IED up and set it at a shallower depth. The fools then decided they needed to check its reception before walking away from the hole. It was not too deep. The IED went off and killed the three foolish insurgents. Our problem solved itself.

The Hibhib Iraqi Police were not the only security forces struggling in their infancy. While the Hibhib station was infiltrated thoroughly, the Khalis station was full of cowards. They operated a checkpoint at the highway junction in south Khalis, a traffic circle with a guard tower built in the middle of it. While the Iraqi Police had a machine gun in the tower and a sizable force, at the first indications of a pending firefight, the checkpoint would turn into a ghost town. Worse, they often abandoned their weapons when they departed. We frequently had to collect their Russian-built PKM. The PKM is an excellent medium machine gun. Extremely reliable, simple to use, and capable of firing 7.62 mm bullets, it was not a weapon I wanted the local insurgents to collect.

An Iraqi Army infantry battalion was based in Khalis. We had a team of about a dozen American officers and senior sergeants, led by Major Bullock, attached to it for the purpose of mentoring them. While I was impressed by Major Bullock, I did not envy those officers. Living with an armed force that was likely infiltrated by the enemy brought them a twenty-four-seven danger that we did not face. Furthermore, the Iraqis were not as skilled in battle, so any firefight involved a whole new layer of risk.

Occasionally, we would raid some enemy fighter's house and use the Iraqi Army soldiers to help us. While they were not as good in a fight, the Iraqi soldiers understood how Iraqis hid things so were great for finding weapons where an American would be less likely to look.

I personally hated raids, but not because of the danger associated with kicking in a person's door in a land where everyone legally owned an AK-47. They were frankly an epic waste of time and effort. We would detain our suspected insurgent in Hibhib, Dojama, Khalis, or wherever and take them back to FOB Warhorse. Turning them over to military intelligence soldiers was such a hassle. The most frustrating part was that as often as not, the detainee would be back on the streets very shortly afterwards. For the most part, we were capturing very low-level pawns.

The system attempted to emulate the American justice system, which isn't perfect, but in introduction to a new culture in a copycat format, it seemed like a colossal failure. Much of our intelligence was based on informants' intel, which any good police officer will warn you to corroborate with hard facts. I suspect that higher level insurgents, the ones that Special Forces targeted, were subjects of more extensive and cross-referenced intelligence gathering.

One raid in Hibhib burned my frustrated soul more than any other. We were supposed to capture a leader of a small enemy cell. The man was allegedly well connected and a financier of enemy operations. That such a man operated in Hibhib was not a stretch to believe. After all, the leader of Al Qaeda in Iraq was killed there only two months before.

It was a big operation. We linked up with the Iraqi Army in Khalis and their attached advisors. In a massive convoy, we sped to Hibhib, cutting west on the main street, our convoy intentionally separating out a bit. The lead Iraqi Army platoon sped up and turned left to cut south on a side street to be in position on the far side of the target house. Our platoon and another Iraqi Army platoon continued to the canal before cutting south directly at the target house. The trailing Iraqi Army platoon drifted back some so they could take a position blocking escape routes to the west and north as we hit the target.

My truck had barely stopped moving when we opened the doors and bailed out, trotting to the gate of the target house's compound. As soon as everyone was assembled, we lined up in a stack to the right of the gate. With a squeeze to the shoulder of the man in front of us, we passed the message up the line that we were all ready, and the lead man nodded to the driver of the Humvee right next to us. Quickly he smashed the push bumper into the gate, flinging it open. We flowed like water released from a dam, peeling different directions inside the compound wall.

"Clear! Stack on me!" An instant later, we were reassembled to the right of the door to the house. There was no need for stealth now. A squeeze of the shoulders, and then the breacher booted the door. Again we flowed into the house.

"*Air-fi Yudik!*" (Hands up!) I yelled when I saw a man in the middle of the room. He was stunned. "*Air-fi Yudik!*" Our yells echoed in the small room as he and his wife and children all put their hands over their heads, clearly terrified.

"Clear! Target secure!" We had our suspect without a shot fired. Quickly, we put flex cuffs on him and led him out to the Humvees. As we did so, some Iraqi soldiers filed in and began a systematic search, leaving no item unturned.

The house was little more than a hovel. The place was so poor that one of our men collapsed the underground septic tank from his heavy combat-loaded weight. The suspect's home was Spartan. A couple blankets and mats, a few pots and pans, and a couple goats were all the man had to his name. The man was taken away, his wife and children distraught. Once on the objective, I found it impossible to believe this man was connected at all, and clearly he was not capable of financing his family, much less a small-scale war.

Later we learned the informant had a grudge against the man. The poor man owed some money and somehow insulted the informant. Unfortunately for the poor man, this led to a faulty raid against him. While I highly doubt the man was ever connected to an insurgent group before we detained him, I was confident he was at least a sympathizer afterwards.

Not all of our operations were as counterproductive. Some were very valuable to the populace. In an effort to buy the hearts and minds, we spent buckets of money financing projects to improve Iraqi life. We funded new water wells in the desert. We funded projects to "pave" streets in small towns. That usually meant paying a man to run a dilapidated road grader up and down the street. In the small town of Mansuriyah, the road grader managed to mix the open sewage in the borrow ditches into the dirt of the street, making a horrifically smelly and muddy road.

One of the more enjoyable operations was a "MEDCAP" mission. We would borrow the battalion's physician or his assistant and some medics and take them out to the people for a brief medical clinic. The Iraqi health-care system was completely wrecked, especially in the smaller cities and towns. Often, the occasion of our clinic was the first time any of the locals had ever been to a doctor for anything. It was the sort of mission that made you feel good all over.

Iraqi life was hard. The people did not have basic health care, and they lived in one of the most heavily polluted parts of the world. The locals ate a lot of fish, often caught out of the canals that crisscrossed the farmland. They also drank the same water. The water was not filtered or purified prior to drinking, and the canals all had multicolored chemical slicks on them. Open sewage was the norm in every single part of the company's battlespace. The resulting effects on the people were incredible. We saw all kinds of birth defects. There were kids with green skin tone, even when not ill. There were some with missing bones and weird growths. It was sad.

As soon as we set up a clinic, we had a huge line of people coming to see the doctor. It was amazing. Best of all, the people were thankful and in a great mood. The kids would come play soccer with us while we stood guard. The operations were usually fun and entertaining for all involved. It was a pleasant change from driving around and waiting to soak up a roadside bomb.

The enemy fired a few potshots during our MEDCAP in Khalis, so when we undertook one the following week in Hibhib, we expected trouble. This time, the headquarters section brought Staff Sergeant Watts and his UAV. Called a Raven, it was the size of the Styrofoam airplane I threw around as a kid, and it would provide a video feed to a small screen on a handheld controller. Before Watts could toss the thing into the air, we had to make sure that every Warlock was turned off. He explained to me that the Warlocks would jam the control signal, and the Raven would then fly away into the sunset. Last time Watts flew the Raven, a passing patrol's Warlocks cut the signal, and a hasty patrol had to be formed to drive in the last known direction until the Raven was able to send its location back to the controller. I laughed.

Hibhib was also the scene of one of our more amusing operations. In August, the local insurgents decided to conduct a war of words. On a compound wall, they wrote in English, *You will die USA Army* in black spray paint. It was hardly terrifying, but it demanded a response. Upon our discovery of it, we planned our poetic response. For our next patrol, we added a can of black spray paint to our kit and, prior to setting out, had our interpreter translate our message into Arabic so we would be ready. With the sun high, and the heat oppressive, we arrived at the wall in Hibhib. After a check to make sure there were no booby traps or other dangers, we were ready for our planned mission. A minute later, our response in Arabic decorated the wall: translated, "Eat shit and die!"

Summer of 2006 saw some of the worst sectarian violence of the Iraq War. The Sunnis and the Shias were killing each other when they weren't too busy killing us. The bloodshed got worse as the summer wore on, and Diyala Province, the southeastern corner of the Sunni Triangle, saw some of the worst in the country. The Sunnis were disenfranchised by our toppling of Saddam and the Baathist government, who were Sunni. The Shia Iraqis who had been disenfranchised by Saddam were out for revenge and gaining power. CNN frequently reported that as many as 100 people a day were dying. That number seemed severely exaggerated to our brigade commander and gave birth to one of the most macabre missions I ever had.

The only way to counter fuzzy facts was to have hard facts. In order to get an accurate count on the daily dead, we had to count the dead ourselves.

Iraqi culture was very orderly about taking care of the dead. The dying would arrive at the hospital to die. Often they were well past dead before arrival, with injuries clearly incompatible with life. The hospital would put them in the morgue to be collected by family in the night. By morning, not one of the bodies from the previous day would still be there. If we visited the morgue during late afternoon or early evening, we could get an accurate count of the daily dead. We would also ask the staff if any had already been picked up from the day's killings.

Since arriving at the Khalis hospital at nearly the same time every day was begging for an ambush, we decided to do it in tanks. The afternoon patrol of the Iron Triangle would simply make a pit stop. However, on the first trip to the hospital, I discovered a new impediment. We pulled off the highway and turned onto the narrow streets to circle around to the front entrance. Houses were powered by electrical lines that ran to the nearest generator. Each house ran its own line instead of the tidy system used in America. As a result, dozens of wires crossed the streets, hanging from the buildings instead of tall poles. An Opel sedan or Bongo truck easily fit under, and even a Humvee could limbo the wires, but at over ten feet high, the tank was too tall.

"Whoa, slow down. Okay, driver stop." I held my rifle by its butt and gingerly hooked an electrical wire with the front sight. *Plastic butt means insulated right?* I then slowly lifted it up to clear the fifty caliber.

"Okay, ease forward. Gentle. Okay, stop." I had lifted it clear of the machine gun and my hatch, but I could not reach far enough to lift it over the tank's crosswind sensor mast. Quickly, I crawled out onto the blowout panels over the ammunition storage and again lifted the wire with my rifle. Once over the crosswind sensor, we were home free—at least, until we got to the next really low wire.

"One thing is for certain; if we ever get hit doing this dance, I'm gonna angle the fifty caliber up and rip down all their wires in return. Jeez." My crew laughed in response.

The morgue at the Khalis hospital was a metal shed in the back of the walled compound. With temperatures well past 110 outside, the inside temperature was similar to an oven. The bodies rapidly deteriorated in the heat and humidity, and the stench was indescribably horrid. Some days I had to examine body parts to make sure there wasn't an extra leg or arm, meaning there was another dead body unaccounted for somewhere. After the first trip to the morgue, I decided to use the same uniform every time so that the lingering stench would not permeate more than one. At the end of the deployment, I burned the uniform. As nasty as it was, at least we had an idea what the body count was. While high, it was never even close to 100 people a day.

After counting bodies, it was time to race back to Warhorse and get to the chow hall for dinner before it closed. One might think that an appetite would be rare after such a task, but I got used to it, and the exertion of the day required significant refueling of the body.

Arriving at the FOB dining facility right at closing time was probably the most volatile thing we did. We developed some seriously bad blood with the fobbits that ran the chow hall. In their defense, they were trying to be efficient and run a clean and orderly place. They just lacked understanding and empathy. Meal times were as punctual as a German train schedule. If you were late, you missed it, no exceptions. A soldier guarded the entrance to the large white building. The purpose was not to protect it from the enemy but to ensure every soldier washed his or her hands and had a clean uniform. Of course, if you had been patrolling all day and raced back in the nick of time, your uniform would be filthy. This would spark a confrontation that often bordered on felony menacing. We were tired, stressed out, and in a foul mood when we arrived at the dining facility after a patrol. We were not to be trifled with.

Once inside, things improved. The food was prepared and served by Kellogg Brown & Root civilian contractors. I've always privately joked that they brought Kellogg in to cut costs. When I was in Kosovo a few years earlier, the food was made by Brown and Root and you could get omelets and steak at any meal, including midnight chow. Not so anymore.

The Army cooks merely watched over things and did who knows what. The contractors served a good spread, though. Napoleon said that an army marched on its stomach. The US Army in Iraq made sure it did so in style. Food was all you could eat, with options aplenty. TVs in the air-conditioned, framed tent offered a taste of home. On the way out, we found prepackaged food we could stuff in our pockets and save for when we missed a meal. Of course, if we missed a meal, we could always eat a Meal, Ready to Eat (MRE), but those were a very poor alternative.

The concerning thing about the dining facility was that it was a huge, white tent of a building, just like the one at Balad. Its roof wouldn't stop a thing and made for a great aiming point for insurgent artillery crews. On Thursday, this concern was at its highest.

Friday was most Iraqis' day off, so if you wanted to have a good time, Thursday night was the best one of the week. The local insurgents were no different. In order to keep their day jobs, they often had to fight in their time off. This pattern led to what we called "Thursday Night Fires." Like clockwork, the insurgent artillery crews would clock out of their day jobs and punch in with their illicit one. Usually about the time the sun went down, they would set up their rockets or mortars and lob a few rounds in at the FOB. Fortunately, the local crews were not that talented. They aimed for the most visible thing in the fading light, which happened to be the burning trash pit at the south end of the FOB. Every now and then they landed rounds somewhere else, but normally they merely blew up trash.

In order to keep the trash pit the best target for the insurgents, the FOB had a blackout policy. No lights were allowed on the FOB. The tall radio antennas did not display their aviation safety beacons. The streets were as dark as a cave. Stumbling around at night was difficult, but falling in a drainage ditch or getting clotheslined by the volleyball net was just the price of admission.

In August, the brigade commander grew tired of the Thursday Night Fires, and we launched Operation Rocket Man to counter them. Every Thursday afternoon, we sent patrols to counter the enemy artillery crews. The primary weapons used by the enemy were 60 mm mortars, which had a range of about two kilometers, and the 107 mm rocket, with a range of about eight kilometers.

Previously, our 3-29 Field Artillery Battalion had conducted counter-battery fire missions to kill the insurgent artillery crews without much success. With US patrols scattered all over the battlefield, our artillery needed to make sure nobody was too close to where they were going to shoot. It would not do to accidentally shell a friendly patrol. Unfortunately, the time it took to confirm everyone was clear allowed the enemy to pack up and be long gone before our artillery rounds impacted.

The new plan was to have ground patrols check the common enemy firing positions prior to them firing. Either our presence would be noticed and would deter the enemy artillery crews from setting up and shooting, or we would catch them in the act. The intelligence section provided us a map of the places to check. Most were fields within two kilometers of the FOB. The enemy rarely fired rockets from maximum range since they struggled to aim them. Fortunately for the enemy, missing the FOB was unlikely to make the locals angry as nothing but fields and a meat-packing plant surrounded us.

As the shadows grew long, we would head out the gate in

Humvees and check the fields. Most were small fields amid large palm groves. I felt like I was in Vietnam as we tromped through dense undergrowth below the palm-tree canopy. It was hard to admit, but the area was beautiful. The lush foliage provided both green and shade. Unfortunately, the humidity was through the roof in the stagnant air, and Iraq is home to many poisonous vipers and insects, so every step was taken with care. Miraculously, I never saw any.

White Platoon was responsible for monitoring a pair of fields just west of the village of Aswad, right across the highway from the FOB. Roads in the area were few, and ambush would have been child's play. Amazingly, we never were ambushed and never hit an IED while crashing through the palm groves. Still, despite our efforts, the enemy artillery continued to fall on the FOB, usually near the trash pit.

One of the platoon's other missions was mentoring the units guarding the pontoon bridge over the Tigris River at As Sindi, the bridge I crossed over when I first arrived. At the time, I had been worried about ambush. In reality, the bridge was probably the least likely place for that. An Iraqi Army company guarded the west side of the bridge. They had dug in positions around it. Their position was only about five miles from the massive Balad Air Base. A thousand feet across the Tigris River, a company of soldiers from the country of Georgia guarded the east bank. Georgia was a former Soviet splinter still living a precarious position in the Caucasus Mountains. The Iraqi company on the west bank and the Georgians on the east bank did not get along at all, and rifle and machine-gun fire frequently crisscrossed the Tigris between them. An enemy unit would be foolish to try to get between or even near them.

One random afternoon, Captain Looney summoned AJ and me to the command post. The mortar platoon's compound at Udhaim needed something brought to them urgently, and we were to take the Humvees and run north with the part.

Udhaim was just south of the Hamrin Mountains and well over an hour north of Khalis. Despite its tiny size and remoteness, the place had strategic importance on the crossroads of smuggling routes from Iran towards Kirkuk, Balad, and many other flash points. Several months prior, the Iraqi Army outpost at Udhaim had been overrun. The Iraqi Army had since added a platoon of T-55 tanks along the sand berms of the compound "walls." We contributed the mortar platoon, which took a couple 120 mm mortar tubes with them so they could provide counter-battery capabilities to the outpost. In the middle of the compound, a stack of shipping containers added an Alamo-like look to the little fort.

In a fight, help was usually only about fifteen minutes away, but Udhaim was a different story. The nearest help was an hour away. An hour on a battlefield is more than a few lifetimes.

Smoothly, the platoon mounted up and headed to the gate. A short stop to charge weapons, turn on Warlocks, and give a last once-over, and we were out the gate.

"Steel X-Ray, White Four; SP. Over." Game time and game faces. Up the highway to Khalis we went, bracing for a possible IED blast on the east leg of the Iron Triangle.

"Steel X-Ray, White Four; checkpoint two-five-one, north on Cheyenne. Over." We left the Iron Triangle and headed north.

The drive to Udhaim was remarkable. As soon as we departed the north side of Khalis, the lush, irrigated farmland was replaced by open desert. A slight climb announced our departure from the historic floodplain, and scattered scrub brush and random goat herds were all that survived. This was the desert Iraq most people envisioned.

"Steel X-Ray, White Four; checkpoint two-five-niner, charlie mike. Over." About halfway to Udhaim, we passed Camp Ashraf, established by Saddam to house the Iranians who fought for Iraq during the 1980s Iran–Iraq war. The poor people could not return to Iran, where they would have been executed, but Iraq didn't trust them either. Now the people lived in a compound similar in nature to something from the World War Two Holocaust, but without the systematic murder. One of the biggest contrasts between the camp and the neighborhoods near it was the tidiness of the residents. Ashraf could have passed for a community in Arizona. From the highway, all we could see was the chain link fence, though. We sped north.

"Steel X-Ray, White Four; RP. Over." Finally, the berms of Udhaim's compound appeared on the left side of the highway, and to the delight of our stiff legs, we pulled in the gate. Despite only needing about ten seconds to accomplish our mission, we stayed at Udhaim for a bit. The mortarmen gave us a tour and showed us on a map where the latest attacks had come from.

As tankers, we had the intrinsic need to climb around the Iraqi T-55 tanks. The T-55 was about the oldest tank still serving in the world. The Soviets had fielded it in the early 1950s, and yet it was still a workhorse of many armies. While its armor and 100 mm cannon were completely inadequate for a clash of tanks, it was more than up to the task of fighting enemy infantry. In fact, when the Soviets invaded Afghanistan, they replaced their modern tanks with T-55s after about the first year. While the T-55 had the same-size crew, it was significantly more cramped than our M1A2 Abrams. I'm not very big, but I did not fit comfortably inside the turret or driver's compartment of the T-55.

We left Udhaim as the shadows grew longer. It had been a fun adventure, but my stomach was hungry. The danger of having a good dining facility is that sometimes the stomach makes decisions instead of the brain. The whole platoon was anxious to get back to Warhorse before dinner was over. As a result, we turned the A/C off to gain a few more horsepower and mashed the gas pedal to the floor. Speed never offers protection from IEDs or ambush, but we gambled anyway. The trip ended without incident.

The enemy was not the only danger we faced on patrol. Despite being very technologically advanced, we still at times had difficulties overcoming the environment. At night, we maximized our technological advantages, driving with our lights off and using night-vision goggles. The danger arose when there was a new moon and overcast obscured the starlight. When the illumination dropped to zero, even with night vision it could be very hard to see much.

On a particularly dark night, we were returning from another fruitless hunt for the car-bomb factory in the projects of northern Khalis. We opted to take a different route home to avoid ambush. Instead of taking the main highway, we headed east into the farmland.

A back road along a major canal led back south and connected with the highway just north of FOB Warhorse. Our plan was take this rarely used road to bypass the city and IED hot spot just south of it. The problem was that a large cell phone tower was at the intersection, and as we drove towards it, the lights on the tower washed out our night vision. It was too dark for us to even see the edge of the road through the washout. With a canal inches away, we opted to walk along in front of the Humvee to guide it and not be in it should it experience a rollover into the drink. It was one of the most stressful drives of the deployment for me.

Lady Luck must have had a crush on me. In a place that was busy trying to kill me and my fellow soldiers, Lady Luck was needed sometimes. You did all you could, but sometimes you were dealt a hand of twos and threes.

One day we went to a meeting with the local leaders in Mansuriyah. The town populace was the most pro-US in our sector, but support was not unanimous, and we still needed to keep our guard up.

My heart sank when we arrived for the meeting at a local tea shop and found we were the last to arrive. The elders had already taken all of the seats against the wall, leaving us seats facing them. This meant we would be sitting with our backs to the street and the massive crowd that had gathered. My time in Kosovo had already cemented the fear of sitting with my back to people. Now I was stuck, and you did not ask an elder to change seats. It was very uncouth.

With our back to the crowd, we had to weigh risks. The crowd was large enough we all felt a direct-fire attack from the enemy was unlikely, but an assassin hiding in close was more likely. For the meeting, we pulled soldiers from the outer perimeter and placed them on guard right behind our chairs. The decision proved to be fortuitous. After the meeting, Staff Sergeant Arleth showed me a knife he removed from a man who pushed his way through the crowd to right behind me. Sergeant Arleth's actions had been smooth and professional, and nobody noticed him disarming and arranging for the man to be escorted out.

BLOOD AND DARTS

IN EARLY SEPTEMBER, WE ADDED another route to our Iron Triangle patrols. Route Vanessa south through Baqubah was becoming a major concern. One of the battalion staff's soldiers had been killed on this road just north of the university. Patrolling the new extension was more dangerous than the rest of the Iron Triangle, requiring us to drive down to the university and then return back up the same highway. The likelihood of hitting an IED designed for a tank was much higher.

On September 15, 2006, I hit one of those larger IEDs—a stack of 155 mm or 152 mm rounds. The plan was probably just to create a large enough blast to affect a tank. However, the rounds did not explode at the same time. The bottom one went first, and one round exploded up in the air. Shrapnel came in through the hatch, some forced through the turret ring of the tank. I took hits from the groin up. Fortunately, my body armor stopped the most dangerous pieces.

I don't remember the blast, but I remember sitting down in the tank and staring at a piece of shrapnel sticking out of my right forearm. Despite my training and common sense, I tugged the jagged metal shard out of my arm. The thing was about an inch long and half an inch in diameter. I didn't feel a thing. There was no pain, just a numb, dazed feeling. I had been knocked senseless.

At the aid station, they stripped me of my Nomex coveralls. Despite having no other holes in my Nomex coveralls, I had taken more shrapnel than I thought. Little bitty puncture wounds dotted my right shoulder. Surprisingly, there was not much blood. The shrapnel had been hot enough to cauterize the flesh. My groin protector had slowed a piece down enough that it was just hanging from the fabric. Without the groin protector, it probably would have ended my manhood or cut into the thigh towards the femoral artery.

A few minutes after my arrival, the battalion commander—Colonel Fisher—and Sergeant Major Rimpley arrived. They told me to hang in there, and Colonel Fisher pinned a Purple Heart on my T-shirt. Shortly, he was joined by Colonel Jones, the brigade commander, along with Sergeant Major Dave List. They said something to me, but I don't remember what it was.

In reality, the shrapnel wounds were not that significant—as a movie would have said, "just a flesh wound." Other than a quick cleaning and a bandage, the wounds required little medical treatment. The concussion of the blast was another story. I was already vulnerable to head injuries as had I suffered many concussions in boxing, hockey, and football earlier in my life, and unfortunately, the head injury required me to get further evaluation. My balance was disrupted and I was puking. Before I knew it, I was on a medevac helicopter to Balad. At the Air Force combat hospital, I was evaluated and then slated for evacuation to Landstuhl Hospital in Germany. I felt like a loser.

In the Balad hospital ward, a large tent with several litters in it, other wounded soldiers and I decided to make the best of the situation and visit the PX on Balad. None of us knew where it was but figured we could find it. We just needed to sneak out of the hospital tent and walk around until we found it. We knew we had a few hours before they took us to the airstrip and loaded us on a C-17 medevac airplane. Without testing the plan against common sense, we were out the door.

We were a motley crew of four. As we all had been evacuated to the hospital by helicopter, we were each missing at least one thing from our uniforms. I somehow was missing my hat, even though I had been given a chance to pack a few things to bring with me before flying. Everyone in our group was missing a hat. One of the guys was on crutches and missing his pants and boots, his leg heavily bandaged. Another was in a sling and missing his uniform jacket. The other had no shirt at all and a head bandage to top it off.

I really have no idea how far from the hospital we got, but we never made it to the PX. We ran into a sergeant major who must have been stationed at Balad for the deployment.

"Soldiers, where are your covers?" A cover is the official term for a hat or helmet, something to cover the head, a required piece of the uniform. *Really?! That is the missing uniform item you are going to fixate on? Not the pants?*

"Uh, somewhere on Route Tampa?" the soldiers on crutches replied. He had been flown from the ambush site directly to Balad. We all had stupid grins common to little kids caught with their fists in a cookie jar.

The encounter ended our little foray. The sergeant major escorted us back to the hospital, which we probably would not have been able to find either. Once back, we ended up with a medical orderly who guarded us to make sure we didn't wander off again and thus miss our flight.

At some point while waiting for the flight, I found a computer and sent an email to Pat to see if he would come to the hospital and visit me. But email is not very quick. Not everyone had access to the internet all the time; soldiers needed to find a computer that was connected and wait their turn to check the email. Additionally, making a trip to a recreation facility that had internet took effort and had to be done in between duties, and usually computers had a thirty-minute time limit for use. In any case, Pat was back home on his mid-tour leave but emailed his roommate to come find me and get an update. Before Cooper came by, I was long gone.

Before we went out to the airplane, we all had to go through a metal detector, and an officer sat down with each and every one of us, asking if we were going to be okay and making sure that we weren't going to hijack the plane. I was insulted and incredulous. *Really, someone on a gurney worries you? Or a guy who can't stand without falling when you turn out the lights?* Later, I asked about this and found out it is the legacy of some guy hijacking a medevac plan back in Vietnam.

A C-17 medevac airplane is a cargo airplane that has been converted into a flying ICU. It is set up to keep critically injured soldiers alive for the long flights from a war zone to established hospitals. A few hours after leaving Balad, we touched down at Ramstein Air Base in Germany. Across the valley and a short drive away was Landstuhl, the primary destination for all medevac flights out of Iraq. The hospital was built to support the large formations of soldiers stationed in Germany during the Cold War. Now it was the first stop for soldiers injured in battle or sick.

The good news was that I was not critically wounded, and thus I was considered an outpatient. At least I did not have to stay in the hospital. To handle the large number of soldiers in outpatient status at Landstuhl, the Army had pressed some barracks into service to house us. Germany had little US Army installations scattered all over, most being fairly small. The installation we were housed at was no exception. In my injured state, I had no idea where the place was and probably would have been unable to find it on a map. But I was still able to read, and I shot an email off to my cousin who was stationed in Vilseck, Germany. Before long, my cousin Andy arrived and spent some time hanging out with me. I'm glad he did because I felt terrible. Getting wounded is not glorious. It is not fun. I was in pain and felt like a complete loser. I was not with my brothers-in-arms, and I did not have any serious visible wounds to "justify" it.

I don't remember much about Landstuhl. I don't remember the appointments or where we ate meals. I'm sure there was a dining facility or something. I remember constantly feeling like an outcast. I was separated from everyone I knew and felt like I was not wounded badly enough to warrant the time away from the company.

After nearly three weeks at Landstuhl and a short visit to Pat, I boarded a CH-47 Chinook in the darkness for the flight to Warhorse. My return to the company at FOB Warhorse in mid-October was far from triumphant. I was about as worthless to the company as a soldier could be. I could not leave the wire on patrols with them. I could not even walk around the FOB when the threat level required helmet and body armor. That meant that on Thursdays and any other random time the enemy lobbed artillery at us, I was not even allowed to leave whatever building I was in. I became a prisoner of house arrest at those times of elevated uniform posture.

What I could do was throw darts in the command post. Twelve hours a day, that is just what I did, though I never really became skilled at it. I spent my time in the command post with the two soldiers assigned to the shift. The command post was responsible for tracking the company's patrols as they ventured around the battlefield. Additionally, we would track and plot reported enemy activity. When a patrol was getting ready to depart on a mission, we updated the patrol leader on the situation on the battlefield. There were many other things tracked and other housekeeping activities, but the two soldiers were more than capable of handling the entire job. I was not needed. So I learned from them.

Staff Sergeant Watts was the sergeant in charge of the command post. He was a field artillery forward observer assigned to the company. The forwards observers, the company "FIST" team, were some of the only non-tank-related soldiers in the company. We had a great team of FISTers. They were characters, but they were also competent. The officer of the team was a former West Point roommate of mine, Silky Cho. The commander used him as the company intelligence officer, and Silky was out on patrol with the commander constantly. Captain Looney was not a lead-from-behind type. The company headquarters section was out and about daily. The other shift of the command post was led by another non-tanker in the company, Sergeant Larrea. He was the company chemical specialist. Despite the lack of chemical warfare risk, he made himself extremely useful as a leader in headquarters and through his administrative talents.

The company command post was located at the northeastern corner of the FOB, nearly a kilometer away from the company's billets in the middle. It was a plywood building common to most Army deployed facilities, built on a standard, tried-and-true set of blueprints. A row of identical buildings were occupied by the battalion's combat trains command post—the home of the battalion's personnel and supply offices—and two other company command posts. The rest of the battalion headquarters were at the far end of the FOB.

Next to our row of plywood buildings was an artillery platoon of M109 Paladins. The Paladins were self-propelled, armored 155 mm artillery pieces. Watching them fire was always fun. It wasn't as cool as the tank because you never got to see the artillery round land on its faraway target. Still, the big guns inspired a bit of awe. In darkness, the muzzle blast would light up the night, and the red-hot projectile would fly away into the distance. The blast from the gun shook the buildings and knocked the dust out of the seams. Often the rounds traveled so far away before landing that we would not hear the impact explosion. At night, the Paladins sent parachute flares out in support of Iraqi units, who did not have night-vision equipment and needed flares to light up the night when the enemy was on the prowl. Watching the flares lazily float downward in the distance was mesmerizing.

Before the artillerymen sent a fire mission downrange, the battalion would "clear the fires." This meant the artillery would give us the coordinates they were planning on shooting. We would then check to make sure nobody was patrolling too close to the spot. Each company command post would let battalion headquarters know we were clear of the area. We did this even for the parachute flares. When those were fired downrange, the heavy canister would still eventually drop to the ground, and it could seriously hurt someone if it landed on them. Also, we didn't want to bathe in brilliant light a patrol of our own trying to hide in darkness.

One dark evening while I was sitting in the company command post, Captain Looney came in and told me to join him on the back steps of the building. I stepped out into the darkness and watched as he lit a cigarette. The glow of the lighter lit up his face. There was a long pause as he stared at me and took a few drags on the cigarette.

"Do you blog?" Captain Looney asked. I had never heard of the term and had no idea what it meant.

"No, sir," I replied, wondering where this was going. Captain Looney stared at me in the darkness and paused.

"Your wounds are pretty minor really. Yes, I put you in for a Purple Heart, but I don't want you talking about getting wounded. You see, it's your fault that you got hit. I talked to your crew. They told me you were up, out of the hatch, and that is why you took shrapnel."

Shocked and growing angry, I instinctively came to the position of attention, my heels together and feet at an angle. I pressed my fists to the sides of my legs, trembling. Biting my lip to keep from saying something, I quietly listened. *I know to not argue, but how does your theory account for shrapnel at groin level? Surely you don't mean you think I was completely out of the hatch?*

"So your injury is your fault. I do not want to you talking about it to anyone. Is that clear?" Captain Looney stared at me, taking another drag on his cigarette.

"Yes, sir. By your leave?" I saluted and did an about-face before he even responded, trying to leave before Captain Looney noticed I was now struggling to choke back tears.

I was incredulous. Surely this was some massive miscommunication. Perhaps my head injury was clouding my ability to understand what he was really saying. I already felt miserable about the whole deal, and this talk further dejected me. As I walked away, I stayed in the shadows to hide the tears in my eyes.

I obeyed him, though. I became a recluse and kept my thoughts to myself for the rest of the deployment. In the two more years I served with Captain Looney, I never once revisited the discussion to find out if that is what he really meant. I didn't want to know. Over the years, I concluded Captain Looney was probably trying to avoid damaging the feeling of invincibility that the young soldiers have. Given the clouding effects of the brain injury, I probably did not quite understand him right anyway.

On another night, I was in the command post well after midnight. None of our platoons were patrolling, so we listened to the battalion radio and chatted about life in general. At close to 2 a.m., an F-16 flying a reconnaissance mission over our area found some men digging a hole in the middle of nowhere. As the pilot reported it to battalion headquarters, I instinctively knew the men were insurgents digging up a cache of buried weapons or ammunition.

The pilot wanted permission to drop a bomb on them. The battalion executive officer was in the headquarters and denied permission. They could be farmers, was his reasoning. *Really? Farmers digging a random hole in the middle of night, well after curfew? In a land where often the women have to do the hard labor?!* My farming background was not sufficient to argue with the major successfully, so I shook my head at the ceiling and never touched the radio mic. The bomb was not dropped, and the insurgents and their cache lived to fight us another day.

One of my jobs in the command post was to run a buffer between Battalion's requests for information and Captain Looney. One day, Captain Looney decided the black-market fuel stands along the Iron Triangle were financing the insurgency. He decided to put them out of business and cut off a source of funding. Of course, the official gas stations were all shuttered, so it would also mean eliminating the only source of fuel in the area. As Captain Looney led a patrol to pour out the black-market gas cans and light them on fire, columns of smoke rose in the distance, visible at FOB Warhorse. Before long, Battalion became curious, and I had to try to explain to them what Captain Looney was doing while he was busing making friends, one gas can at a time.

Some of the cyclic administrative tasks fell to me during this period of uselessness. Part of the Army's property-accountability program was a monthly counting of items. Since I had nothing better to do, I helped with the inventory, verifying every piece of property on the property books. We had our "organic" property, the stuff we brought from Fort Carson. We had our "TPE, or Theater Provided Equipment" that we inherited when in Iraq. We also had our "installation" property. This included the CHUs we lived in, the air conditioners, and other household-type property. All told, it was a lot of stuff to find and verify. One by one, each platoon linked up with me with all their assigned equipment, and I found the property on the paperwork and checked it off as the soldiers read it to me.

As I neared the end of my inventory, there was something big missing: an entire HEMTT truck. A HEMTT is an eight-wheeled, four-axle beast of a truck. They are huge—and we were missing one. You would think it wouldn't be that hard to find a massive truck on a base that only measured a couple square miles. I told Captain Looney about my problem. The company's leaders collectively scratched their heads trying to remember the last time the truck was used. We didn't take it on patrols, after all. Eventually, someone remembered loaning it to a small detachment to carry supplies to the Iraqi Army post just down the highway. A check of that post's parking lot turned up successful, and the truck was returned.

Not only were some things hard to find, but we also had items that didn't show up on the books. I would write down the serial numbers for the things we physically had but didn't have on paper. In particular interest to me was a shotgun and a fifty-caliber machine gun. I took the information to the supply sergeant, who then tracked down the assigned owners of the weapons. Both had been deleted from the system as lost by their units. Now we had the "lost weapons." A few forms later, and we had them back on the books of the Army inventory.

A few evenings after I completed the inventory, I was back at the company command post, looking over my latest administrative pile of work. This time I was investigating the loss of property resulting from a Humvee in the engineer company catching fire. I went through the sworn statements and my notes from the interviews of the crew members while I waited for a section from Red Platoon to finish their patrol on the Iron Triangle. They were on the home stretch, coming up the highway in front of the FOB, so I started packing up my stuff to get dinner.

"Steel X-Ray! Red Four! We just took friendly fire from a convoy and are diverting to the main gate." *What the . . . ?!?!?!?* Before I could even say a word or jump to my feet Sergeant Larrea was already working the radios.

"Steel X-Ray, casualties?"

"Negative!" The anger was evident in his voice.

"Sergeant, get six and seven and I'll pass it up to Battalion!" I was already across the room to the radio stack. We now had three very excited radio conversations going. On the Icom handheld walkie-talkies, Larrea reported the issue to Captain Looney and First Sergeant Gonzalez while the company net was still busy with Red's account of what happened. I added to the racket when I told Battalion. A lot of anthills were kicked over, and soon Humvee after Humvee went screaming down the road as leaders rushed to defuse the brewing fist fight at the gate, speed limit be damned.

Finally, everyone separated and a weary but angry-looking First Sergeant Gonzales stomped into the command post. He sat down, shaking his head. Then he relayed what he had learned. A convoy was arriving at the gate, and one of their security vehicles had taken a position to block the highway south of the gate. It saw the headlights of Red Platoon's two tanks and did not recognize them as a friendly vehicle. Apparently the crew couldn't see the outline of the tank and flashed a green laser at it. Red Platoon did not see the laser dot on the front of the turret and didn't react because they were looking at the world using the thermal viewers. The lack of a reaction cause the security vehicle's gunner to open fire with his fifty caliber. Fortunately, the crew was down and nobody got hurt and the tank shrugged off the bullets with barely chipped paint. The same could not be said for a few faces and fists, though, inside the gate.

I wondered how I would have reacted to that. *But also, how can you mistake a tank for anything? It's like having a house coming down the road at you!*

As October came to an end, we began the exciting process of packing up to go home. The end was near, and each task related to ending our deployment was worth it. Equipment needed to be counted, much of which was accounted for by individual serial numbers. There were bags to pack and CHUs to clean out. Soon, we sent a couple soldiers home to assist with our reception back at Fort Carson. Morale went up. When the first of the soldiers belonging to the unit that would take our place in Diyala arrived, morale soared.

October also brought the beginning of the rainy season. At first, it was pleasant relief from the heat and dust. As the rain continued into the morning, FOB Warhorse slowly became a quagmire of thick, slippery, gooey mud. It was difficult to walk in and would also stick to your uniform when you fell. By afternoon, large puddles were forming throughout the FOB. After a few days, the rain stopped, and the sun baked the top and a sandstorm dumped more moondust, creating bizarre dusty, muddy roads.

October 2006 saw a significant change in the Iraq War. After more than a year of escalating violence within the country, it was clear our strategy was not winning and actually barely keeping a status quo. President Bush ordered the "surge" to begin that fall. The number of US combat units in Iraq went up drastically. Deploying units would stay for fifteen months instead of twelve in order to keep more soldiers in Iraq. Baghdad was the first area to see the massive increase in US forces. While this was good for Baghdad, it was bad for Diyala at first. The US pressure in Baghdad created an environment too hot and dangerous for large insurgent forces to remain. As a result, many enemy forces departed Baghdad and flowed north into Diyala. Before long, the enemy in Diyala was powerful enough to feel aggressive.

To counter the influx of enemy forces coming out of Baghdad, the battalion created an outpost in Khan Bani Saad. Destroyer Company moved down there along with a portion of the battalion command post. The battalion radio net came alive with reports of violence in Khan Bani Saad. As we continued to prepare for our departure, the neighborhoods of Baqubah became more violent.

Additional reinforcements arrived. A light cavalry troop from the 82nd Airborne Division joined our battalion. One of the platoon leaders was a friend of mine from West Point, John Ryan Dennison. I had been a plebe in his company at West Point and went to church with Ryan. It was good to see him and a great reminder of how the bonds forged at West Point and in the Army never broke. Ryan was still the great positive influence I remembered him as. Sadly, four days after I returned to Fort Carson, Ryan was killed in Diyala by the enemy.

One chilly night in late October, the battalion's engineer company got in a large firefight in the neighborhood of Tahrir. Tahrir was on the east side of the Diyala River and had become a dangerous place for any human. As the battalion radio squawked the play-by-play, it became clear the fight was larger than normal. Soon the battalion forward command post on the edge of Tahrir was involved in the fight. With that, Colonel Fisher decided some tanks would change the tone of the fight and directed us to send a section of two tanks to aid the Humvee-mounted units in Tahrir.

In the company command post, I sat in a metal folding chair and listened to my platoon sergeant's section depart the FOB. Sergeant Rinder's tank made it all the way to Tahrir before the enemy sprang an ambush. Shortly after crossing the river, Sergeant Rinder's tank was hit by a massive IED. The blast put a huge hole in the pavement and broke the left track. Immobile, Sergeant Rinder's tank would not be able to take the fight to the enemy attacking the engineers. Instead, the enemy brought the fight to Sergeant Rinder. As the RPGs and machine-gun fire sought out his tank in the darkness, he lit up the night with cannon fire, following it with more machine-gun fire. His wingman joined the fight, protecting his rear and flank. Before long, the enemy gave up and left the tanks in charge of the cratered battlefield.

After a long mission to recover the tank, along with all of the pieces knocked off, we were tired. Ironically, we were supposed to empty the tank out within the week and load it onto a truck to turn it in for the end of the deployment. When the sun came up, we surveyed the tank. The large IED had blown the left track apart, ripping huge holes in the metal and rubber. The road wheels were heavily damaged from the blast. In the process of dragging it home, some of the damaged wheels didn't turn and were as a result ground down by the friction of asphalt. The metal decking on top of the track had huge holes ripped in it. Amazingly, the hull was not pierced into the crew compartment. It was dinged up, but nothing had given it a direct hit. The M1A2 Abrams was not invincible, but it was a tough beast. Under the power of a strong winch, Sergeant Rinder's tank was loaded up on a trailer, and we never saw it again.

Around this time, C Company's executive officer (XO) departed to return to Fort Carson to prepare our return. Since I was still unable to patrol, I inherited his duties for the company. This included going to meetings with the battalion staff and other company XO. The battalion XO, Major DiGiambattista, intimidated me more than any other officer. He had very little patience with us and would not tolerate mistakes or failures of any kind. I dreaded the meetings, but sometimes the staff provided a reason to smile. During one meeting, the battalion intelligence officer pointed out that there tended to be more IEDs during the full moon. Another staff officer quipped, "Yeah, because werewolves plant them." Even Major DiGiambattista laughed.

Our equipment was steadily getting put on trucks and transported to Balad Air Base, the major logistical hub in the area. This sent large convoys up the Iron Triangle and down the narrow road to the Tigris River pontoon bridge nightly when there had been significantly fewer convoys in previous months. It was a recipe for trouble.

October 2006 also saw the arrival of a new danger. Previously, IEDs had been made primarily from artillery rounds left over from Saddam's regime. Saddam had one of the largest stockpiles of artillery rounds in the world, and since he did not let his soldiers fire them often during training, there were plenty left for war. The rounds made for nasty IEDs, but they were not specifically designed to penetrate armor.

A new IED arrived in October. The new bombs were a reflection of the enemy learning and, at the same time, running out of artillery rounds. The new bombs were made out of copper or steel cones, backed by plastic explosives. These did not send nasty shrapnel in all directions like before. Instead, the explosives turned the metal cone into a super-fast jet of molten copper or steel, capable of penetrating thick armor even at a distance.

The explosively formed penetrators were not a new concept. Warheads using this concept had been widespread since World War Two. Land mines built around these warheads were developed decades ago. Now the Iraqi insurgents turned to the penetrators to counter our armored vehicles. When one of these penetrator IEDs hit an armored vehicle, it would pierce the armor and send spall fragments into the crew inside. They were lethal beyond anything we'd encountered thus far on the roadside.

The battalion scout platoon was the first in our brigade to find one. Part of the platoon accompanied a patrol from Blackhawk Company as it made the trek to Balad. They traveled up the Iron Triangle without incident. We were still spending a lot of effort patrolling it. At Khalis, the patrol turned west towards As Sindi's pontoon bridge. West of the town of Jadidah, the narrow road made a sharp series of turns as it crossed a canal. As the patrol entered this natural chicane, it slowed. A vicious blast announced the presence of the roadside bomb amid the tall grass at the edge of the pavement. When the dust settled, three young scouts were dead, the penetrator killing the entire crew of their Humvee.

The loss of three soldiers so close to the end of deployment was heartbreaking. The sudden change in IED lethality was a major shock. Nobody wanted to get killed or hurt trying to leave Diyala. While the intelligence section worked to identify the enemy team responsible for the IED, we changed our efforts, focusing on improving overwatch on the narrow road. The most drastic reaction to the IED was what I personally called Operation Slash and Burn. The company escorted several fuel tankers to the narrow road. As the large tanker trucks slowly rumbled down the road, a soldier sprayed fuel on the grass next to the road. Behind them, another systematically lit everything on fire. Massive black-and-white plumes of smoke marked the patrol's progress on the horizon as it burned the borrow ditches along two miles of road. As dusk settled, only ash lined the road, and the enemy would not be able to hide their new penetrating IEDs there. Fortunately, the enemy did not yet know just how far away they were effective from.

The battalion quickly gained intelligence that the culprits of the IED strike were staying in a house near the site. The house had good fields of fire towards the only road approaching it. Any attempt to attack by vehicle would be without the element of surprise. There was a farm field on the other side, and we opted for an air-assault raid to capture or kill the enemy sapper team. We started planning. During this planning period, the leaders of the company that would replace us arrived to begin learning the area.

The day before the operation, the pilots who would fly the Black Hawks flew to Warhorse. My contribution to the operation was picking them up and driving them from the landing zone to the command post for the operations briefing. The incoming company commander from the 1st Cavalry Division was obviously impressed as Captain Looney laid out the plan. Captain Looney had thoroughly planned the operation, complete with fine-tuned timing and well-considered contingencies. The Black Hawks would touch down in the field just before the Humvees in the ground column turned off the highway. Once actions on the objective were complete, everyone would leave by Humvee.

That night, the raid went off perfectly. The timing was impeccable and the assault smooth. All three enemy fighters were captured alive. When the guys returned, they were flush with excitement and gave me the blow by blow, including the arrival of Colonel Fisher shortly after the house was secured. True to reputation, he arrived with a cigar in one hand and a coffee cup in the other. I began to understand why the men called the Colonel the "Big Fish."

As October turned to November, the 1st Cavalry Division unit replacing us took over control of the battlefield and the FOB. We moved out of the bunkered-in CHUs and into our temporary home in the large gym. Like the dining facility, the gym was a large, unprotected building with a white roof. Inside the gym, we set up rows and rows of cots. We would live there until it was our turn to ride a helicopter to Balad. Despite turning over control of things, we were still busy. Tasks related to packing out equipment and preparing to depart kept us fairly busy. When we weren't busy, nobody wanted to just lounge on a cot right next to the next one.

Within a day, it was obvious a new unit was running the show. The new brigade decided our blacked-out FOB was not very safe. We had very tall towers reaching into a sky full of helicopters coming to land. Just in time for Thursday Night Fires, the aviation safety beacon lights were turned on. These towers were set up between the brigade headquarters on the west, the dining facility on the east, and the gym on the north. When the weekly dose of artillery fire flew in, I was not surprised that all of the rounds landed right in the vicinity of the three most important buildings on the FOB. One of the mortar rounds hit a porta potty outside the gym. Our impatience to leave and go home only got worse now that the enemy had our position dialed in.

Finally, our night to fly away came. Just north of the gym was a large landing zone the CH-47 Chinook helicopters used, and luckily the distance from the gym was short. While I had been in Landstuhl, the company had loaded unneeded personal equipment into a shipping container and sent it home early. Because I wasn't around for that and nobody thought to pack anything up for me, I missed the opportunity. As a result, I had more than double what everyone else had. The bean counters in the Army would make you pay for anything you left behind, so I had to drag everything home. As I staggered to the Chinook in my body armor and helmet I wasn't supposed to be wearing, I had my large rucksack on my back. A duffle bag rode on top of that. My smaller pack was strapped to my chest. My rifle dangled on its sling. Both hands carried another heavy duffle bag. I probably had more than 200 pounds of stuff to carry.

Not a second too soon, the Chinooks lifted off in the darkness. *Popping smoke, yeah baby!* A huge sense of relief overcame me as we soared over the Iron Triangle, crossed the Tigris, and settled down at Balad Air Base. At Balad, we would spend some more time hurrying up and waiting. Often, it could be a week before getting a flight to Kuwait.

The time was not wasted for me. Pat was back from his mid-tour leave, and spending my time with him was poignant. One night after dinner, Pat and I were walking back from the dining facility to his company's compound on the west edge. We were both shivering with cold but too proud to admit that we were freezing. We were in Iraq; how could we be cold? As we walked into his compound, we noticed the puddles had iced over. Apparently it really was cold, and we laughed. I spent nearly the entire week with Pat when he was not on patrols.

From Balad, a C-130 carried us to Kuwait. The flight south was not nearly as painful as the C-130 that carried me north months ago. The joy of heading home made discomforts bearable. The sun was coming up in Kuwait as we piled our bags and headed to get breakfast. We would not be there long enough to need billets. After eating, we formed up to go through customs. Navy personnel trained by US Customs and Immigration dumped our bags out and rifled through everything. The sailor going through my stuff even unrolled my socks.

"Dude, seriously?" I asked. It had taken so much time and effort to get all of this stuff to fit.

"Sorry, sir, but yesterday we found a frag grenade, so, yeah." The sailor shrugged and continued. Finally, I got to stuff all my things back into their bags and add them to the pile of checked luggage. Impatiently, we milled around in the secured area for our flight's boarding time.

"Everyone with a Purple Heart come to the front corner now!" a sergeant yelled over the din of excited voices. *Great, probably another screening to make sure we don't freak out on the plane or something.* I went to the front warily along with several others.

"If you got a Purple Heart, you get to sit in first class," the sergeant announced to the small gathering. I looked at the brigade commander and several other staff officers sitting nearby. *Sit with them? Thanks, but no. I'll stay with my guys.* I turned and started to leave.

"What did you get your Purple Heart for? That chipped front tooth?" the first sergeant from another company sneered, looking at me obvious disdain. Clearly he noticed my dental work and couldn't notice anything else since I was in full uniform, complete with hat and gloves.

"Very funny, First Sergeant," I replied as I walked past him. *I knew it. Getting a minor wound makes you a pariah.*

We climbed aboard a charter jet that would carry us back to Colorado Springs and Fort Carson. I moved as far back on the airplane as I could get. The sun was just setting over Pikes Peak when we touched down. The slap of crisp air welcomed us home as we climbed down the stairs to the tarmac and shook hands with the welcoming committee. A bus ride and a couple hours of putting equipment away kept our anticipation on edge. All we wanted was to see our families, go home, eat a good meal, and sleep in our own safe beds.

We formed up outside the Fort Carson special events gymnasium and listened to the sounds of thousands of excited and joyful people inside. The doors opened, the crowd hushed, artificial fog rolled into the air, and Toby Keith's "Courtesy of the Red, White and Blue" broke the silence. As we marched in through the doors, the crowd went wild. Someone gave an appropriately short welcome-home speech, and the command to fall out unleashed us to our families. Appropriately, it was November 11, Veterans Day.

The little things in life make the biggest difference. I took an hour-long shower simply because I could. There was nobody in line and hot water aplenty. My sister, Kate, and cousins Jessie and Carrie had a big bowl of chili waiting for me. A cold beer topped off the perfection of home. A four-day pass gave me the opportunity to unwind and settle into my own home.

    I think the nearly two months of not patrolling helped avoid some of the jumpiness that most combat veterans experience upon returning home. I did not enjoy crowds and avoided them. The only time I experienced a flashback was driving home and seeing a car hit a box in the road. The box must have had a bunch of construction dust in it because a poof of dust exploded up. I freaked and stopped my car in the middle of the busy street until I remembered it was okay; I wasn't in Iraq.

INTERMISSION

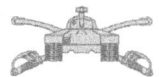

BEFORE WE STEPPED OFF THE plane on Veterans Day, we already knew we were heading back to Iraq in the coming summer. After spending a year in Iraq, we would have less than eight months to regroup, rebuild teams, and train for a fifteen-month deployment. We didn't complain about the fairness, or complain that it wasn't long enough to prepare; we just buckled down and got to business.

I was returned to full duty in early January 2007. AJ moved from White Platoon to become the executive officer of the support company. I did not envy him at all. Blue Platoon's leader, Lieutenant Brown, became the executive officer of the battalion headquarters company. Red Platoon's leader, Lieutenant Fogerty, departed the battalion. The company executive officer, Captain Twilley, went to battalion staff. Lieutenant Zackary Nesary took his place. By January, the soldiers and sergeants in the platoons experienced nearly as much turnover.

I was assigned to Blue Platoon. My platoon sergeant would be Sergeant First Class Ron Winning. He was very experienced, crusty sergeant and a pragmatic leader. I was happy with the assignment. Nearly all of the other sergeants of the platoon departed for other assignments. Only Sergeant Edwin Edwin, my gunner, was staying. Edwin was from Kosrae, Federated States of Micronesia, in the Pacific and was an extremely hard worker.

Many of the soldiers also departed. Specialist Kennedy, who was severely wounded in Baqubah, would not return. Specialist Norman wrecked his motorcycle the day after he returned, crippling himself. He shortly left the platoon and the Army.

Of the soldiers that served on the Baqubah deployment, only "Tex" Kincaid, "Will" Williams, Cody "Soda Pop" Reece, and Cory "Big Red" Bushell remained in the platoon. Tex and Will were best friends and both very resourceful. Soda Pop made up for his size with a double-sized personality. Cory was as loyal a young soldier as you could find. We had a good core, but we needed a lot of rebuilding.

To replace the departing sergeants, Blue Platoon got Sergeant Danny Key from headquarters and the newly promoted Sergeant Mike Elledge. Mike was much wiser than his new rank suggested. In Baqubah, he had been part of Red Platoon. Every time I saw him around the company's compound, he would ask me when I was coming to Red. Mike was the oldest member of the platoon but easily the most physically fit. Danny, too, was wiser and more experienced than his rank. Danny fought in the first Gulf War with Ron before getting out of the Army to make the dye Yellow Number 5 until September 11, 2001.

We promoted Tex and Will to corporal, making them gunners. Unfortunately, it looked like there was no way we would get replacements fast enough to rebuild the team before our summer deployment date. Some of the coming replacements would miss the entire train up and likely be fresh out of basic training. It was less than ideal as the situation in Iraq became increasingly ugly.

The other platoons in the company experienced the same turnover. My West Point classmate Todd Allison joined us to lead Red Platoon. Todd actually ranked me, but I was still considered the senior platoon leader in the company because of combat experience. While I had made the deployment to Baqubah, Todd had been a victim of the Army's often interesting decision-making. The Army decided to convert a combat brigade at Fort Riley into a brigade of training teams for the herculean task of training Iraqi and Afghan units to a level of competency. That meant the brigade needed lots of senior sergeants and experienced officers. New lieutenants were not useful to the brigade. Since the decision was rapidly made, many new lieutenants had already been assigned, arrived, and now needed reassignment. By the time Todd escaped the silliness, he had already been promoted to first lieutenant. I was happy to have Todd join our company. He was a great leader and loved tanks, a perfect match for Team Steel.

A classmate from my Armor Officer Basic Course arrived to the company to lead my old White Platoon. I was admittedly not as excited to see him. His performance at Fort Knox had not impressed me much, and I was worried about my old platoon. The lieutenant came off as arrogant, seeming to refuse to listen to all advice. Fortunately, Sergeant First Class Rinder was still the bastion of White Platoon and could even out the leadership.

The mechanics also had a change in leadership. Sergeant First Class Tony Corona, who had led our mechanics during the deployment, was selected to help run the battalion's rear detachment for our coming deployment. He was replaced in the maintenance section by Staff Sergeant Danny Bowden, who had been with our sister company. Danny was a great fit for us. He was incredibly hardworking and a savvy mechanic. Above all, he cared for his soldiers. In the coming deployment, he became one of the most important players in the company and a great friend.

Our artillery forward observers had only minor leadership changes. The only change was Silky Cho departed and First Lieutenant Clint Rush took his place. Clint was passionate about his job. He was as excited to understand artillery as I was tanks, working hard to help the company out anywhere he could and becoming a great asset as a leader. Clint teamed up well with Sergeant Watts, and the two led the company's forward observers to come out on top of the brigade-wide artillery competition. It was nice to know we had top-notch quality in the team.

In the midst of changing out key players, our equipment, which had taken the slow boat back from Iraq, started to arrive, kicking off one of the most stressful garrison periods for me. When our sensitive-items container arrived, supposedly full of all of our radios, weapons, and such, we had to inventory it as we unpacked it and put the items in the secure storage room at the office. Two more containers full of equipment arrived shortly after. It was a complete debacle. The arms-room sergeant and arms-room officer who had prepared the packing list and supervised the sensitive-item-container loading at Baqubah did a terrible job. The packing list for the other containers were equally poorly done.

We were missing a lot of items that were closely controlled and some items that were considered high risk for pilferage. These were items that prevented anyone from going home until found. Each day we opened and unpacked a container turned into a late night as we searched for missing items. While we counted and counted again, quadruple-checking serial numbers, our supply clerk contacted the unit that replaced us in Baqubah to see if they could find the missing items. Some of the items were found back in Iraq. Some never turned up. Heads would roll. The arms-room sergeant was tried, busted down in rank, and transferred to another company.

To ensure this type of disaster would never happen again, Captain Looney made me the arms-room officer, with the already busy supply clerk as the arms-room "sergeant." Captain Looney made it clear to me that while my platoon would function just fine without me, the arms room would not, and it was to be my primary focus.

It was a good thing I was single because I soon spent every evening at the office until nearly 8, working to get the arms-room situation in hand. The Army does not like to lose things and placed a lot of very strict regulations. The last thing it wants is for a machine gun to walk off and turn up on the streets of America. Not only are the sensitive items accounted for daily, weekly, and monthly, but the paperwork of those inventories are inspected.

When I started, I found we didn't have 99 percent of the *current* paperwork required, much less the historical records of that paperwork that was supposed to go back years. Some of it I could generate, but the historical records were not something I could fix. For every piece of historical record we were missing, I had to type up a memo as to why and then have the commander sign it. A simple "Oops, it's missing" would not suffice. Every time I went to Captain Looney with a stack of memos to sign, he would get angry. Being the messenger sucked.

The amount of paperwork associated with an arms room is amazing. I had to create weapons cards that soldiers would turn in to us in exchange for their weapon when they came to the arms room. When they returned the weapon, they got their card back. You could only put one thing on the card since it was by serial number. Since modern soldiers have a lot of stuff, we had a lot of cards. Every soldier had an M4 rifle. Each rifle had optics, flashlights, and such. Nearly every soldier had night-vision goggles and a pistol. One soldier would get the items assigned to each vehicle. Each tank had one fifty-caliber machine gun, two M240 machine guns, two voice radios, a data radio, a GPS, binoculars, chemical-detection equipment, a muzzle boresight device, and more. It was more than enough to fill a shopping cart. Of course, this is only the equipment that we stored in the arms room for the vehicles and soldiers.

In addition to exchanging cards for weapons, every single item had to be individually signed for by the soldier. When they returned, each item again had to be individually signed for. To speed up the process, we created prefilled ledger forms with the items and serial numbers and the soldier's printed name. When drawing the weapon, all they had to do was sign. We would fill the date en masse on the form.

Of course, another step was required by regulations. Each soldier signed a hand receipt for the items they were taking from the arms room. This was on top of handing a card and signing the massive ledger of items. When the soldier returned the items, we gave them their receipt back, and they would be free and clear. Just like the ledgers, we prepared typed hand receipts that only needed to be signed and dated each time.

Weapons draw before a training exercise was a major event. The first time the company rolled out for training, it was a minor disaster. Our prefilled forms had not been perfected yet, and our system of physically finding the items and handing them out the window was inefficient. Our methods for transporting all of the stuff across the street to the motor pool were slow. Both Captain Looney and First Sergeant Gonzalez grew white hair and wrinkles as we battered ourselves against our own system. Before we were even half done, it became apparent that coming in at 3 a.m. was not early enough for a 6 departure. Now we would have to wait until after the morning physical-training road closures lifted before we could roll. As we refined our systems and practiced with each training event, we became efficient and could get everything out of the arms room in under forty-five minutes.

In addition to getting all of the weapons and other sensitive items to tanks, the soldiers needed to load all of the other needed equipment. Some things like camo netting, lubricants, and tools could be loaded and stored ahead of time. Some things that were bulky and went in the bustle racks would get loaded up as we mustered for the training event. I was always amazed at how much stuff we could cram onto the tanks and still be functional and not an overloaded gypsy wagon. Finally, with everything and everyone loaded up, we would stage the tanks on the road behind the motor pool for our convoy to the training site.

When we were done training and returned from the field, everything needed to get back where it came from after being cleaned. Once everything was back in the arms room, I had to account for everything. Regulations required that a different person of at least staff sergeant rank did the by-serial-number inventory, with soldiers who were not assigned to the arms room reading the numbers off items. After each number was read off the item, the sergeant would find it on the inventory paperwork and check it off. To expedite the process, we organized everything so it would be in order, and assigned the items so they too would be in order of crew when going out the door. When they were done, then I would count items and make sure everything matched up. It was a lot of work. The flag and the sun were both down long before we were able to go home.

To maximize our short time to prepare for the coming deployment, the officers and senior sergeants gathered in Captain Looney's office and thoroughly planned our training. We were to get our new tanks in late January. We expected to spend some time getting them in good shape. February would be focused on individual skills, full of weapons ranges and classes. March would be the battalion's field exercise, pitting platoons against different scenarios. We would then go straight into gunnery, ending with just enough time to pack everything up to head to the National Training Center at Fort Irwin in May for the brigade's pre-deployment certification. We would come back and get all of our equipment fixed up and repacked for Iraq, with a deployment window of July or August.

Captain Looney wanted to make sure that we would be successful in all we did when we deployed. Despite the counterinsurgency focus on partnerships and developing relationships with the populace, Captain Looney understood that we needed to be able to fight and win. We often joked around the company that any monkey could drink tea and listen, but it took a well-trained warrior to win a firefight. Captain Looney knew the best chance to bring us home was to make sure we were dominant when trouble came our way.

Captain Looney's training plan focused on the difficult tasks related to shooting, moving, and communicating under stress and fire. We would not waste our soldiers' time by training them to stand around for long periods of time, watching for trouble. After all, if they could master the difficult things, the easier related subtasks would develop naturally.

In addition to ensuring we would be well trained in combat, we wanted to make sure we had the physical stamina and strength. The trend in Iraq was for companies to live in the neighborhoods in company compounds instead of big FOBs like our last deployment. This meant we would need to patrol on foot. Physical training every morning was geared to this mission requirement. Once a week, we conducted ruck marches, walking several miles with our full combat kit and weapons. Additionally, we would wear our rucksacks, loaded with another twenty to thirty pounds. On the other days of the week, long runs, sprint workouts, and homemade weights kept us sweating for an hour and a half before it was even breakfast time.

Our new tanks were hand-me-downs from the 1st Cavalry Division. The battalion we got our tanks from had just deployed to Iraq. Knowing they would leave them behind, the battalion chose to use their limited available time training and not doing maintenance on the tanks. It showed.

I was very excited to sign for the platoon's tanks. In the motor pool, we laid each tank's tools out on the tarp in front of the tank. One by one, I would call out the tool name, and the crew would find it on the tarp and hold it up for me to see. I marked down what was missing on the paperwork before turning it in to the company supply clerk. We were missing a lot of tools, but across the platoon, we had at least one of every tool we needed to work on the tanks. It would have to do. The supply clerk would order us more tools, and eventually, those tools would arrive.

The mechanical situation was worse than the tools. Every tank was "dead lined." Dead lined meant that it was not mission capable because something important was broken. The tanks' issues ranged from broken laser range finders to broken engines. Captain Looney's C66 tank even had a broken sprocket. All of the tanks needed new tracks. The list of broken parts was so extensive that the entire brigade's annual maintenance budget was not enough to cover it. Furthermore, many of the parts were not readily available anyway. With combat in Iraq demanding parts and taking priority over units training, it would be a long time before we got some of the parts. Sergeant Key's C33 tank did not come off the dead-line report until we got to Kuwait and caught up with the war stocks. We spent nearly every working hour in January and the first week of February scrambling to fix the tanks.

The company's weapons were also in poor shape. Many of the machine guns were so worn out they had to be completely replaced. Most of the rifles needed new barrels. Many of the ACOG rifle sights were broken; some were even leaking their radioactive tritium. The weapons were so battered that I spent more time at the company office working on weapons than out with my platoon working on the tanks.

One of the collective decisions the company made was to increase each soldier's basic combat load of ammunition. The Army prescribed 210 rounds of ammunition in seven magazines to soldiers. One magazine was in the rifle, and three on each side of the belt or vest. When I was in Kosovo, this always felt like enough, but in analysis of fights in Diyala, we wanted to increase the load to 300 rounds in ten magazines. My cousin Andy had shown me how to transform the issued load-bearing vest into a rack-style harness that allowed another magazine pouch in the centerline. Most of the soldiers, including me, bought their own kit as there were many options that were superior to the issued system.

In the meantime, we collected magazines. My goal was not just to get every soldier to ten magazines, but to have a large collection of spares. One day, one of our soldiers found a few hundred "broken" magazines in the scrap-metal bin. We collected all of them, and I went through them to make as many good magazines as possible out of the parts. Soon I had enough to issue every soldier ten magazines and have another forty for each platoon to use as desired. Additionally, nearly every soldier had his own private stash of personally owned magazines. We wanted to be ready for anything during our next trip to the Iraqi sandbox.

As a young leader, I worried my troops would feel slighted that I was not working next to them in the motor pool. In time I realized they knew I was equally busy at the office and that it was the natural lot of an officer. Not once did the men make a comment in my hearing about me slacking or being back at the office to avoid the weather. Besides, any time they were assigned to help in the unventilated arms room, they were sweaty within an hour.

During this very busy period of training, we still had to perform all of the Army's traditional garrison duties. In between training exercises, the men took turns sitting at the company and battalion duty desks; grass needed to be mowed, and someone needed to hand out towels at the gym. As an officer, I got to take my turn as the battalion duty officer about twice a month. During the duty day, the duties was fairly unobtrusive, with the only requirement being to eat at the chow hall and report back on the quality of the food. At night, the burden dramatically increased. Every locked door had to be checked. The motor pool needed inspection to make sure every vehicle was properly put away for the night, tarped, and locked, with drip pans under the engine. Barracks needed to be walked through to check for trouble and maintenance.

In the event of a soldier getting in trouble and arrested, the duty officer had to make sure that the proper chain of command was notified and start the paperwork for the serious incident. In case you actually managed to finish everything and had any chance to rest, the battalion XO wanted a book report completed on whatever book or paper he felt needed reading. In the morning, the duty officer had to report to the battalion XO and submit the report on the night and the book report. Once complete, it was back to the company for physical training and the start of another duty day.

Each platoon was responsible for operating different training ranges for the company. One of the ranges I was responsible for was the company's machine-gun range. Since we knew that we would likely be using Humvees and machine guns to guard an outpost, we needed to train and qualify every soldier in the company to shoot the machine gun without it being part of the tank.

To prepare for the range, my sergeants and I pulled out the manuals for the machine guns and looked at the exercises required.

The Army makes things simple, having already figured out how many bullets it takes for each exercise and what those exercises should be. The only thing left to do was to find a range that had the right targetry.

Of course, ammunition and ranges are hot commodities on a busy Army post where everyone is slated for deployment. Many of the other lieutenants planning ranges had their ammunition requests modified to much lower quantities because they didn't do enough work to justify their amount requested. One of my mentors at West Point taught me how to crack the code and get exactly what I wanted. The trick was to attach a copy of the manual's list of exercises we were doing and the ammunition requirement for each exercise. Then you had to attach a by-name list of soldiers who would be shooting so nobody would question the number you were asking for. I did this for the machine-gun range and received the entire 120,000 rounds of ammunition I requested, more than six times what other lieutenants got for their requests. I wasn't very popular with my peers for a while.

Careful planning was required to make sure the range would flow smoothly and not waste soldiers' time. Time was planned working backward from the finish. We had to calculate how much time was needed to run every soldier through the tasks, to reset the range between groups of soldiers, and to set up. Some tasks needed daylight and some darkness. Certain tasks had to be executed in the correct order. Logistics needed planning. We had to plan for getting the ammunition, food, and transportation. Mounting up on the tanks to go to a rifle range was out of the question. Some ranges could be walked to; most were too far away.

Our machine-gun range itself was entertaining. It was early March, right before the battalion exercise. Fort Carson is very dry and often warm in March. The only mounts we had that were similar to a Humvee were on the tops of our tanks. The company did not have a single gun-truck Humvee, but we knew we would use them when we deployed. With satisfaction, we headed out into the training area in the few tanks we could get running, the first tanks to rumble out onto Fort Carson in more than a year. We were heading to the northernmost tank range. The targets on the range were more difficult than the manual called for, but I was happy with that. If we could hit targets at longer ranges, we could hit targets at closer ranges.

We set up the range and started shooting. The civilian target operator in the range tower with me was ecstatic to have tanks on his range again. It had been too long for him since the last tank visited. Even more exciting for him was the prospect of gunnery, when we would shoot "big bullets" from the main gun instead of just 7.62 mm and fifty-caliber machine guns. The civilian was concerned that we would have problems with fires during gunnery. The large tracer rounds tended to cause fires easily when the grass had been allowed to get thick. Prairie needs to be burned periodically to remain healthy.

The civilian gave me instructions. "If we get a fire today, let it burn." He wanted to allow the overgrown grass to burn some before we called in the report to Range Control.

"Okay, if you say so." When it came to ranges, Range Control civilians ran the show. He used his radio to let his superior know about the fire possibility so the northern range complex crew could assemble a firefighting crew.

Sure enough, as the day got hotter and drier, the wind picked up. As we fired thousands of rounds after thousands of rounds, the inevitable occurred. A small wisp of smoke announced the grass had caught fire.

"Let it go for a couple minutes before you call it in," the civilian reminded me. As I began the process of identifying the exact grid of the fire and its size, a gust of wind came up. Within moments, the fire was off for the races. With flame lengths in excess of four feet, it raced towards a neighboring range on a rapidly growing broad front. A huge plume of gray smoke rose from the fire, high into the air.

"Range 105, Range Control." The central Range Control office was calling us. They probably could see the smoke.

"Do you have a fire?"

Yes, they see the smoke.

"Roger, I'm working the report right now." I was stalling for time for the civilian.

"You need to report those immediately!" They were not impressed. My reply that the fire just started did not seem to impress them either. Oops.

Within a few more minutes, the fire was rapidly closing on the grenade-launcher range just west of us. The military police unit shooting there frantically loaded ammunition and weapons in their vehicles so they could get out of the way. My career flashed before my eyes. Then the wind shifted as the fire reached their firing line. Now the fire was racing east just as fast as it had gone west. Just a mile away were the coal piles for one of the Colorado Springs electrical power plants. My stomach knotted up even more. Fortunately, the fire was stopped before it really caused problems, but not before it burned a lot of ground and got me thoroughly in trouble with Range Control.

With training time and ranges a hot commodity, we needed to maximize everything we did. When we went to the rifle range, we did not just do the standard zero, qualify, and simple exercises. The range our company was able to get for rifle marksmanship was a simple flat range. There were no pop-up targets. The range had foxholes in a line and target stands twenty-five meters away. Most units merely shot at paper targets from the generic firing positions. We took it a step further.

As we prepared for the range, I went on my hands and knees to Range Control to get permission to deviate from the standard use of the range. We wanted move-and-shoot scenarios in addition to our rifle qualification. A civilian from Range Control met me at the range one morning and I walked him through the plan and my risk-mitigation controls. He was appeased by the plan and thought it was a creative use of the simple flat range.

The range day was a cold one with a layer of snow on the ground. After everyone zeroed their rifle and fired their qualification table, we were ready to have fun. The normal qualification involved shooting at pop-up targets at ranges from 50 to 300 meters. When that wasn't an available option, there were paper targets that had silhouettes to scale to match those pop-up targets.

The next sets of exercises were reflexive-firing drills designed to work on rapidly identifying the target and shooting from the standing position. Soldiers engaged the indicated target from all different directions. Included were engagements while walking forward, to the side, and backwards. I wanted my guys trained to return fire while moving instead of doing only one or the other. Additionally, they needed to know when to use different rates of fire. To train this, we placed objects on the range to represent cover instead of undertaking the engagements on an open piece of dirt like most units did. We trained to use rapid rates of fire as we moved to cover and then to slow down and aim more carefully upon reaching cover.

The last exercise we did was designed to push the soldiers even harder, mixing in the need to communicate and work as a team. I had the soldiers begin their engagement, reacting to contact. Then I made my platoon sergeant play the role of a wounded soldier and had the guys treat and evacuate him under fire. While the platoon aid-and-litter team stopped shooting at targets, the rest of the guys had to pick up the slack in fire. The aid-and-litter team dragged Sergeant Winning to cover and then put a bandage on his wound, started an IV, loaded him on a litter, and began to move him to the designated landing zone. The team leader had to call up the report and request for a medical evacuation helicopter over the radio while doing this.

The range we were using was very wide, and I started them on one end. As the guys carried the litter, the guys providing security had to bound down the range one by one to keep up the fire on the enemy. The maneuver was a variation on what the infantrymen called an Australian Peel. The exercise was both physically and mentally exhausting. It was worth it and would pay dividends later.

The battalion training exercise in late March provided a chance for platoons to maneuver as a whole. In the Army, platoons plan and do training for crew and below. Companies train squads and sections. Battalions train platoons, and brigades train companies. In March of 2007, we were still severely undermanned, needing about 20 percent more soldiers. I did not mind because if we could accomplish the mission shorthanded, I knew we would be able to accomplish the mission when soldiers were gone on mid-tour leave or because of casualties.

The battalion exercise, named Lion Triangle, was geographically huge. We had nearly the entire training area to ourselves. Our "FOB" was in the southeastern corner of Fort Carson's training area. I could see Pueblo West from the hill next to the FOB. From the FOB we did route-clearance missions on the roads running west towards the bombing range. The "village" we did our training raids and meetings/ambushes in was halfway back to Fort Carson but on the west edge of the training area. Just getting from the FOB to the village took an hour of driving. The village was a product of the Iraq War changing the focus of the Army. With only two existing urban-training sites on post and many units needing to train, the Army got creative. Additional villages sprang up as the Army bought Tuff sheds and turned shipping containers into buildings and arranged them in a third-world manner.

In order to get practice using gun-truck Humvees, the scout platoon—owners of all five of the battalion's gun trucks—loaned them out. It was not enough to equip the whole company, but it was enough to train a couple platoons if we ran "split section." For our missions to the village, we would have two crews in tanks and two crews in Humvees. The tanks would provide the lead and trail vehicles in formation and would be the primary security vehicles. We loaded up guys to dismount and go into buildings in the Humvees. The tactical risk of only having four guys to go into buildings was offset by having tank cannon fire in support.

The raid missions were straightforward: planned raids on the enemy house in the village. We would have a long approach march and attack straight onto the object. Soldiers from our sister company provided enemy and innocent-civilian role players in the village. Another platoon leader and platoon sergeant provided observer/controllers. They would give us critical feedback on our performance so we could learn and improve. The "meeting" mission was really to train us to react to ambush. We planned a mission to visit with the local civilian leaders, and while we were doing this, the enemy would ambush us at some point. We would then have to fight our way through the ambush, either on the road or even in the village itself.

After we completed Lion Triangle, we had a very short turnaround before we headed right back to the field for gunnery. Complicating things, we had changes of command for all of the battalions and the brigade right before gunnery. The Big Fish was replaced by Lieutenant Colonel Pappal. Very quiet and reserved, he was a night-and-day difference in style from Colonel Fisher.

Gunnery is the Super Bowl of armored training, so we were excited. It was not necessarily the most difficult aspect, but it had scores, and with scores come bragging rights. Honestly, I had no illusions about our scores going into gunnery. We were experienced with our rifles and warfare in general, but only my platoon sergeant had fired gunnery before. All of our gunners and the rest of the platoon tank commanders were shooting gunnery for the first time as trigger pullers. There is a huge difference between loading or driving and being the gunner or tank commander. To further hinder our performance, the training schedule had been incredibly packed, so we all had the bare minimum of time in the simulator; but as true-blood tread heads, we were passionate about gunnery. Passion would be our key to success.

To avoid the hassle of Fort Carson convoy rules, we did not roll as a company. Instead, we broke the company up into small convoys of five or less vehicles. Six vehicles invoked all kinds of rules. The platoon was still shorthanded, so we shared drivers and loaders. The men didn't mind since it was gunnery. As Blue Platoon rolled out, we only had three tanks and were joined by two of the vehicles from the maintenance section. The company regrouped at the first range on the northern range complex.

Range 104 was a dry-fire range. Since no bullets flew on this range, it was positioned behind the other ranges, using a slice of land between the northern range complex and a creek. There was only one lane for crews to use. On the east side, a tower overlooked the range, though you couldn't see the targets on the far end from the tower.

As soon as we got to the range, each tank pulled up to the boresight line. This was a low berm on the south edge of the assembly-area parking lot. Twelve hundred meters to the south was a square black-and-white panel we used to calibrate the fire-control system of the tank. Boresighting the tank was a process that no matter how many times you had done it, you always read the steps out of the book. Skipping or messing up any step would result in significant accuracy errors. Despite not shooting anything on Range 104, we still went through the full process.

The race was on. The range was first come, first served. We carefully but quickly completed our boresight and preparations to fire and then got in line. Tradition and leadership expectations meant that the company leadership should be the first tanks to go. The platoon leaders had to take turns being the range officer in charge, so one would always be pushed to the back half of the firing order.

Tank gunnery was designed to do more than just test a crew's ability to hit various targets at various ranges. It was also a test of the crew's ability to do so while minimizing its own exposure to enemy fire and its ability to handle malfunctions. Every second the tank was exposed instead of hiding behind cover counted against the score. Each engagement tested the crew in a different way. Each member of the crew had a specific task to perform, and it had to be exactly correct and in the exact order, or penalties added up. If the error was safety related, the crew could be disqualified on the spot. Failure to qualify on the first try was a shame akin to forfeiting the Super Bowl.

The next major event during gunnery was "screening" the tanks. After yet another boresight alignment, the tanks would rumble up the hill to the next range. Screening is the big-boy version of zeroing a rifle.

Each tank crew would radio the tower their data inputs from boresight, as well as inputs regarding temperature, ammo type, and more. Up in the tower, the company master gunner would verify their inputs and make any adjustments necessary. Once the book work was done, the master gunner would have the tank crew fire a single 120 mm round at a bullseye target. Depending on where the round hit the target, the master gunner might have further corrections for the crew to make. Accuracy is critical in tank warfare. When shooting at distances of a mile and a half, the slightest error can produce major misses.

After screening, gunnery got exciting. The next ranges involved series of exercises to test the crew's ability to fire machine guns and cannon under various conditions. "Fight the tank!" is the armor community's version of the Navy's "Don't give up the ship!" A knowledgeable crew can fight on despite significant damage and degradation to their tank. If something unexpectedly broke during your gunnery run, you had to find a way to continue and succeed anyway. Gunnery was our chance to prove ourselves. My favorite engagement was the use of manual controls and sights to shoot a moving target and two stationary targets. It is a physically demanding challenge for the gunner to hand-crank the tank turret from target to target. A smart driver can pivot the whole tank to make it easier on him, but the communication between the driver, gunner, and tank commander has to be good or they end up countering each other's efforts.

During these engagements, the crew would have their radio rigged to transmit everything said on the internal communications so the evaluators knew what was going on. In the tower, a zoom-capable thermal camera recorded the action to discern whether the tank crew hit their target or not. Tank crews not on their run waited on the approach road, listening to the radio and critiquing performance in hopes of improving their own. Each range had two lanes tanks could complete their run on. We exercised the wingman concept on the range because we would in combat. As one crew went through an engagement, the wingman crew would scan for targets and call them out on the radio. While this may seem like an unfair advantage, it served to train crews in the art of accurately describing targets so someone could find it from another perspective.

Each "table," or series of exercises, had a mix of day and night engagements. Both day and night included stationary defensive engagements and moving offensive engagements. Of course, *stationary* isn't exactly literal in this context. The tank crew would tuck their tank into defilade behind their firing position so that just the gunner's and commander's thermal viewers could see over the top of cover. As the two viewers could scan independently, the crew would divide the battlefield into areas of responsibility. If the engagement conditions allowed, the loader would pop up out of the hatch to help look for targets.

Once the target operator in the tower started the engagement, the clock was ticking. The targets would only stay up for a specified amount of time. Again, the critical part was the crew's exposure time. This clock directly affected their score and started as soon as the commander gave the command for the driver to move up into firing position. In a defensive engagement, the crew could remain tucked into defilade for long periods of time and not get a bad score from the time—assuming they were able to hit all of the targets before they went down. Offensive engagements did not afford any protected time as the tank was already exposed.

Everyone was on the edge of their seats when a tank crew began an engagement. The radio allowed everyone to hear the high-pitched whine of the tank in tactical idle and the crew in anticipation.

The commander would begin the fire command while aligning the gunner's sights to target.

"Gunner, sabot, tank!"

The gunner then announced he had the target in his sights: "Identified!"

The loader would signal the cannon was armed and he was out of the way of the recoil: "Up!"

"Driver, move out!" With the weapon ready, the commander ordered the tank out of defilade so the cannon was exposed. The driver would move forward until either the cannon fired or the driver could see the target. A good crew would fire the cannon as soon as it cleared the ground instead of waiting for the driver to brake and thus throw the sights off as the tank pitched forward and tossed the gunner.

"Fire!" The commander's order allowed the gunner to fire. Of course, the gunner could hold off the trigger if he did not think the gun was clear yet.

"On the WAAAY!!!" the gunner would sing out, pulling the trigger in the middle of "way." The intense crack of the cannon shook everything around it, knocked dust off the tank, made a large ring of fire around the muzzle, and picked up lighter items in front and tossed them into the air. From outside the tank, it was awe inspiring. Inside the tank, the cannon breech snapped back about eighteen inches and spat out the aft cap of the round, the cannon blast muted and barely louder than the metallic clinks of the breech.

As soon as the breech snapped forward into battery, the loader slapped the arming lever down and began to reload the cannon. The loader pressed his knee against a switch to open the ammunition-compartment blast door and pulled out the correct type of round. In one deft move, the loader flipped the round up and over and fed it into the cannon breech, then pushed the round home with his fist until the breech block slid up and locked. As the loader moved out of the way, he would slap the arming lever back up. Once done, the loader checked to make sure the ammo door closed before yelling, "Up!" A good loader would complete the entire process in just a few seconds.

While the loader fed the cannon breech, the commander and gunner checked on their fired round's effects. If the target was still up and a threat, the commander would order, "Re-engage!" If the target was hit, the commander would order, "Target cease-fire. Driver, back down." As the tank backed up, the commander and gunner resumed searching for targets.

Some engagements were tests of the loader and tank commander's abilities to hit with the topside machine guns. The commander engagements were fun. Up in the hatch, I would scan for the targets, not needing to worry about moving the tank out of hiding when it was time to shoot. As soon as I saw the target pop up, I aimed and announced, "Caliber fifty." With arm-rattling power, the gun jumped in its mount as I depressed the butterfly trigger.

As exhilarating as gunnery was, it was also exhausting. Every morning, the crews woke with the sun and began their daily preparations for firing. Morning LOGPAC—logistical package of fuel and ammo—waited on nobody. The company's goal was to have first rounds downrange within minutes of our earliest allowed time. As the company was short on soldiers, loaders and drivers made multiple runs, doing maintenance on the tanks in between. For the gunners and commanders, there were also additional tasks to perform. We took turns evaluating other crews' runs and performing the chores of the range. Between it all, there was no time for rest. After the last tank completed its day run, there was just enough time for evening LOGPAC and another round of boresighting the cannon before the darkness crept in and night runs began. Often, the last crew would be done sometime after 2 a.m.

My crew's night run for Table V was the only run I remember vividly a decade later. The first engagement had troop targets for the gunner to use the coax on. Prior to beginning our run, we test-fired our coax machine gun and got the tank settled into position. Everything was ready and looking good. When we started our run, disaster hit. We started our movement down the road towards the targets, scanning for the little groups of pop-up infantry targets.

"Troops!" Edwin called out upon seeing one of the two groups of targets.

A short and crisp fire command rang out in the turret, and Edwin called, "On the way" as he pulled the trigger. About six rounds in, the coax had a different pop than normal, more like a string of black cat firecrackers. The M240's feed-tray cover flew up, and pieces of ammunition bounced around the inside of the turret.

"Cease fire! Cease fire! Is everyone okay?" My orders to the crew were unnecessary; they all knew something went wrong and were working to stop the machine gun. After each crew member announced he was okay, I told the tower we were okay, but our machine gun was done. We pulled off the range and worked to see what had happened and if we could repair it.

As the bolt stripped a round out of the belt and pushed it towards the chamber of the machine gun, the round went off early. Hot fragments from the casing went through the casings of several more rounds in the belt, causing them to go off in the belt-feeder chute. The culprit of the malfunction was a primer not fully seated into the casing, which caused the round to go off when the bolt struck it. A couple hours later, we completed our run, swapping out the coax with the loader's M240.

After completing final qualifications, we conducted a few more non-firing exercises to prepare for the platoon live-fire exercise. While the actual missions went well enough, the company movement to the northwest portion of the training area was embarrassing. White Platoon was to establish an assembly area in a large open field on top of a plateau. The only thing in the way was a power line that ran along the road. As the platoon moved into a coil formation, where the four tanks all face out in a circle, the platoon leader somehow managed to back his tank into a power-line pole. The pole snapped, and the tank backing up dragged the power line down until it sparked out on the commander's hatch. Had the platoon leader been any taller than the very short height he was, the power line would have killed him. Instead, he lived but cut the power to half of Fort Carson. When I arrived at the site, I could not figure out why he had backed up anyway. To position his tank for the coil in the open field, he just needed to turn left ninety degrees and stop. How he failed to see the pole was beyond me.

The battalion also planned a live-fire exercise to certify platoons. We were heading to the National Training Center in May, and platoon live-fire certification was required. The live-fire exercise would be a raid. The enemy compound was constructed by the battalion's engineers. They made some rudimentary wooden buildings in the middle of the valley that served as a tank-maneuver area. To force platoons to approach in a manner that sent all bullets in the safe direction Range Control wanted, the engineers dug an anti-tank ditch. The ditch would make it so that there was really only one approach and good location to set up the vehicles for the raid.

Digging the ditch was a major undertaking for the engineers. They did not have bulldozers. Instead, the engineer company was equipped with the M9 Armored Combat Earthmover. The machine is a combination of a dozer and a scraper on one small, fast-moving, armored tracked vehicle. Like all jacks-of-all-trades, it excelled at neither function. The ACE was a better scraper than dozer, though, and the machine was best used in conjunction with a real dozer. Best practices called for a dozer to push the dirt out of the ground, and the ACE would scrape up the loose soil and move it to the desired location. Despite nearly twenty years of knowing this, the Army in its infinite wisdom did not equip the engineer companies in heavy brigades with dozers when it reorganized the Army. Digging the anti-tank ditch abused the ACE, and mechanical breakdowns resulted, delaying the project significantly.

The battalion furthered the realism of the exercise by making the targets reactive. We were training our soldiers to engage until the target was no longer a threat. Unlike the standard range targets, where any hit anywhere on the target "kills" it and the target lies back down, we wanted targets that were hard to kill. We placed paper targets presenting a threat or a civilian on a cardboard box. The box hung from the ceiling of the shoot house by a string tied to a balloon inside the box. The balloon's placement and size corresponded with the lethal areas of the paper target. Only a lethal shot would pop the balloon, allowing it to pull through the hole in the cardboard and dropping the target to the floor. To simulate people that just don't die easily, some targets had multiple balloons tied in series.

When it was Blue Platoon's turn, we borrowed the scout platoon's gun-truck Humvees and approached the objective from the south. The second each truck came to a halt, the TC and dismount (normally the loader from the tank) jumped out and ran towards the door to the plywood house. As we ran, we fell into our stack formation, and immediately upon reaching the door, our breacher booted the door open. The stack rapidly flowed through the door, the lead two firing their M4s at the targets. Within half a minute, the whole house was cleared and all the targets were on the floor, strings with popped balloons hanging from the ceiling like sad vines.

As quickly as we declared the objective secure, the officer acting as the observer and controller designated one of our guys to be a casualty. Our aid-and-litter team snapped into action and extracted the "wounded" soldier to the platoon medic while the platoon's enemy prisoner of war (EPW) team began to search the target bodies and building for intelligence.

In under five minutes, weeks of planning, building the site, a day of mission planning and preparation, and hours of checks and triple checks culminated with an official blessing to go to NTC. Such is the way of training.

In true Army fashion, I got a new platoon sergeant right before we departed for NTC. Sergeant First Class Jay Weatherly arrived to us from Germany. Jay was a superb tanker and a great leader. While I was sad to lose Ron, Jay was a great addition to the platoon.

FINAL BLESSINGS

AS SOON AS WE RETURNED from our live-fire exercise, we began preparing our equipment to ship off to NTC. All of the tools and equipment inside the tanks came out and went into twenty-foot shipping containers. Each one had to be loaded carefully so the heavy items would not damage anything. All of the radios and weapons from the arms room went into 300-pound cages inside a container. As the company's arms room wouldn't fill it completely, we shared the container with other companies. My packing list of items was checked, double-checked, and triple-checked by both us and a battalion staff member. There could be no discrepancies. Each cage was padlocked, and then a serial-numbered seal went on it to ensure nobody tampered with it. Serial-numbered one-time locks went onto the shipping container. When we got to NTC, the same collection of people would open it together and go through the same processes of verifying everything was still in place.

Finally the day came to load our equipment onto the train. The railyard was at the north end of Fort Carson. The tanks and other vehicles were organized into carloads and then staged in the order they would get on. Once the order was confirmed and everyone was ready, we drove the tanks to the loading ramps. With only the driver in, each tank was eased up the ramp and onto the railcars from the rear. Dozens of flatcars were pushed into place at the ramp. One soldier would carefully guide the driver from the ramp to the farthest railcar. Railcars are pretty high off the ground, and the gaps between them are also significant. Fortunately, tracked vehicles can span gaps even wider, though it is still unnerving to watch a seventy-ton tank inch out over the gap and then eventually grab the edge of the next car.

As soon as the tank was in place on its designated car and its paired tank joined it, a team scrambled onto the railcar and tied the tanks down with heavy-duty chains. Their goal was to keep pace with the vehicles getting loaded. The soldiers guiding the tanks into position didn't care about racing. All they cared about was safely getting the tanks into position. With tanks as wide as the railcars, there was no margin for error. Planning and preparation had to be well done, or a mess would result. Throughout it all, Todd had to make sure that nothing was on the wrong car when compared with the manifest he would provide the railroad.

I enjoyed railyard operations. You could see your progress, and it was not something we could train for or do often. Besides, the railyard illustrated just how much combat power we had as an armored brigade.

With our equipment in the capable conveyance of the Burlington Northern Santa Fe Railroad, we prepared to travel to NTC. We lucked out. Instead of the daylong bus ride, we were going to fly by chartered jets to an old Air Force base near NTC and then bus a couple hours the rest of the way. The air base we flew into was one of many places where old aircraft went for final storage. The boneyards were amazing to see. Some of the aircraft had already been cannibalized.

The NTC at Fort Irwin is literally in the middle of nowhere. Nearly every military installation in the nation is on the edge of town, or even surrounded by city. Not Fort Irwin. From the time you pull off I-15, it is another forty-five minutes of driving through empty desert before you see the buildings of the main post. The rocks along the way are painted by different units who have rotated through the training center.

Upon our arrival to the infamous Dust Bowl—the area where units assembled and prepared to move out into the desert for their rotation—we each found a cot in our massive assigned tent shared with more than a hundred other soldiers. We had less than a week to load all of our equipment onto the vehicles, get everything equipped with MILES gear, and plan our operations. Since we were focusing on counterinsurgency, the platoon would use two of our tanks and borrow two Humvees from Fort Irwin so we could conduct dismounted operations better.

Fort Irwin's training fleet of vehicles it loans to rotation units is one of the Army's biggest and most annoying frustrations. The vehicles are used and abused—driven like a rental car. Not every unit uses everything, though, so some of the vehicles sit neglected for long periods of time. When you borrow one, it's usually in bad shape, on the verge of some expensive breakdown. When you return it, you have to somehow bring the hunk of junk up to perfect working condition or pay out of the unit budget for repairs that will take too long to complete before departure. The wise soldier photographs everything upon receipt to prove the damage isn't new when you return it.

Every vehicle and every soldier gets equipped for the greatest game of laser tag—MILES. Strips with laser sensors are Velcro'd onto the vehicles, and soldiers wear a harness and a halo of sensors. Every rifle gets a laser transmitter. The vehicles get a more sophisticated transmitter. Everything is linked together so at the "Star Wars" room on main post, they can tell who shot whom and when. Contractors are hired to install the MILES gear onto the vehicles under the shade of a building. Everyone scrambles to get their vehicle in line quickly, and then crews take turns resting with the vehicle in line while others work on other tasks. Sometimes the line takes days to get through.

While we were in the Dust Bowl, we had a mini epidemic. Some unknown soldier decided to access the water trailer ice block, contaminating the water with dirty hands. Soon, the whole battalion was very, very sick, and the porta potties had a line rivaling the

MILES gear line. The medics figured out the problem and dumped the contaminated water, ending the crisis.

Finally, we departed in convoys to our FOBs for the rotation, with 1-68 Armor assigned the eastern end of the central maneuver corridor for operations. I was happy with that; even though it was my first time on the actual ground, I had fought numerous simulator battles using the map and terrain, so it felt like home turf to me. We would not be fighting any clashes of mechanized forces, but I knew I would have fun in the wide-open expanses of NTC.

For our operations, we again task-organized the battalion. Team Steel traded Todd Allison's platoon for a mechanized infantry platoon. While I can't remember who the platoon leader was, I remember vividly the platoon sergeant, Sergeant First Class Iron Eyes. Sergeant Iron Eyes was an intimidating warrior and already a legend in the battalion. During a gunfight in a suburb of Baqubah, he had been shot in the thigh. Without a word, he bandaged himself and kept going without slowing down, not seeking treatment until back at FOB Warhorse.

Sergeant Iron Eyes strove successfully to emulate the warrior tradition of the Sioux, and he made his whole platoon live by the mobile mindset of mechanized warfare. Every day, the whole platoon packed up every last thing as soon as they were awake. They were not tied to any piece of ground or comfort, ready to strike off in an instant. While Sergeant Iron Eyes was generally quiet, he had a great wit and sense of humor. Above all, he was a professional.

During the first week, we ran a series of scripted scenarios to ensure every platoon and every company could demonstrate its ability to fight through critical incidents. One included working with a helicopter team to practice the fine art of describing targets and locations so a completely different perspective could understand. The exercise took a sobering turn in the afternoon when one of the OH-58 Kiowa scout helicopters crashed. I was glad I didn't witness the crash.

During the last week of the exercise, Team Steel was assigned the task of preventing the enemy from infiltrating fighters and weapons through an area called Hidden Valley. Hidden Valley was a scenic byway from the main post to the village just south of the battalion FOB. It was known as an important bypass of the Four Corners by scouts and those with multiple trips to the NTC. The southwestern entrance to the valley was hard to discern from the main valley. A few wadis gave access, disguised by the spurs and wadis extending off Tiefort Mountain. Hidden Valley offered two eastern exits. John Wayne Pass went into the next major valley south of the central corridor. A small, steep-walled cut emptied Hidden Valley right into the village.

To achieve our mission, we took turns setting up OPs and patrolling the valley. We were busy. The soldiers playing the enemy in the village often made runs back to the main post—representing a large city—to shower and resupply. While we were stuck in the "box" for the entire exercise, they rotated back constantly. Daily, we would encounter minivans and SUVs sneaking through Hidden Valley. For the most part, they were clean, but every now and then, we found someone we were looking for. Barely a couple days into the exercise, we managed to catch the number one enemy leader, much to the chagrin of the OCs. He was on a run to shower and get more beef jerky when we caught him in the wadi road.

We found a small bowl that was big enough to hide a tank and a Humvee near the west exit of Hidden Valley. Once tucked in there, people on the road wouldn't be able to see us as they drove by. I had Bravo Section hide there and took my section to wait in plain sight in the valley. We waited.

A 1986 Toyota minivan slowly came up the valley from the village. As it drove past us, I noticed the guy in the front right seat was supporting his head with his right hand on his cheek in such a manner that I couldn't see his face. Then it hit me: everyone in the van was doing something to hide their faces.

"Blue, Blue One; we are stopping this van in the wadi. Alpha, move out and follow. Bravo, stand by to cut them off." We were bouncing over the sand to the road before I even released the push-to-talk button on the radio hand mic. The Toyota picked up speed and we matched. *Let them commit. Patience.*

"Blue, execute!" I called out as the Toyota entered the top of the wadi road where it would not be able to turn around. Sergeant Weatherly's section came around the bend, and the Toyota instantly knew they were trapped and stopped.

Smoothly, efficiently, the guys pulled everyone from the van and searched them. There were no weapons, but everyone had their identification cards. I radioed in the names and waited for the command post to get with Battalion for any possible matches.

When I got to the front-seat passenger's name, I noticed our platoon OC looking frustrated and talking into his radio.

"Blue One, Steel X-Ray; he is wanted list number one." *Gotcha!*

"Detain him. Actually, detain them all." I was grinning. With satisfaction, the guys put zip tie flex cuffs on them. As we did so, our OC came huffing down the small rise he had been watching from.

"LT, you guys have to let them go," the OC announced loudly.

"Why?" I wasn't backing down without a challenge.

"They are out of play. We can't let you ruin the whole exercise script because you got lucky. Good find, but it doesn't count. They are out of play. Release them."

"Wilco." I nodded to the guys and then grinned, pulling the platoon camera from a pouch. "Take pictures first, guys." We took our small victory pictures and shared them with everyone so we knew what our number one bad guy looked like.

Our attempts to intercept an enemy vehicle usually turned into a frustrating pursuit. Officially, the box had a speed limit, but the enemy would always take off at high speed to avoid us unless we really had a good trap on them, like the trap we sprang in the Hidden Valley wadi road. Any time we matched speed to intercept them, the OCs yelled at us on the radio to slow down. Our response was always "We will when they do." Of course, the tank will always beat a wheeled vehicle in a cross-country, bone-jarring, ditch-jumping race.

A few days into the exercise, Blue Platoon got a change of orders as 4-10 Cavalry was planning a major operation way up in the northwest corner of NTC. They wanted some tanks to help them, and we supposedly were the nearest ones available. Their plan required the tanks to approach the objective from the north while the scout platoons approached from the south. It was a hammer-and-anvil type of plan, but it had a huge problem. In order for us to reach our specified position, we would have to drive more than seventy kilometers, all of which was not patrolled by friendly forces—"Indian Country" at its finest.

Seventy kilometers (over forty miles) is a really long approach march for mechanized forces under the best of conditions. It is an impossibly long distance for a platoon to attack solo. Of course, the route was not a nice paved highway but rather dirt roads that climbed two major passes along the way. The passes would force a higher consumption of fuel, all before we got to the fight. As Sergeant Weatherly and I did the math, we realized we were going to need to bring our own fuel truck just to make the march there and back. If we had a breakdown, we would have significant difficulty recovering ourselves back. Once we pointed out this problem, the whole plan got scrapped, and some staff officers learned the difference between cruising range and operational range.

The last day of the exercise was supposed to be the grand finale. A big event in the village was supposed to get attacked by a large enemy force, and we would be hard pressed to stop it. As the sun came up, Team Steel set out to seal off the village exit of Hidden Valley. The whole team had about 100 meters of concertina wire to work with, and we planned to stop all vehicles by setting the wire across the narrowest place. White Platoon was in charge of placing the obstacle, and Blue Platoon would provide security in the valley while they set up. We would help drop off wire, though.

Unfortunately, White Platoon's leader again came up short by changing the wire-obstacle location to a wider spot, thus running out of wire. When he called me to come help with the wire, I was angry that he completely failed to follow the plan. I ordered him to collect up the wire and move it all back to the correct location and stomped off. I didn't get very far before looking back in time to see the stubby lieutenant throw a roll of wire on one of my soldiers pulling security from the back of a cargo Humvee. At a dead run, I returned, getting in his face just as he was getting ready to toss another roll of wire. After a short exchange of words, I took over fixing the wire and sent him off to find the commander and a new task. I was livid. Nobody takes frustrations out by throwing razor-sharp wire on another soldier. That was probably the straw that broke the camel's back, and it was the last time that lieutenant led soldiers in 1-68 Armor.

Shortly after getting the wire sorted out, Blue Platoon was sent to the other end of the valley where enemy forces were attacking a platoon just off the main road. By the time we arrived, the fight was over, but now we were near the main highway and decided to commence interdiction operations there. We didn't have to wait more than ten minutes before getting into a series of firefights with enemy forces heading north. Any vehicle that stayed on the highway got stopped for search. Those with weapons opted for losing a one-sided fight. I had six guys and two machine guns at the search point, but the most in any vehicle we fought was two guys with weapons. The enemy vehicles that tried to bypass us into the desert were merely hunted down by the tanks waiting for just such foolishness.

We had a blast, but before the sun reached its zenith in the sky, we got the word the exercise was over. It was time to come in and begin the process of turning stuff in, packing up the rest, and leaving. Units everywhere had been chomping at the bit for this news. The last shots had hardly stopped echoing off the hills when the first convoy of support vehicles streamed past our battlefield en route to the main post. Soon we joined them.

While we were at NTC, someone in the Big Army figured out that sending us back to Iraq in early August wasn't fair. Starting a fifteen-month deployment just nine months after returning from a twelve-month deployment would stretch families to the breaking point. On top of that, we still had not received enough replacement soldiers to get close to full strength. Some replacements were not scheduled to arrive until October. Our deployment was pushed back a couple months.

The delay gave us time to review our lessons learned at NTC and train to address those areas. Training for the most part was conducted inside the platoon. Resources to put together larger training exercises were not available as they had been allocated to other units under the earlier assumption that we would be packing and heading out the door to Iraq by this point. I was happy for the extra time. Many of our guys missed major training events because they were at schools across the Army at the time.

Additionally, we had some last-minute personnel changes. AJ Boyes came back to the company to become our XO. Specialist Cody "Soda Pop" Reece moved to headquarters to be the XO's gunner, and Mike Elledge went to be the commander's gunner. Still within the company, Soda Pop and Mike maintained the tight friendship with the platoon.

A collection of new privates brought us up to full strength. PFC Nick Monks, and Privates Billy Bailey and Jake Jacobsen rounded out Blue Platoon. Nick was from Massachusetts and had the accent to match. He was tough, putting up with the teasing he got. Billy "Beadle" Bailey was a wiry kid from Appalachia who also got more than his fair share of teasing. Jake Jacobsen lucked out and did not collect as much ribbing since Nick and Beadle took the spotlight.

As the summer wore into fall, our deployment date kept getting delayed until it finally settled on the one-year mark since our return. Each time the date pushed back, we ended up with different missions to plan for. I'm sure the staff officers kept very busy constantly having to redo all of their work. The one thing that was very clear to us was that the surge was working, yet the dangers from the EFP roadside bombs were very real. Several of my friends from West Point had been killed or severely wounded by them. To counter the risk, the Army rapidly fielded heavier, better-armored vehicles for patrolling. The downside to these vehicles was that their weight was often too much for the canal roads. One of my friends from West Point was killed when his vehicle collapsed a canal bank and rolled into the canal. War is filled with all kinds of different dangers.

To keep us from losing the knife edge we trained to, we undertook another round of exercises in early fall. This time, brigade ran the exercise so whole companies could operate together, and we actually got prime real estate to train on. One mission was in the well-built mock town complete with sewer systems and a wide range of realistic buildings. Another live-fire mission used the live-fire city range. The men performed well, and I was confident in our readiness. In addition to going through the missions with Team Steel, I got to be an OC for 1-8 Infantry. It gave me a chance to provide feedback—but more importantly, to see others' methods and learn free lessons.

As we neared our deployment date, we made our preparations and cherished the time with our families. It was bittersweet. Before we knew it, the evening of our departure arrived. The majority of the company was on the same flight. Many families joined us in the company offices as we undertook our final weapons draw out of the arms room and said our goodbyes.

Knight Company training. Sweaty, dusty, tons of fun.

Dinner in Iraq with my brother Pat. Stuff legends are made of.

Keith Hanson's dry humor never failed to make me smile.

White Platoon in Diyala. Welcome to the jungle.

Dusk route clearance patrol Down Route Vanessa in Baqubah.
We ran echelon left formation to give traffic a chance to get out of the way.

Author in the tank commander's hatch. Baqubah, 2006

Beida, 2008. Taking a break from the march of a foot patrol. Left to right: Daniel Garcia, Jay Weatherly, Billy "Beetle" Bailey, Juan Perez, RJ "Will" Williams

Hawasem, 2008. Sadr is in the background. This is from the roof of Office Max.

COP Ford, Baghdad 2008. Once a week, we took a morning off from patrols to conduct maintenance on the vehicles.

C32 rumbling down Kumeil Elashteri Road, Route Florida.

Sadr, 2008. A view of the wall on Jamila Street towards the end of the fight.

Continuing the attack on Route Gold

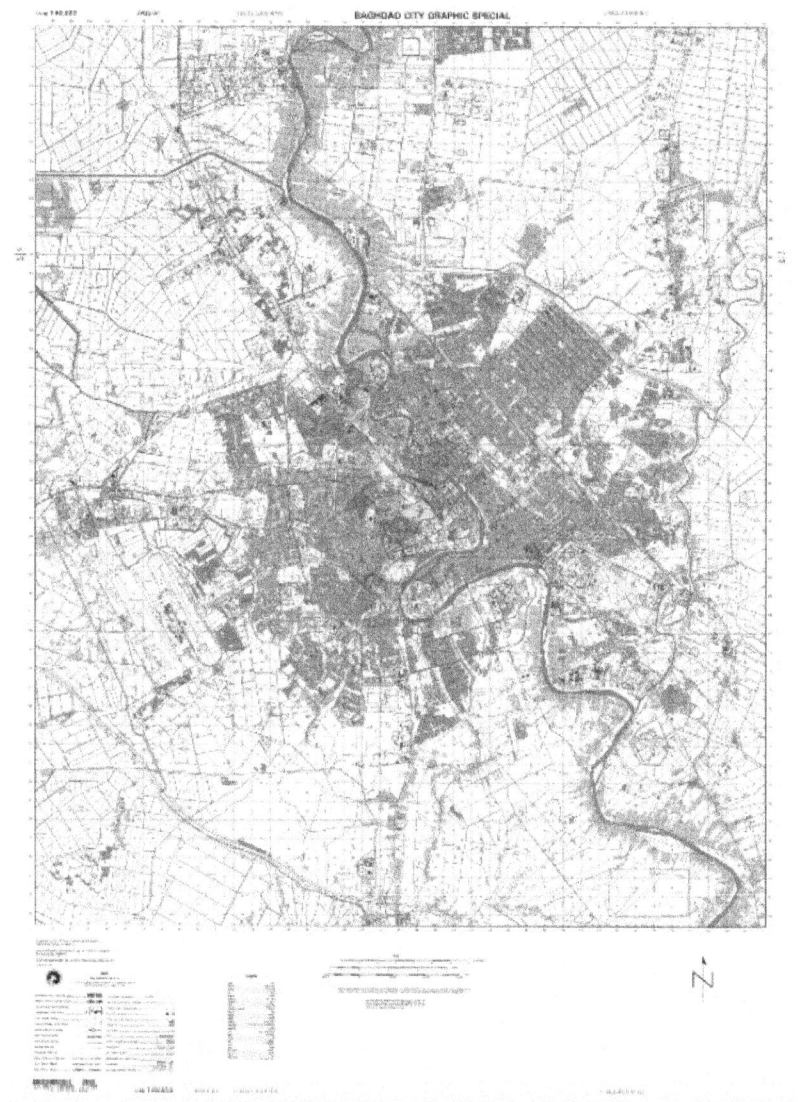

Map of Baghdad City

Part 2
SADR

Hail Mary, full of grace.
The Lord is with thee.
Blessed art thou among women,
and blessed is the fruit of thy womb, Jesus.
Holy Mary, Mother of God,
pray for us sinners now,
and at the hour of our death.
Amen.

HALF-BAKED PLANS

WHEN WE DEPLOYED BACK TO Iraq at the end of November 2007, only about 380 days had passed since we had gotten home from Diyala. It was the beginning of the sixth year of the Iraq War and a year into the surge. A cease-fire agreement with JAM—Jaish Al Madhi, the Shiite army—had generated relative peace in eastern Baghdad and the Shia-dominated areas of Iraq. Part of the deal was the creation of a huge sanctuary for JAM in Sadr City, a large, crowded neighborhood that was home to about 2.4 million Shiite Iraqis. The "Sunni Awakening" had brought the other large demographic of Iraq to relative peace also. Local, US-funded "Sons of Iraq" security groups manned checkpoints throughout the country. It was an optimistic time, but everyone knew the country was still on a knife's edge.

Blue Platoon was finally at full strength when we arrived in Kuwait for last-minute preparations to move north. Sergeant First Class Jay Weatherly was our platoon sergeant, the foreman of the outfit. Staff Sergeant David Rocha and Staff Sergeant Danny Key were the section sergeants. Each of us was also a tank commander. My crew, the C31 crew, was filled out with gunner Sergeant Eddie Edwin, Specialist Cory Bushell, and PFC Nick Monks. The C32 crew with David Rocha included Sergeant Kyle "Tex" Kincaid, PFC Derek Quinn, and PFC Jake Jacobsen. The C33 crew with Danny Key included Sergeant

Juan Perez, Specialist Daniel Garcia, and PFC Billy "Beatle" Bailey. Jay Weatherly's C34 crew was rounded out by Sergeant RJ "Will" Williams, Specialist Adam Wallace, and PFC Josh Butler. The platoon medic, PFC Ryan Earnst, rode with the C34 crew most of the time.

C33's missing part was finally on hand, and we fixed it as soon as the tanks arrived at the sprawling Camp Buehring in the desert wasteland of Kuwait. To increase the misery, every day was marked by wind and drizzling rain. It was cold. After fixing the tanks and getting them unpacked from their transatlantic voyage on a ship, we headed to a range in the middle of the desert to confirm their weapons systems. Each tank would fire a couple training sabot and HEAT (high-explosive anti-tank) rounds to make sure everything was working before loading up wartime ammunition.

At the range, we discovered my tank, C31, would not superelevate the gun for some unknown reason. When the gunner uses the laser to find the range of a target, the ballistic computer figures out what adjustments to make to the cannon for it to provide the correct trajectory to hit the target. C31 would not adjust the gun at all. After the master gunner and mechanics unsuccessfully fiddled with it, we decided it was not worth worrying. After all, the cease-fire conditions in Iraq meant we would not use the tanks. If for some reason we needed the tanks, we would be firing at near point-blank ranges, less than 400 meters. Superelevation at those ranges was irrelevant.

Now that we were in theater, we got additional equipment to fully enable us to operate as infantry, including a M249 Squad Automatic Weapon, and night-vision goggles for those without. Every night at Camp Buehring, we patrolled the camp to get everyone used to their goggles. These walks were marked by lots of stumbling and running into things. With the reality of pending combat sinking in, the men became more focused and nervous. To counter this, we trained battle drills and formations to remind them of their competence and to keep minds from wandering to worry. My goal was to find the balance between keeping them busy and allowing enough time to process their own stress.

One afternoon, I had finished a round of battle-drill practice with Blue Platoon and returned to our tent. Sean approached, looking frustrated.

"LT, can you talk with my platoon leader? He is refusing to come and train with us. The guys are concerned that our leader is not taking our lives seriously. They worry he won't perform and need to have confidence he knows the battle drills and actions on. It's also hard to keep them motivated to train when he is propped up on his cot playing computer games."

"Sure, I'll have a word." I went over to White's tent. The lieutenant was sitting on his cot with his laptop in his lap.

"Hey, your platoon is outside doing battle drills. Why aren't you with them?" I asked. The lieutenant looked up at me. His face showed annoyance and perhaps a bit of condescension. He pointed to his combat patch on his right sleeve.

"I was in Iraq in 2003. Don't you remember? They can do their thing without me. I'm going to stay right here."

Yeah, you were in a long-distance communications unit, not a combat unit, I fortunately thought silently without saying it. "You are a platoon leader now. The guys need you. They need to be able to trust you and recognize your voice giving instructions. Grab your kit and go join them." He put his headphones on and put his feet up on his cot. Conversation ended. Disgusted, I went out to tell Sean his platoon leader was too cool for school.

The one nice thing about Camp Buehring was that other units heading north were also there getting their last-minute preparations. The result was bumping into friends who had gone to other posts after leaving West Point. Every meal in the dining facility was a mini-reunion that went a long way towards temporarily easing the stress of looming combat.

While we were in Kuwait, I realized how poorly planned our deployment had been. Before leaving Fort Carson, we were slated to deploy into eastern Baghdad, on the southeastern side of Sadr

City, and move in to an old factory that had been converted into an outpost. Upon our arrival in Kuwait, this changed. We were instead going to Camp Taji, a massive base just north of Baghdad, to wait for an assignment. The unit assigned to eastern Baghdad did not need to be replaced yet. For that matter, no unit really needed replacement. Furthermore, there was not a fleet of Humvees waiting for us.

AJ headed north with a collection of officers and supply specialists to search for Humvees. The battalion found some for us—in a junkyard near Ramadi. As they were shipped to Camp Taji, AJ fired off an email warning us of their condition.

The battalion also found a temporary assignment patrolling the small Istiqlal Province, just north of Baghdad. Istiqlal was bordered on the west by the Tigris River and on the east by the Diyala River. The southern boundary was the canal at the north edge of Baghdad. The northern boundary was my platoon's old area from last deployment. Hussainiyah, sometimes called "Little Sadr City," was the major city in the middle of the province. Home to some 700,000 Shia Iraqis, the city was a large rectangle. Currently, a field-artillery battery patrolled the entire province. We would be dumping five companies—some 930 soldiers—into an area currently patrolled by less than 100. We would live in converted warehouses at Taji and patrol from there.

With our last-minute preparations complete and a plan in place, we loaded up onto C-130s for the trip north to Baghdad International Airport. From there, Chinooks flew us to Taji. Taji was the largest military base in Iraq. It had been a major logistical hub for Saddam's army, and now it was a large hub for both US and Iraqi forces. The eastern side was the Iraqi Army's, and the western side was the US's.

My first impression of Taji was that it was a dump. Literally. The bus route to the PX was lined with destroyed armored vehicles. Huge piles of trash and debris lay everywhere. The warehouses we lived in were filthy. Pigeons lived in them and rained bird poop down. Ventilation was nonexistent, so the buildings were cold, dark, and dank. About 200 soldiers lived in each building. To afford some level of comfort, we used wall lockers to divide the warehouse into "rooms." Since we all had different schedules, the lights were almost always on, and there was always noise. Winter is the rainy season in Iraq, so thick, gooey mud clung to boots and pants. Within a week, everyone was sick.

The state of our Humvees was equally depressing. They made our tanks' arrival nearly a year ago seem like a gift on a silver platter. Once again, the entire fleet was dead lined. It was so bad that the division's deputy commanding general showed up to see the problem firsthand. The only good news was that parts were easier to come by. The soldiers labored daily to repair them, and by mid-December, we were back in business.

When the platoon took an Iraqi interpreter, he rode with the C31 crew. The interpreter assigned to Blue Platoon was an older gentleman, "Steve," a Sunni Iraqi from north of Baghdad. He never told me exactly where he was from, or his real name. He did, however, make it very clear to me that he had been a major in Saddam's air defense forces before the invasion. Steve was used to giving the orders and doing what he wanted. Being relegated to parroting a mere lieutenant chaffed him. I spoke and understood enough Arabic to know when he was not translating my words or a local's words correctly, something Steve did often. I did not like letting people know I understood them because I would lose the ace up my sleeve, though Steve often forced my hand.

Steve seemed to be on vacation a lot, and when he was, the platoon borrowed one of the company's other interpreters. Normally, it was a young man named "Z." Z did not have the same prejudice as Steve, but he was not as fluent in English and was easily scared.

The battalion task-organized the tank and infantry companies. Blue Platoon started out our patrols under B Company, getting renamed Green Platoon for the duration with the mechanized infantry company "Blackhawk," led by Captain Matthew Jensen. I respected him greatly and enjoyed working for him. B Company was assigned to relieve the artillerymen operating out of Joint Security

Station Istiqlal—a tiny compound a few miles south of Hussainiyah that combined US, Iraqi Army, and Iraqi Police into one shared command center. The idea was to coordinate efforts and mentor the Iraqis directly. The main Iraqi Army barracks for the battalion were a couple hundred meters farther east of the compound, and the police had a station on the west side of the JSS. A much larger police station was under construction about a mile north up the highway. We would live and operate out of the JSS.

I was nervous when the artillerymen arrived at Taji to pick up the company leadership and take us to the JSS to begin the handover process, known as left-seat/right-seat ride. It would be my first patrol since getting wounded last deployment. The artillery unit had MRAPs—large, heavy-armored cars specifically designed to better withstand IEDs—instead of the Humvees we were equipped with. We rumbled out Taji's east gate and crossed the Tigris to a small island on a pontoon bridge. The water level was a bit low, and the weight of the vehicles caused the pontoons to bottom out. It was weird going from the mushy-waterbed feeling to a jarring bottom out.

The small island had a dirt runway for small airplanes, though it was not used. On the island, we stopped and lowered the rhino devices into place—heated black boxes on poles in front of each truck, meant to trigger infrared beams of IEDs early in hopes the penetrator would sail harmlessly past the truck's engine. The other side of the island had an old truss bridge that didn't look particularly stout. From there, we meandered through palm groves and small hamlets until we reached Hussainiyah, where we headed south on Route Dover to the JSS.

As we pulled "in" to the JSS, my heart skipped a few beats. The compound was too small to park vehicles inside of it, so we parked out front and then walked in. A single strand of concertina wire and a couple soldiers were the only things protecting the compound "gate." The whole compound was less than an acre, enclosed by a wimpy-looking cinder-block wall. The building was pretty small. The roof was host to sandbag guard "towers" at each corner. To my horror, I did not see a machine gun in the one facing the gate.

The sad fate of a friend from West Point, Jake Fritz, came to mind. His JSS had been overrun and he taken prisoner before being killed. The enemy had rapidly overwhelmed their defenses, and my understanding was their defenses had been properly prepared. Now I was getting ready to live in what struck me as extremely poor defenses. I hoped my eyes were not bulging out of their sockets and my jaw was still attached.

"Gents, can you excuse us for a moment? Is there a room I can use to talk to my men in private?" Captain Jensen asked the artillerymen.

"Sure—down the hall to the right just before the shower is your room." Captain Jensen led us into the room and closed the door. Quietly, he addressed us.

"Obviously the security here leaves much to be desired. I can see on your faces that you know this. Believe me, as soon as we have the reins, this will change." Captain Jensen paused, looking each of us in the eye. "That being said, it is vital that you do not say a word about it to these artillerymen. They have been here and patrolling for quite some time now and they know this place. We need to learn everything we can from them. We must learn how to run a JSS and how they are working with the Iraqi Army, Iraqi Police, and the National Police. This isn't Diyala, and the war has changed, so we need to know how they're doing things. If you mention or hint that we disapprove of how they are doing things here, you are going to piss them off. Do not mess this up."

Again, Captain Jensen paused to let this sink in. "Now, in the meantime, we will do a few things. You will be armed at all times no matter what. Additionally, we will keep an internal guard rotation here on our quarters. First Sergeant, make that happen. Any questions?" There were none, and we filed back out of the room to return to the artillerymen.

The JSS, aside from feeling exposed, was fairly cozy for a combat outpost. The U-shaped building was well built by Iraqi standards and kept clean and tidy. The Iraqis had a command post in the front room, and the US command post was in the room next to it. A small conference room doubled as a dining room. A series of small rooms down each wing were turned into packed barracks rooms. The platoon's sergeants and I shared a small room, while the other half of the platoon shared another. The small courtyard was the weight room.

An Army field kitchen trailer lived behind the building, cranking out two hot meals a day for us. Lunch was usually provided by the Iraqi Police, and most company leaders joined them for it. In the back corner of the compound, a field-artillery counter-battery radar was set up facing Baghdad. Its crew had their own little shack to live in.

Along the side wall was a row of modified porta potties. Since we were in the middle of nowhere, we had to burn our waste. Each of the plastic porta potties had a big hole cut out of the back, and part of a metal drum was slid into the tank. Each day, platoons would take turns hauling the drums out to the field in front of the compound and stirring the shit as it burned. It was a time-honored combat tradition to burn shit. We dumped our trash in a pile out near the shit-burning site. We tried to burn the trash also, but some things won't burn. A family that lived nearby would come and rifle through the trash every afternoon, looking for anything of value.

Over the next two weeks, the artillerymen shared everything they knew about the area, the people, and how to avoid the nasty IEDs. They taught us how to get around Hussainiyah, something easier said than done. The biggest gift they gave us was a map that had every street roadblock or weak bridge marked. They also were eager to answer our questions.

"What is with the PVC pipe on the trucks?" I asked, pointing at one of their MRAPs. A sixteen-foot PVC pipe about a half inch in diameter was bolted to the front bumper and then tied with a rope to the back corner.

"Ah, that is how we get under the power wires without snagging them. Back when the Iraqi national soccer team was playing in the World Cup, we accidentally snagged a bunch of wires during the game and killed the power. You want to talk about some very pissed off people . . ." The sergeant trailed off. "But it sure makes it safer for the gunners too."

The artillerymen gave us a first-class left-seat/right-seat ride, and we were grateful for the lessons they shared. Before we knew it, they were gone and we were on our own. The first thing we did was improve the defenses at the JSS. We added more obstacles on the approaches and put machine guns in all of the positions. Still, we always kept our pistols and rifles loaded and had one with us at all times. Even in the shower, we kept a gun near us.

To ensure that every platoon would be able to quickly respond to a fight anywhere in the company battlespace, Captain Jensen did not assign platoon areas and instead had us all patrol the entirety of the company battlespace. This was a different method than under Captain Looney, but it made a lot of sense to me. When I was patrolling the Iron Triangle last deployment, I would have been hard pressed to name some of the towns Red Platoon patrolled, much less find them and know how to get to them in a hurry.

Just south of Hussainiyah was a massive hospital. The main building was about the size of four football fields and four or five stories tall. The campus had a few other buildings. One day, Captain Jensen had me take him to the hospital to see how we could improve it. I wasn't sure what to expect when we rolled through its gate.

Of the sprawling hospital, only a small fraction—the first hallway and a few rooms off it—was in use, and by a tiny staff. Despite the building's size and outward appearance, it had not been very functional since 2003 when looters ripped open walls to strip out wiring and copper pipes. They didn't just take what was easy to steal; they systematically gutted the building. Squatters then moved in. Cooking and campfires occasionally got out of control and burned rooms and even a whole wing of the building. The doctors and staff working it had pieced the front entrance area back together to provide minimal services to the public. Only a massive amount of money and a committed project would restore the full hospital. It was heartbreaking.

Hussainiyah had about 600 police officers for its population of 700,000, with a district station for the west half of the city and another on the east side. Nearly every day, we would pay a visit to one of the police stations to compare notes and mentor them. One of their problems was with accountability of equipment, particularly weapons. It was no wonder that the insurgents were able to arm themselves. I often deliberated how much of that was related to insurgent infiltration of the police department. The city, and naturally the police department, were almost exclusively Shia and leaned heavily towards supporting Shia militias. The city even hosted an imposing, government-looking headquarters building for the political front for the Badr Brigade, very similar to the Provisional Wing of the Irish Republican Army of the 1970s. I'm sure that Jaish Al Madhi also had its own political headquarters of sorts in Hussainiyah.

One afternoon, I led a patrol to the central market. Making the people feel safe in the market was important; it was the hub of Hussainiyah life, and it was massive, the largest I ever saw in Iraq—a warren of narrow corridors jam-packed with hundreds and hundreds of small vendors. Indiana Jones would have been at home. Getting lost was easy. Forcing your way through the shoulder-to-shoulder crowds was anything but. We would grab a strap on the soldier in front to avoid getting separated in the crowd.

The most amazing portion of the market was the fish market. It was half a football field's worth of fish of every type and size imaginable, all laid out in the hot sun and dust. I couldn't help but consider the fact that we were more than 350 miles from the ocean, a distance that took days to travel in Iraq. My stomach churned at the mere thought of all that seafood baking in the sun for a couple days. Just north of the baking seafood, a large garbage pile also contributed to the smell. Six feet tall, as if made by a dump truck, the mounds offered cover in the event of a fight, so they needed to be patrolled also. As we trekked across the stinky mounds, we often had to move through herds of goats grazing on the food scraps.

In the process of patrolling the market one day, we gained intelligence that a weapons deal was going down in the parking lot just north of the market. The parking lot served both the bus terminal and the market, but it was tiny compared to the typical lot for a modest business in suburban America. The intelligence was very specific and promising. We even had the license plate of the vehicle being used to hide the weapons. The seller had parked the vehicle, and the buyer would simply drive it away, having exchanged cash for keys somewhere in the crowd.

Wary of a trap, we carefully worked our way up to the parking lot. Sure enough, the car was there. It was a white van. I compared how the vehicle was sitting compared to other vans in the lot—whether it was loaded heavier than normal. Nothing worrying stuck out. I had a Humvee approach the van so our Warlock would provide some protection. After a careful search for booby traps, we opened the door. As promised, we found the weapons. One of the AK-47s bore markings from the western police station, something we would follow up on. Despite not catching the smugglers, the foray was worth it to capture the illicit weapons and track them to their origin.

On the north side of the city was my favorite building in all of Iraq. We found it while on a patrol to check on some old IED factories that had been raided a few months ago. Since the occupants were all in jail, we were curious about who had reoccupied the factories, both residential buildings in the northeastern part of the city. We entered the city on the southwest corner and zigzagged to avoid ambush.

At the building, it appeared that nobody was home. After checking the door for booby traps, we booted it and cleared the first floor. It had a dirt floor instead of the common concrete and tile, unnerving me a bit. Next we checked the second floor. At the top of the staircase was a metal door that went out onto the roof. As the fourth man in the stack, it was my job to breach the door for the team. I moved up and kicked it right below the latch. Instead of the door flying open, my foot pierced the rust-fatigued metal, and I was trapped in the door up to my thigh. Without missing a beat, someone shoved me, and the whole door, including me, went flying out. After a few minutes of belly laughing, the guys helped me free my leg.

The second factory site was also empty but not as amusing. From there, we snaked our way to the northern outskirts and began our return to the highway. About halfway back, we found my favorite building. It was an engineering marvel, though small in scale. The entire building was made from jerry cans—the cube cans designed for mass stacking in military logistics. If you look at pictures of the World War Two German Army in northern Africa, you might find a truckload of them. Instead of gas, these cans were filled with dirt and then stacked. The doorway was a simple rug hung across an opening. The poor farmer that built it was very proud of his work and ecstatic to tell me about it. The home was proof of the spirit of mankind.

The grand opening of the new Iraqi Police station across the highway was a big event. To make sure it went well, the whole company attended to provide security, along with the police chiefs from both stations in Hussainiyah and the national-level chief. The Iraqi media showed up in force. Everyone had to park outside on the highway's shoulder because the parking area had been used to lay out a huge banquet. Despite the size of the spread, it was not for the average policemen or us. We watched from the roof as the media and big cheeses mingled and feasted.

During this time, a new threat emerged. Instead of relying on armor-piercing IEDs, the enemy added massive, deep-buried IEDs, placing them a few feet under the road or in culverts. Instead of piercing armor, the shock wave from the enormous blast would kill the crew. Some also had accelerants to catch everything on fire. The fact that the bombs were deeply buried meant they were controlled by wire, so our Warlocks would not protect us at all. Nobody in the company hit one while we were with B Company, but other patrols passing through our area did, with several soldiers killed. This new variant was worrisome, but there wasn't much we could do about it.

Another day found us heading back to Taji to refit. We periodically returned to do laundry and vehicle maintenance as the JSS was too small for quality maintenance. While we were at Taji, Captain Jensen called and informed me I needed to run an errand for the battalion. On my return trip, I would swing down to Baghdad to pick something up from the battalion headquarters responsible for the area south of us. COP Callahan, located just off Dover in the heart of the Shaab neighborhood of Baghdad, was home to 2-325 Airborne Infantry of the 82nd Airborne Division, which was responsible for Shaab. I planned our route carefully; we would be traveling a great distance for a combat patrol, heading down the fabled Route Tampa before turning east to the Tigris River and into Baghdad, then returning back up Route Dover to the JSS.

Since 2-325 Airborne had been busy dropping barriers along routes, blocking off numerous streets, I had to call ahead to get directions to their gate, despite Callahan being right next to Dover. I did not want to play blind man's bluff in a neighborhood known for deadly IEDs. Also, we did not want to be at Callahan long. It had a reputation as being one of the most dangerous places for indirect fire. Just a month or so earlier, a massive barrage destroyed some thirty Humvees and other vehicles and almost brought the tall building down.

As soon as we crossed the Tigris River, I switched radio nets to contact 2-325 Airborne.

"White Falcon Main, Blackhawk Green One, over."

"White Falcon Main. Over."

"Entering your AO on Plutos en route to Callahan. Can we get directions to the gate? Over." I sounded silly, but not as silly as getting blasted by an IED because I got lost.

"Roger, stand by on that. We need you to delay your RP for a bit. We just got hit and need some time to get things under control. Out." Callahan had just taken a rocket attack. After a bit, they called me back and gave directions.

When we arrived at Callahan and I went up the massive staircase to the command post, the acrid smell of smoke lingered. Inside the command post, soldiers were busy reinforcing a patch in the wall. The enemy had managed to hit the command post itself, not just the building. I was more than happy to quickly pick up what we needed and get out of Dodge. Little did we know that in a couple weeks, we would be working for 2-325 Airborne, and our little foray had served as a leader's reconnaissance of where we would soon be patrolling.

CHANGE OF MISSION

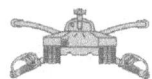

IN JANUARY, BLUE PLATOON RECEIVED a massive change in mission. We were cut free from Captain Jensen and Blackhawk Company and returned to Team Steel. White Platoon replaced us, something Captain Jensen was not pleased with. It wasn't a secret that White's platoon leader left much to be desired. Team Steel was reassigned from working in the Istiqlal Province and given to 2-325 Airborne, who wanted a tank company. Even though we would not be riding into Baghdad on our tanks, at least we had the beasts in storage. Team Steel as a whole had already proven itself. The company had been in a firefight on the banks of the Tigris and gained a reputation as a solid performer.

The move was exciting and greeted with a fair amount of fanfare. We even had a reporter from the *Colorado Springs Gazette* on hand as we gleefully packed up our stuff and got out of the pigeon-infested warehouses of Taji. No matter what we were getting ourselves into, we knew we could count on each other, and it was hard to imagine living conditions less appealing than Taji.

Team Steel would move into Combat Outpost (COP) Ford, near the western corner of Sadr City. We were replacing the Airborne's anti-tank company, allowing them to take some area from yet another company needing help. The anti-tank company was hardly bigger in size than our tank company but lacked the firepower potential we brought to the table.

Team Steel consisted of Red Platoon, Blue Platoon, an infantry "Gold" platoon we traded from Blackhawk Company, the headquarters section, and the maintenance section. We were aggressive, well trained, and above all, close knit. Team Steel was my home, my family. Since the war was going well, the M1A2 Abrams tanks and M2 Bradley infantry fighting vehicles were left at Camp Taji, an hour north of Baghdad. Team Steel rode into Baghdad in Humvees.

The headquarters section and the platoon leadership from each platoon headed to COP Ford first. We would begin the left-seat/right-seat ride with the Airborne. As I had been to COP Callahan before, I led our team's patrol to COP Ford. It was nice to feel relied upon. Our patrol was uneventful, though finding the actual entrance to the COP proved tougher than I anticipated. It was fairly nondescript, blending into the school next door.

The COP was a decently sized compound. Once inside the gate, we saw a helicopter landing zone that appeared big enough to sit two Black Hawks down at the same time. A row of concrete barriers protected an area for vehicle parking. Next to that was the COP's firing range, though we were told not to go shooting. It also served as the dud-explosives pit. On the other end of the vehicle parking was a barrier-protected maintenance workshop. Next to the maintenance area was our large generator. The engine was bigger than a tank engine and quite finicky. The living area of the COP was an old Baathist YMCA–type building protected by yet more barriers, and machine-gun bunkers dotted the roof. It was a stark contrast to our arrival at JSS Istiqlal.

Inside the building, a collection of larger rooms had been turned into platoon living quarters. Whole platoons shared rooms. All windows had been bricked over to prevent enemy fire from entering. The "lobby" of the building was the lounge and, every other day, the dining room. A basketball gym offered overflow housing. The company command post was in the back corner of the building. The Airborne had stuffed about as much as they could possibly fit onto a collection of folding tables. In one corner, they had the controls and monitors for the pan-tilt-zoom CCTV camera on top of a tall pole. From that, they kept an eye on the immediate surroundings. Maps and such liberally covered every inch of surface. It was clearly a working man's command post.

In a separate little building behind the command post was the supply room and the living quarters for an EOD detachment, led by Staff Sergeant Peterson from Fort Carson's 71st EOD Group. It was convenient to have EOD guys in-house, though we did not have control of them. They came and went with route-clearance patrols. Next to their building was a large military water bladder to supply our non-potable water needs. Water was pumped from the bladder to tanks on the roof where it fed the showers and sinks. Around the corner of the building was a row of porta potties, pumped out every few days by a local Iraqi contractor.

Part of the building was also home to a platoon from the neighboring Stryker infantry company. The platoon was bigger than both of our tank platoons combined. The Strykers rotated their platoons between COP Ford, Taji, and JSS Sadr City, which made it difficult to keep track of faces or get to know any of them well. The Strykers were from 2nd Cavalry Regiment of Vilseck, Germany. My cousin Andy was in the 2nd Cavalry, but Andy was up north in Diyala, and it was very unlikely I would run into him.

COP Ford had an inner-city hubbub. Something was always going on. Each platoon went on at least two patrols a day, usually for several hours at a time. Building upkeep suffered. The building was dark, dirty, and dank. Despite being in the middle of Baghdad, it was not cushy. Electricity was unreliable. Supplies, including a hot meal, only came every other day. To prevent the soldiers from the unpleasant necessity of eating MREs for all of the other meals, chest freezers were placed in the hallways, one for each platoon. Frozen pizzas and meat filled them. Each platoon had a microwave, and the courtyard was equipped with a charcoal grill. Airborne was happy to provide massive quantities of charcoal.

Much to our glee, we discovered the anti-tank company soldiers were masters of hoarding ammunition. They had stockpiled an entire twenty-foot container full of it. We had several basic combat loads of small-arms ammunition on hand when usually the most we could expect was a double combat load. They were prepared for a rainy day, even though the last year had been relatively quiet in the neighborhood. After all, Sadr City, home to the most organized insurgent force in Iraq, was just a few blocks away. We would soon be especially thankful for their ammunition stockpile.

Our left-seat/right-seat ride was much quicker than earlier ones. The rest of the company came to join us in a large convoy. The enemy gave them a housewarming gift, detonating an IED literally the second they entered the neighborhood. Fortunately, it only lightly damaged the HEMMT it hit, and nobody was injured.

I was happy to see the guys arrive. As they moved into our platoon's room, the Airborne troopers moved out. The room was pretty dirty. As it was barely big enough to fit the platoon, they had a hard time keeping it clean, and some surprises were found, like a box of dusty hamburger patties. We really couldn't blame them; the room was just too crowded and cluttered to allow constant cleaning. Instead, we planned ways to improve our lot.

The first night, we discovered another problem the Airborne had been living with. The Iraqi metal-frame bunk beds were incredibly flimsy and required delicate movements to avoid collapsing them. Our guys wrecked three the first night. When skinny little PFC Bailey broke one, we knew it was just a bad lot of beds. We designed beds that would not only be stout enough to support adults but also allow us to get the room more organized. The room had a very high ceiling, so if we got some vertical-space development, we would be golden. We just needed wood and nails.

Sergeant Weatherly and I shared a small side room off the main platoon room. It was very convenient as a platoon office. Runners from the command post would not accidentally wake any of the guys since the door was just inside the main-room hallway. I had a modified bunk bed with a desk underneath. Sergeant Weatherly had a bed and just had to put a laptop in his lap when typing. We built a partition wall to shield the room from hallway light whenever the main door opened. On this wall, we placed a large satellite image of the neighborhood. Next to it a dry-erase board kept the guys informed of the upcoming tasks and timelines.

Having a cozy home for the platoon was key as the soldiers were working hard, under a lot of stress, and living with very disruptive daily schedules. Even between patrols, there was much to be done. Our platoon was responsible for manning one of the guard posts on the roof, the small bunker facing the south. The bunker was made from a stack of sandbags with a roof. To protect the soldier from snipers, a piece of ballistic Humvee windshield covered the firing port. If the soldier needed to fire, it would push outward with ease, but a sniper's bullet would not be able to knock it in or penetrate it. This extra protection was vital as an enemy soldier would always have the advantage. There were just too many ways for one to sneak into position to shoot, and no matter how amazing the soldier is, he can't instantly notice the most subtle changes or movements when on guard for long periods of time.

I let the sergeants take care of the guard roster. They were more than capable and probably better at it than me. I also let them take care of maintenance, though I helped work on our Humvee. One day a week we scheduled a full morning of working on the vehicles and equipment. The preventative maintenance would ensure our equipment was working when we needed it, and even when we weren't taking damage in combat, machines just break. The heat and the sand never helped much either. Even though we had a weekly session scheduled, the equipment needed work every day in some manner or form. All of this had to happen between missions. Even when you discounted being accidentally wakened, nobody got more than about three hours of uninterrupted sleep a day.

While we were learning the ropes under the tutelage of the Airborne, the enemy left us alone. The Airborne explained that COP Ford was pretty safe from mortar attacks. With a school on one side and two mosques near it, there was little margin of error for the enemy artillerymen. Once, they missed Ford and hit a mosque. The locals immediately killed the enemy mortar crew and left the bodies, mortar, and getaway vehicle in the street for a patrol to collect.

The sniper threat was different, and the Airborne encouraged us to be very vigilant. Sergeant Weatherly and I decided we would try to never be stationary for more than fifteen minutes; that was about as fast as a sniper team could set up on us.

The previous few months had seen a concerted effort by the US to place barriers down all of the major streets. Each barrier was about six feet tall, ten feet long, and more than eighteen to twenty-four inches thick. Small, people-sized gaps were left on almost every small street to allow people to cross, but these barriers forced all cars to pass through checkpoints. The idea was to make it more difficult for the enemy to get around the city with weapons and ammo. The barriers also served to make it more difficult to place IEDs anywhere the enemy wanted.

On the other hand, the barriers limited our ability to get around, making us more predictable in our routes and hampering our maneuver when a fight did occur. Our first mission as a platoon was developing a detailed map of where we could get through with vehicles and where a person could squeeze by. After every patrol, I updated the large satellite-image map in the platoon room with a green marker.

Our arrival to COP Ford meant we inherited the job of placing more barriers. We still had stretches of road where the barrier walls were not yet complete. Barrier-placement missions were a major operation, involving combat units to secure the area, engineers to oversee the civilian contractor operating the crane to place the barriers, and logistical units to bring barriers. In a typical night, we would place hundreds of "Colorado" barriers along the curbs.

These missions were extremely long and boring. The enemy ceasefire was holding, and once the route-clearance team checked the area, the primary threat was mitigated. Blue Platoon was only responsible for the security, not the actual construction. The operations were conducted in the middle of night when there was no civilian activity, which meant we did not even have people to watch. Copious amounts of coffee were an essential logistical requirement for the platoon on these missions. The nice thing about the barrier missions was that results were visible, and we could actually track our progress.

Blue Platoon's area of responsibility was tiny compared to what I had patrolled on my previous deployment. The neighborhood of Binook in Beida measured about one kilometer by two kilometers— slightly less than one square mile of mixed-density commercial and residential buildings. Our area of responsibility was bordered on the northeast by the very busy Jamila Street, a main thoroughfare between Sadr City and Shaab that we called Route Gold. On the northwest side was Highway 23, the artery connecting the Ur and upper-Shaab neighborhoods to the freeway. For reasons unknown, we did not have a name for Highway 23. The freeway, with the Army Canal running down the median, was the southwestern boundary. Depending on which map you looked at, we called the freeway Route Pluto, Plutos, or Pluton. (The correct version was "Pluto S" for southbound and "Pluto N" for northbound.) Another four-lane, divided arterial street was the platoon's southeastern boundary. COP Ford was a block to the south of this street, which the locals called Palestine Street and we called Route Raniers. Near COP Ford, Palestine Street ended in a massive pile of dirt. Eventually, it would become an overpass and interchange with the freeway outside the neighborhood, though there was no work done on it while I was there.

Binook was divided almost equally into quarters by divided-lane streets running northwest to southeast. The middle street was not a thoroughfare because the Methaaq Market occupied it, and barriers had been placed to protect shoppers from cars trying to cut through.

Previous barrier-emplacement missions limited access from the boundary streets to a handful of locations. The martini glass–shaped intersection on Highway 23, also a major market, was one checkpoint. The intersection next to the defunct gas station was another, though we soon blocked it off with barriers and consolidated the checkpoint with the martini-glass one. Next to the university compound on the east corner was the only other entrance. An additional checkpoint was nearer COP Ford.

The neighborhood had a suburban feel with the majority of homes being the standard townhome with much of the extended family living in it. For the most part, the families were upper middle class. Most commuted daily to the financial sector across the Tigris River. We even had an Iraqi government minister living in the neighborhood. We did not go to local governance meetings, but a retired general living in the middle of the neighborhood was the de facto leader, and we went to him when we needed to work with the neighborhood. Each house was clean in appearance, and date palm trees provided shade to the front courtyards. The side of every house's gate bore a white tile with blue numbering marking its address. Back at the COP, we had an Iraqi postal map that showed every street name and every house number. The streets were as clean as any major US city's. Open sewage was rare. Many locomotive-sized electrical generators dotted the few vacant lots. It was an orderly neighborhood.

Apartment buildings were scattered throughout the area. A cluster of them stood near every market and above nearly every commercial building in the neighborhood. Most of them were three or four stories high, though a few five-story buildings were on the north end. Most of the apartments measured less than 400 square feet but still housed large numbers of people. All of the apartments kept their stairway access locked, presenting a challenge for any operations. The tops of all the apartment buildings had pigeon coops and water tanks. Many sported cell phone towers.

A large Iraqi Police station with some 250 policemen was on the north corner. A US Military Police unit could usually be found there, mentoring and partnering with the Iraqi Police. A block away stood a small medical clinic. Unlike the Hussainiyah Hospital, it was in good condition and seemed well staffed. Six schools educated the neighborhood children, including an all-girls high school. A medieval-looking church, St. Mary's, quietly sat on a major intersection at the western corner. While relatively undamaged, it did not host Masses as the car-bomb threat was too dangerous. A pair of mosques stood at opposite ends of the neighborhood. Red Platoon had the neighborhood immediately around the COP, which was home to many more mosques and schools. Gold Platoon had the neighborhood north of Binook.

On the eastern corner of the neighborhood was part of the University of Baghdad. The fenced compound reminded me of Camp Ashraf and was a collection of homes for professors. Closer to COP Ford was a run-down, multistory, multi-building project that had been occupied by a large number of squatter families. The area was called the Hawasem.

In February 2003, the Hawasem had been a massive construction site intended to be an extension of the University of Baghdad. That dream fell apart with the war, and squatters quickly turned it into a complex, four-story shantytown. The Hawasem was a dangerous and creepy place, home to a constantly changing population that included likely enemy fighters. Furthermore, its construction was clearly not to code, and the risk of injury from structure failures was ridiculously high. Jutting rebar, broken glass, and sharp metal scraps were more common than stable footing.

Just to the west of the Hawasem, the university was building a massive five-story dorm building that dominated the entire northeast half of the platoon's area. Its colors reminded us of Office Max back in the US, and we nicknamed the building such. The academic buildings were southeast, in Red Platoon's area.

The hub of the neighborhood, coincidentally exactly in the middle, was the Methaaq Market. It was much smaller than the Hussainiyah Market and less intimidating. The vast majority of the market was inside a large building, but many vendors set up in stalls lining the street in front, and several businesses occupied first-floor venues, extending the shopping area down the street, nearly all the way to the southeast border. I enjoyed our many patrols in the market. While we needed to have a strong presence in this hub, we also had shopping needs.

Our haphazard diet at the COP grew boring, and we felt the need to supplement with some local food. Fortunately, plenty of bakeries in the market made delicious bread. One made really good khubz, a flat round bread, and another made outstanding samoon, a diamond-shaped, hollow bread that was perfect for stuffing with other food. To avoid potential poisoning, we only bought bread that had already been made. We would walk to the market, five dollars in my pocket, and at some point stop by a bakery. Five dollars would buy enough bread to feed the platoon for a couple days.

Another shopping need revolved around our improvements to our home at COP Ford. Since we'd taken over the place, the sounds of saws and hammers were constant. Many soldiers on Team Steel were former carpenters. As soon as we moved in, Captain Looney and First Sergeant Gonzalez made it clear that the command post had priority of all construction materials. Requests to 2-325 Airborne Infantry for plywood, two-by-fours, and nails were filled sufficiently to make a first-rate command post. Soon it was the poster child for improving a position, and its design allowed for smoother operations when we got into firefights.

The platoon also wanted to improve our position in the COP. Getting lumber for bunk beds was a challenge. Every time the platoon went to Callahan for anything, we found a way to pick up lumber, but eventually the bean counters caught on, and Sergeant Weatherly and I noticed the big tower camera often watching our soldiers when we were at Callahan. After one trip, I was shocked to see that Sergeant Key had brought back several full sheets of plywood. He must have figured out how to sling them under the vehicles, because we definitely did not have any lumber showing from above.

Nails were a different story. Finding those at Callahan was too difficult, and requests went unfilled. Again, we turned to the local economy. One hot afternoon, we went on foot patrol as normal. We plotted our route so that our return would bring us by the hardware store about a quarter mile away from COP Ford. It did not sell lumber, but we bought a twenty-pound box of nails, and the guys took turns lugging the heavy box home.

While we enjoyed success in improving our room's furniture, improving the electricity was a different story. The generator that provided electricity to the living areas was worn out. We had an Army five-kilowatt generator to provide electricity for the command post, but it was not enough to take care of the entire building. The large generator by the maintenance area tried, and generally failed, to provide for the rest of us. Several times a day, our lights would flicker and then go out as the generator shut down.

I often joined Danny Bowden and Keith Hanson as they worked on the generator. Danny was a skilled mechanic, and Keith had worked on large engines with the railroad prior to enlisting in the Army. I couldn't tell you how many times they took the engine apart, cleaned it, and rebuilt it. Each time, they were able to coax a few more hours of life out of it, but it really needed new parts. A market in Sadr City specialized in generator parts, but because it was in Sadr, we had to ask Iraqis to go and then hope they would bring us the correct parts. Hope is not a method, and eventually we got a whole new generator in May.

The suburban aspect of our neighborhood included rush-hour traffic jams that would have impressed even Atlanta. Checkpoints were the culprit. Every morning, hordes of cars departed the neighborhood, returning mid to late afternoon. Patrols requiring Humvees often got us stuck in the jams also.

The tactics used in 2006 of keeping locals at their distance had been replaced by allowing them in close. This served two purposes. First, they provided a great early warning. If the locals stayed away from you, it was because they knew a fight was coming. Second, it allowed us to interact with the people more. We were more the friendly neighborhood cops and less the impersonal aliens occupying the county. Despite this, we still maintained the right-of-way as we needed to keep moving to accomplish the mission, and the locals were more than happy to grant it. The problem was that there was just nowhere to go. Traffic always filled in every possible gap and lane or sidewalk. You just can't win them all.

I was always amazed that in a country with pretty nonexistent traffic laws, we did not see many car crashes. Of course, there were some crashes, and one involved us. During our curfew patrol one night, we were driving through the martini-glass market when, without warning, a sedan rocketed out of a side street and T-boned Sergeant Key's Humvee. There wasn't a scratch on the armored Humvee, but the sedan was heavily damaged.

As soon as we all came to a stop and established security, our aid-and-litter team ran to the car. The driver was in rough shape. He had not been wearing a seat belt, and the steering wheel left a massive mark on his chest. The man's face was bloody, and he was unconscious. As we extracted him, I couldn't help but note the smell of alcohol on his breath. We did our best to treat the man for his obvious injuries while a crowd formed. A man soon arrived and stated he was the brother of the driver. Without fanfare, the brother grabbed the still unconscious driver by a wrist and dragged him off, yelling at him for bringing shame on the family. We shoved the mangled sedan to the sidewalk and continued on our patrol. The car had already been removed by the time we returned to the market the next day.

Of course, it was still a war zone and not a pleasant suburb, something the enemy sought to remind us of. We hadn't been in charge of COP Ford very long when the enemy decided to test us. Blue Platoon was between patrols and I was trying to catch a little sleep when it happened.

BOOM! A heavy stream of fire from a M249 SAW immediately followed the explosion. The loud explosion and gunfire could only mean one thing, and without a moment to fully wake up, I rolled off my bunk and tossed my body armor and helmet on. As I snatched up my rifle and ran out of the office, I was joined by the whole platoon flooding up the staircase to the roof. Our platoon's role for defending the COP was to take up positions on the south and west sides. As soon as Will Williams reached the top of the stairs, he aimed his M203 nearly straight up and fired a flare round into the sky. It was the prearranged signal to our local checkpoints to lock down the neighborhood—we were under attack. With Sergeant Weatherly confirming our guys were established into fighting positions on the roof, and satisfied there was no enemy in view, I ran to the command post for orders.

The silence that followed the initial machine-gun fire and rush to arms was deafening. Within minutes, everyone on the COP was accounted for. We had no casualties and no damage. The enemy had done a drive-by RPG attack on the guard bunker facing north. It was manned by the Stryker guys, and their guard had performed perfectly. The immediate volume of return fire deterred the enemy from following up the RPG.

A few minutes later, Blue Platoon assembled a patrol to check the immediate neighborhood. As soon as we rounded the corner to the northeast side of the compound, it was clear the enemy was long gone. Locals had come out to see what happened. They did not appreciate the enemy much.

The enemy must have been a bit leery of our defenses. A drive-by shooting is an inaccurate method of attack but offers minimal exposure and a rapid retreat. The RPG they fired didn't even hit the COP. Instead, it smoked a BMW parked fifty meters down the street. It was an impressive miss considering the gunner had only been a football field away from the COP. The attack was a great test for us, giving us a good evaluation of our own reactions and plans.

A week or so later, the enemy tested us again, shooting an RPG at the gate of the COP. Perhaps it was the very same crew, because they were clearly concerned for their own safety. This time, they launched the RPG from so far away it took us a while to figure out they were actually trying to hit the COP. The RPG impacted the corner of a house some 400 meters distant and on the other side of Palestine Street. Despite the RPG's wide miss, the enemy gunner still received a healthy dose of return fire from the infantrymen guarding the gate. The optic on their M240B allowed their rounds to get a lot closer to their mark, and the enemy ducked away quickly.

AMBUSH

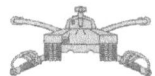

THE NORTH CORNER OF THE neighborhood was on the edge of an area Battalion referred to as the Triangle of Death. The major streets obviously made a triangle shape, and they happened to be one of the major IED hot spots. The north corner was a crossroads of major traffic, and the barriers forced patrols onto the main thoroughfares. To counter the enemy efforts, Battalion wanted me to conduct a lot of ambushes.

Planning and executing an ambush in the middle of a dense and busy neighborhood was quite the challenge. Getting into a decent ambush position without the enemy knowing demanded all of the creativity we could muster. Many ambush patrols in the past had been compromised and counter-ambushed by the enemy. To ensure that I had put enough effort into planning the operation, Battalion required a massive ambush-patrol packet—a seven to nine-page document that required me to spend hours preparing. I complained while preparing them, but in hindsight, the packet did force me to revisit every last detail in every contingency.

The area we were targeting was slightly larger than three or four football fields with only a handful of good positions. A few apartment buildings provided elevation to see over the barriers. A battered parking garage in the heart of the triangle was not bad. We did not want to use the same position more than once a month, so we needed a lot of options.

During the daytime patrols, I concentrated on reconnoitering potential ambush spots. As the area was also a major commercial hub of activity, our real purpose was easily masked by business visits and systematically visiting every single apartment. Once the sun went down, we would return and evaluate the lighting. After a few days, we knew every lock that wasn't locked and every home that nobody called home.

While we still did not have a large range of location options, we at least had good information on which to plan our methods of infiltrating and exfiltrating each one. Additionally, the people grew accustomed to us going through buildings, and we did not turn as many heads on patrol in the area.

The pressure to execute an ambush patrol forced me to conduct our first ambush prior to completing our thorough reconnaissance of the area, so we still had some questions about locked doors at night, but we knew enough to get into a good position. I was also simultaneously planning follow-on ambushes; Battalion wanted at least two a week.

About noon, we completed our morning patrol, and as we gathered around the trucks immediately after pulling back into COP Ford, I gave them the warning order.

"Guys, we will execute an ambush patrol near the triangle. Briefing will be at thirteen hundred hours. SP will be eighteen hundred. The rest of the timeline will be on the platoon board. Check it as you download your kit. Special equipment list is also posted. Questions?" There were none. Before taking my kit off, I wrote the required information on the dry-erase board. I finished and saw Jay looking at it. "Did I miss anything, Sergeant?" I asked him. He smiled and shook his head no.

"I'll go get with Gold and make sure the guys they loan us for tonight are at the briefing." Jay turned to go into our room.

I followed Jay in and stripped my kit and body armor off. My uniform blouse was soaked in sweat, so I took it off and hung it on my bunk to dry. Grabbing a water bottle, I sat and fired up my laptop, opening the ambush-patrol packet I had submitted to Battalion earlier. Quickly, I copied important pieces of information into my field notebook and then went back out to the platoon room.

My orders process by now was pretty well known to the platoon and part of a good rhythm. I did not believe in surprises or theatrics in briefing. I wanted the guys to know as much as they could. Everyone on the patrol would hear the briefing. This meant whoever stayed behind to man the guard post while we were gone would also man it during the briefing. I also did not mind the guys watching as I copied information from my notebook onto the board and posted the graphics on our blown-up imagery map of the neighborhood. I encouraged them to ask questions if something they saw did not make sense. A hole poked in the plan at this stage was fixable still.

At 1 p.m., the platoon gathered around our map board. Some were still munching on lunch, but everyone appeared interested. Tonight's patrol was a changeup.

"Okay, guys, everyone is here. Thank you for joining us." I nodded to the infantrymen before resuming. "The only change to our load out is the infantry fire team will split up to ride where there are seats. Sergeant, add your names to the trip ticket as soon as I'm done briefing. We will be the only platoon out in the area, and route clearance is not scheduled to come through this area tonight." I looked around at the platoon's faces.

"Weather and light: Clear sky tonight. Sunset is eighteen twenty three, moonrise at twenty-one fifteen, with eighty-five percent illumination. Gonna be pretty bright.

"We are targeting the IED cells. They have been operating in the triangle, as you know, and have been planting EFPs mainly in the medians, but also on the tops of the barriers and in the gaps. Typical tactics are for them to make a drive-by first to check the area. They have been using sedans mainly. We can expect four guys in the team. The driver will stay in, the TC will have a PKM at most, more likely an AK or RPD. There is a good chance he won't bring it out unless he is going to shoot. The driver will stay in the car, likely with it still in gear. The sappers will be in the back seat. From the time they stop to the time they are done planting can be as little as ten seconds. If they have to prep a spot, it could go maybe a minute max. I believe the most likely spot tonight will be in front of the generator where the wires can blend in with the rat's nest there. If they show up, they will show up close to curfew. Questions?

"Okay, Blue Platoon will establish an ambush at mike-bravo-four-four-six-five-niner-five-eight-four"—I pointed to the building on the satellite photo—"no later than twenty hundred to destroy enemy IED cells in order to allow company and battalion freedom of movement.

"Concept and scheme of the operation: We will move out in the trucks to the rally point. From there, all dismounts will conduct a presence patrol through the commercial district. We will go in and out of every building. String it out, mix it up, make it hard on the head counters. At the ambush site, Tex, Will, and Garcia will stay with me. This gives us the 203, the SAW, and another radio. More than enough firepower for any IED cell that tries to fight back. Everyone else will continue the patrol to the end of the block and then return to the trucks. Once we are established, the truck will conduct a mounted patrol in the area near the Hawasem.

"When the enemy shows up, we will wait for them to show us a weapon or the IED as our rules of engagement require. I will initiate the ambush. Will, you will pump HE into it until cease-fire or the car catches fire. Garcia, you will target the driver until cease-fire. Tex and I will get the sappers, then target anyone left. Sergeant Weatherly, have the trucks establish a SBF facing north on the street as soon as you hear us shooting. Once you are set, the four of us will come off the building and assault across the kill zone.

"Actions on contact prior to splitting off the ambush team are per SOP. If we get compromised, we will immediately break contact to the rally point and meet the trucks there. Alternate linkup point will be the clinic. If we are attacked, we will hold on the roof, and the rest of the platoon will attack to us. If the trucks are attacked, SOP battle drill. We will leave the ambush position and move to a rally point of the mounted element's choosing, but name the point immediately so we know where to go.

"See the timeline on the board. I want to highlight actions-on-contact drills at fifteen hundred. Special considerations: Tex will also have his radio on platoon net, and all four of us will have an IR strobe on our helmets activated, plus a spare. No change to medical or recovery. Sergeant Weatherly will explain that to the infantrymen. No changes to signals. Questions?"

I moved back so anyone with questions could step up and show me on the map. Several of the guys came up and started discussing things amongst themselves. I quietly watched the platoon. Some of the guys would study silently, then ask their sergeant a question about individual tasks for their piece of the mission.

While the guys got ready, I went to the command post to check for intelligence updates. There were none. Back in the room, I ate a big dinner and worked on tomorrow's plans until it was time to get ready. Periodically, I stepped out into the platoon room to look around and check preparations.

Soon, the platoon room got loud as our pregame, traditional singing of War's "Low Rider" accompanied the music blasting. With grins on faces, the guys danced while kitting up. Morale was high. The song ended, and the guys finished. They checked each other and walked past me, giving me a chance to inspect them as they went out to the trucks. *We have a good thing going in this platoon. Our systems and routines are working well.* I followed the last soldier out to the trucks.

About five minutes prior to schedule, the platoon departed COP Ford. After zigzagging north, we parked near the medical clinic and dismounted eleven of the twenty members of the patrol. Our plan was to string our patrol out so it would be harder for enemy observers to keep track of everyone. We walked through businesses and into apartment buildings.

Once the sun went down, we prepared our infiltration. The whole foot patrol went into a large four-story apartment building. I had selected it for its commanding view and some palm trees that broke up silhouettes on the roof. It was also even with what was in my mind the most likely IED placement site on Highway 23. After talking with nearly every occupant of the building and going in and out of different apartments with different numbers of soldiers, four of us peeled off from the patrol and occupied the roof. The rest of the patrol snaked back through more buildings before returning to the trucks. Once at the Humvees, Jay led them on a patrol route that kept them within about a five-minute response time but away from the ambush zone.

On the roof, we became very still and very quiet and settled in for a long wait. Any noise heard by residents would likely get relayed to the enemy or, just as bad, the police. If anyone saw our shadows on the roof, the same result was inevitable. I was just as worried about a passing police or Iraqi Army patrol seeing us and shooting at us as I was the enemy launching a counter-ambush. Up in the night sky, I saw the infrared strobes of drones and Apache gunships passing in my night vision. Down on the streets below, not a soul stirred. Curfew was in effect and obeyed. Every now and then, a random police patrol would go by. Iraqi Police were always easy to see at night. Their rotating blue lights seemed to be linked to the transmission. If the truck was moving, the lights were on.

I was equally worried about fratricide from US forces. Each of us had an infrared strobe in our helmet band, blinking to anyone with night vision. Additionally, we made sure that Battalion knew exactly where we were. Jay monitored the fires net for any aircraft calling our position as suspicious armed men. Our paranoia was well founded as I watched a pair of Apaches begin a gun-run orbit oriented on our position. It was impossible to tell if they were just looking at us or evaluating us as targets. The thought was nerve wracking. Efforts to ensure everyone in the area knew we were friendly paid off, and the danger from the Apaches passed.

A few hours later, well after curfew, a sedan approached from the northeast. Instantly, the hair on the back of my neck stood up. The sedan passed us very slowly and traveled the full length of the street to the western corner of the neighborhood. As we watched, it turned around and then came back with its lights off. *This is it!* I had no doubt at all the sedan contained an enemy IED sapper team. I radioed Jay that we were about to be in contact. As the sedan continued towards us slowly, we positioned ourselves and readied our weapons. I just had to wait until I saw the IED before we could open fire. *These rules of engagement suck. It is obvious these are enemy, but I have to physically see the IED. Stupid. Focus. Patience, Galen.*

My thumb rested gently on the rifle safety switch in anticipation as the car finally made a U-turn and came to a stop about seventy meters short of our position. The car was on the far side of the median, facing away from us. It was perfect. The range was not too far for us to accurately engage, but it was far enough to be more difficult for the enemy to shoot back. Best of all, it was unlikely the slugs of the IED would travel to us if the IED blew up in the fire.

The back doors of the sedan opened and the trunk popped up. Two men in dark clothing got out of the sedan and looked around. One went to the median and started moving paver stones. The front passenger door opened, and another man got out and took over looking around. The angle and the distance prevented me from seeing what was in the trunk. *If they pull anything out of the trunk, I will call it good.* Both of the men at the back of the sedan went to the trunk. With a flick of my thumb, I moved the safety switch to fire.

I whispered to Tex which enemy sapper I would shoot. "I have right."

"I'll take left." Tex was on the same plan.

A small shout came from the lookout next to the passenger door, and suddenly the enemy slammed the trunk closed and they all jumped into the sedan. Without hesitation, it rapidly drove off to the north as an

Iraqi Police truck slowly came up the street in the distance. Furiously, I realized a random Iraqi Police patrol had just blown our ambush, and there was nothing I could do about it. The enemy would not try this spot again tonight. It was time to leave.

Defeated, we went to the door to the stairs. It was now locked from the inside. Despite the building being nearly impossible to get onto from a neighboring one, the residents apparently also locked the roof door in addition to the street door. We weighed our options. We did not want to damage the door and cause hardship on the residents, but we needed out.

As a pair of Apaches flew over, I had an idea that bordered on comical. We all took turns jumping as high as we could so we would make a lot of noise when we landed. Then I took out my pistol and used the butt of it to bang on the roof. After a couple minutes a sleepy man opened the stair door and looked at us with bewilderment. He asked if we had come from the sky. I grinned and nodded and asked if we could come in. The man let us in, and we went down the stairs and out the street door. I always wondered if the rumor took hold that Americans were dropping out of the sky at night; I figured it wouldn't hurt if it did.

Our linkup with the rest of the platoon and our return to COP Ford went without incident. I was frustrated. There was zero doubt in my mind that we'd had an enemy IED sapper team in our sights. I had been the dutiful officer, waiting for the conditions required by our strict rules of engagement. The result had been the enemy getting away and living to place more IEDs and likely kill more US and Iraqi soldiers. I had done exactly as ordered, following the law of warfare and legal orders, but it did not feel like the right thing. Had we been fighting a uniformed enemy, I would have been free to engage the second I recognized them as enemy. Here I had recognized the enemy, yet had been unable to engage. I found myself regretting my failure.

Two nights later, we returned to the Triangle of Death for another ambush patrol. This time, I brought a fire team from the infantry platoon to add firepower to the ambush. I worried the enemy had gotten word of our previous ambush attempt. I figured the people would tell them that US forces had somehow gotten onto the battlefield where their lookouts and early-warning system had failed to detect the incursion. If I were the enemy, I would increase my firepower and vigilance.

Our newest ambush patrol would use the old parking garage next to the mall on the opposite side of Highway 23. The ramps had collapsed, so there was no easy way to get onto the upper levels, but it also meant the cars up there would always be there, providing cover and concealment to us. This time, we faked a patrol to COP Callahan for our infiltration. We did a quick drop-off from the Humvees north of the ambush site. From there we carefully approached the parking garage. We had brought a collapsible ladder that folded up into a backpack. At the wall, we got it out and set it up, planning on climbing into our ambush position; but as Cory tried to climb it, the ladder broke, dropping him the few short feet back to the ground. After kidding him about being too big, we cleaned up the pieces and found another way into the parking garage.

Once in position, infrared strobes blinking away like Christmas-tree lights, we settled in for the enemy to show up. I was still worried about fratricide, and every time a US patrol went by, we got as low as we could. Sergeant Weatherly shared my concern and did everything in his power to ensure everyone in the battalion's area knew where we were.

After a mind-numbing wait, my worst fears came true. A US route-clearance patrol came by from the west. The patrol used plenty of white light from headlights and spotlights to make spotting IEDs easier. Even the machine guns mounted on the trucks had spotlights. With all of the light, I knew they would not be using night-vision goggles, and that meant they would not see our infrared strobes. Furthermore, our position relied on nobody shining light on us to remain hidden. As the lead truck entered what would be our ambush kill zone, it stopped. The fifty-caliber machine gun pointed directly at us, bright white light blinding us. A second truck swung its machine gun to point at us. My life flashed before my eyes as we all tried to press into the concrete. With a Hail Mary going, I fumbled with my radio to the battalion's radio frequency.

"White Falcon Main, Steel Blue One; we are about to take friendly fire from a patrol using white light, mike-bravo-four-four-three-seven-niner-five-eight-two! Make them go away before they shoot up my ambush team! Out!" I didn't care about noise discipline now. I was way too loud to stay hidden from the enemy, but maybe the gunners might hear English. *Fat chance of that.* "Get low and pray, guys!"

Jay sent text messages on the Blue Force Tracker to every icon in the area in hopes of helping get the message across before we were shot. He also jumped onto the battalion fires radio net to try to get the message to the unidentified unit. After an eternity, the route-clearance patrol stopped pointing their machine guns at us and drove away.

The incident severely shook me. I decided we were done for the night, and if I had my way, forever, and we left the parking garage and linked up with our Humvees. Back at COP Ford, I unloaded my frustrations on Captain Looney. I was furious and wanted him to find an explanation as to why we nearly got killed despite the ambush packet and all our efforts to ensure everyone knew where we were.

After weathering my barrage of anger, Captain Looney called Battalion. It turned out the route-clearance unit that normally patrolled our area was in the middle of being replaced by another unit. Tonight was the first night the new unit was using their equipment and call signs, so the message never got to them. A minor and routine event caused a near catastrophe, and the risk we were taking weighed heavily on my shoulders.

About a week later, a Stryker was hit by an IED next to the Hawasem. Battalion asked us to concentrate our ambush efforts on this area, which was more challenging. The buildings were not as convenient, and there were more people sympathetic to the enemy. Still, we did our duty.

As the checkpoint at the Hawasem was not manned during the night, we set up nearby. We had heard rumors the enemy was planning on disrupting the checkpoint itself. Placing an IED in the checkpoint would accomplish that and more. From a pile of rubble between the nearest Hawasem building and Office Max, we quietly watched the street. Our wait was rewarded. A couple hours after curfew, a man with a World War Two–era Soviet submachine gun came walking down the street from the direction of Sadr City. The weapon was not issued by the government, making the owner unlikely to be friendly. The man's path would take him within fifteen feet of me. In the near pitch black, I was not worried about being compromised and decided we could try to capture the man instead of killing him. The excellent cover and dispersion of our team gave me confidence it could work. When he got directly in front of me, I sprang the trap.

"*AGUF PARA ARMAE!*" I yelled, ordering the man to stop and put his hands in the air. The man dropped the submachine gun and complied.

"EPW team!" My command set in motion well-rehearsed drills, and two of my men quickly searched and flex-cuffed the enemy fighter. The weapon was cleared and inspected. It was a PPSh-41, an antique weapon that fired relatively rare ammunition. The man only had about twenty bullets for it in a rusty drum magazine. Soon we delivered our prisoner to the battalion intelligence section at Callahan. Our ambush's catch had been amusing, but it was nothing like the enemy we had lost on our first try.

A few days later, a runner from the command post summoned me. A Stryker had gotten hit by an IED just a few blocks from COP Ford, down the street from St Mary's church. Quickly, the platoon loaded up our Humvees and responded to the scene. Danny Bowden and one of his mechanics joined us. By the time we got there, the Stryker soldiers had already prepared the damaged Stryker for towing and were ready to roll out. A quick discussion with their platoon leader, Kenny, a West Point classmate of mine, and my guys set out to find the triggerman's location. We found an abandoned building with some fresh footprints in the dirt on the second floor. Looking out the window gave us a perfect view of the exact spot of the IED's detonation. The triggerman was long gone, and there were no clues left behind. I did not feel like we were winning the IED battle. Still, we were fortunate. The number of IED strikes on US vehicles was low, even lower when compared to what we experienced in Diyala.

In addition to our ambush patrols, 2-325 Airborne was very adamant that we conduct a lot of foot patrols. It made sense to us; they were light infantry, after all, and they like to kid tankers about being fat and lazy. True to their requests, we often conducted our patrols completely on foot, traveling to the far corners of our neighborhood. Walking a couple miles does not seem bad until you add on the weight of the combat load, a few hundred flights of stairs as we went into many buildings, and the oppressive heat and humidity of Baghdad.

On one of our patrols to the southern corner of the Triangle of Death, we were busy checking on the businesses when Battalion requested us to respond to aid another platoon on the north edge of Shaab. They knew where we were and figured we would be the closest and thus fastest patrol available. Battalion requested we talk to them on their radio frequency to coordinate the response. When I told them it would take us some time to walk back to COP Ford to get our trucks for the drive to north Shaab, the response caught me off guard. The Airborne responded they never expected us to walk that far from the COP because they wouldn't. So much for the reputation of being fat and lazy tankers.

Shortly after that, we stopped conducting patrols without any truck at all. Gold Platoon was undertaking a foot patrol near the northwest corner of our neighborhood when they were hit by an IED made from a 57 mm anti-aircraft round designed specifically to hurt personnel. Gold took some casualties, but they had a Humvee to evacuate the wounded back to the aid station. Jay and I discussed the incident and decided that we wanted to have at least two Humvees with us no matter what. They would provide the means for evacuating wounded and would also give some Warlock protection against the IEDs. Still, all but four soldiers, the absolute bare minimum needed to drive and gun the Humvees, ended up walking on patrols.

About this time, 1-68 Armor took over the whole area from 2-325 Airborne. Our sister companies replaced the Airborne companies and their responsibilities so the Airborne could return home to Fort Bragg. They had been in Baghdad for fifteen months.

One night, while on patrol in the north area of Binook, an Iraqi citizen flagged us down with a frantic request for help. His neighbor, a wealthy banker, had just been attacked in his house by insurgents. While he was not severely injured in the attack, the enemy had kidnapped his daughter and slipped through a footpath gap in the wall lining Jamila Street. We quickly raced over in hopes of catching the enemy, but they were long gone. All that remained was a very distraught family. They knew it was unlikely they would ever see their daughter again, even if they paid the ransom. JAM used kidnappings for ransom as a method to fund their war against the government.

Another night found Blue Platoon serving as the battalion's quick reaction force. As the QRF, we had to be ready to roll out the gate in under five minutes in support of anyone anywhere in the entire battalion's area. Captain Looney had successfully lobbied to get us permission to serve as the QRF from COP Ford so we could work on planning other missions while we waited around. We were very thankful for this. QRF was a very boring affair most of the time.

This night was different. A checkpoint on Route Dover where it crossed the canal on the north edge of Baghdad was in trouble. They had called Battalion to report someone placed an IED in their checkpoint. It seemed a bit dubious, but Battalion wanted us to go find out.

The mission required us to travel up Route Dover through Shaab to the canal. I was not excited about it as the route had seen some nasty IEDs lately. Matt Vigeant had a close call earlier. The armor-penetrating

EFP had been a dud, causing a half-hearted poof instead of killing him and his Humvee's crew. Others had not been so lucky.

We rolled carefully up Dover. If there was an IED at the checkpoint, it was likely south of it to target a responding unit, so we stopped the trucks a few hundred meters south of the checkpoint. There was not a soul in sight. *Something's wrong.* I dismounted our fire team, and we worked our way on foot towards the checkpoint from the west. A tall chain link fence prevented us from getting more than twenty-five meters from the highway. At the checkpoint, I still could not see any of the irregular forces that were supposed to man it twenty-four seven.

Finally, I noticed a head sticking over a berm farther north. Leaving the rest of the team in positions to cover me, I walked over to the man and found the rest of the forces. The leader of the checkpoint informed me the IED was literally in the checkpoint. It had been somehow placed there while surrounded by guards. Even more doubtful now, I asked him to show me the IED. The man led me back to the checkpoint and then suddenly stopped out in the open. There, not twenty feet from me, was an IED, the steel plates of two charges clearly facing me.

I dove for cover on the west shoulder of the road. The man suddenly realized the stupidity of standing in the kill zone and took off running north. The IED was placed on the east shoulder, between me and the rest of the platoon. The rest of the dismount team was still in danger. I told them to start low-crawling past the IED. While they started that long and slow task, I told the checkpoint crew to return to their berm and stay there until we could remove the IED. I added that I needed them to stop any friendly forces from driving south into the checkpoint.

"One, Four. Six wants you on the radio."

Captain Looney wanted to speak to me. Unfortunately my MBITR personal radio did not have the range to speak to him, so I needed to get to a Humvee. I too began to low-crawl away from the IED.

"One, Four; Six wants to know what's taking so long." I asked Jay to let him know I needed to low-crawl out of the kill zone and it would take some time. Finally, I was safely out of the kill zone and jogged the remaining distance back to the Humvee. As I sat in my Humvee, a blatantly obvious answer hit me in the face. *Why didn't you just have a truck flip the platoon radio to retransmit to company? Duh.*

While we waited for engineers to show up with the bomb squad, we set off to find the triggerman, following the command wire from the IED to a run-down industrial complex east of it. The other end of the wire was not connected to anything. The enemy triggerman likely took his detonator with him when he fled. As long as it took for us to get to his position, he had ample time for disassembly and escape. We were still not making progress on the IED battle.

Captain Looney loved raids. That was his passion, and he spent a lot of time developing intelligence to find a target to raid. Raids were a big production. It took at least two platoons and lots of planning to execute one. One night he had us undertake a raid just northeast of Methaaq Market. In the middle of the night, we snuck out on foot. After quietly reaching the house, we were forced to become super noisy: the gate was way better built than anything we had worked with before. Finally, some of us were shoved over the front wall into the front yard. The gate easily opened from the inside, but the front door was just as difficult, and before we could breach it, the man of the house opened it and let us inside. It was a very anticlimactic raid. We failed to find the enemy we were looking for. The whole time we were there, I couldn't help trying to remember which house belonged to the government minister. It was somewhere on this street.

Another raid came with no notice. Captain Looney had seen some suspicious activity on the camera after curfew. Someone with an AK-47 had peeked out of a gate near the mosque east of COP Ford. Quickly, Blue Platoon formed up with some of the headquarters-section soldiers and snuck out of Ford. It was Red Platoon's area, so I wasn't completely familiar with it. When we came around a corner next to the target house and ran into a bunch of concertina wire, I was a bit puzzled.

Wire can be difficult to see in night vision on a dark night, so what happened next didn't surprise me, but it gave me a huge smile.

I stopped the platoon to conduct a leader's recon of the target house. As Captain Looney came up to me in the formation, he didn't see the wire and walked straight into it. Looking thoroughly embarrassed, he carefully pulled the wire from his pant legs and tried to pretend nothing happened.

Avoiding looking at him lest he see my smirk, I continued my recon. *I bet this is the same sadistic happiness my guys enjoyed when my foot was stuck in the door.* Quickly and smoothly, we assaulted the house, careful not to damage anything or unnecessarily harm anyone in it. It turned out the man we saw was the leader of the checkpoint and thought he had heard someone outside his house. He went out with the AK-47 to make sure his family was safe. All's well that ends well. While the raid was a bust, watching the commander get tangled in wire was worth the price of admission.

Some of the raids we conducted were with the help of military intelligence soldiers, who used highly classified methods to target the higher commanders of the enemy. While those missions tended to have a much higher success rate, they were incredibly frustrating because the military intelligence soldiers were so hush hush about everything. It's hard to navigate and set up on a target when you don't know even the most basic information. One of the raids ended up targeting a house just a block away from COP Ford. It was crazy to think the enemy was comfortable living and operating that close to our base.

In early March, Captain Looney became convinced the enemy was hiding leaders in the Hawasem. I was also pretty sure enemy fighters were living in the Hawasem, but I did not think any were high level, and rooting them out from the squatters would be hard. One afternoon, AJ told me they were putting together a raid on Office Max since it was the only nice building in the Hawasem and thus had to be the location of the leaders. Such logic failed to register with me.

Office Max was huge. It was five stories high and had a ton of rooms. The operation would take the whole company to pull off. The assumption that enemy leadership was staying there did not make sense. On patrols, we had noticed the same two guys guarding the building every time we passed it, which did not suggest the alert posture one would expect from enemy leadership.

The next morning, I decided to patrol the Hawasem. We would visit the professors compound, the squatters, and Office Max. By visiting everything, we wouldn't reveal our true focus. Instead of raiding Office Max and risking damage to it, we walked in and asked for a tour. The two men gladly consented. They let us look at every room, inspect their weapons, and I took a picture with them so we had their faces captured. Our afternoon patrol systematically went through the neighborhood across the street, doing more of the same.

That evening I told Captain Looney the view from the top of Office Max was impressive. I showed him the pictures and described everything we had found. He didn't say anything to me, but later Clint told me Captain Looney and AJ were furious with me for ruining the raid. I was okay with that.

AWAKENING THE DRAGON

MARCH OF 2008 WAS THE month I aged a decade in a couple weeks. For Blue Platoon, the fighting associated with the Sadr uprising of 2008 started on March 17. The uprising in response to the Iraqi Army offensive in Basra officially started on the twenty-third, but on the seventeenth the war turned uglier for us.

The evening of March 16 brought a change of mission for the platoon. We would take a break from patrolling the Beida neighborhood and drive our M1114 Humvees to Taji to trade them in for newer M1151 Humvees. The M1151s were supposed to have slightly better armor. They also had improved air-conditioning, electrical systems, and even a power turret traverse. While we had inherited the M1114s from a junkyard in Ramadi and breathed life into them and made them ours, the M1151s had been used by the Airborne infantry battalion we were attached to for a couple months before 1-68 Armor moved in to their old sector.

Instead of the headquarters section traveling up as a whole and being away from the COP, one crew was attached to a platoon for the mission. Mike Elledge was going to return to the platoon in a couple weeks as part of a larger personnel rotation, so he would join Blue Platoon for the trip to get Captain Looney's M1114 replaced. This would let Mike get into the swing of being a truck commander and allow Captain Looney to stay behind and run the company.

In order to minimize downtime, each platoon was going up to Taji in the afternoon. There they would spend the evening preparing the old Humvees for turn-in and readying the new ones for combat. The next morning would involve final combat preparations and then the return to COP Ford. All of the tools and components had to be accounted for and recorded. Thousands of rounds of ammo had to be transferred from one to the other and carefully stored. Medical kits, stretchers, pyrotechnics, camo netting, and spare batteries rounded out the list of items to change over.

Little things that personalized our trucks had to be undone and then redone on the new truck. I ran a piece of cord across the ceiling of the truck to hang my radio hand mics from. This allowed me to find them more easily and put them in reach of both the driver and the gunner if they needed to use the radio. I also taped a pad of luminescent plastic to the dash and hung a dry-erase marker on a string next to it. This pad allowed me to write notes even in pitch-black night. Reference cards went on the visor. A Plexiglas map board went on the right side of the radio stack with the computer screen holding it in place. Bandoleers of rifle magazines hung on the backs of the seats. Two rolls of concertina wire sat on the hood, and a medical backboard was strapped to the trunk, which was filled with medical and other supplies.

By midmorning, we were ready to return to COP Ford. There was just one last task: shopping at the PX store for necessary items unavailable at Ford. With last-minute personal needs attended to, we lined up inside the west gate to Taji. As a platoon, we got out of the Humvees, loaded and charged our weapons, went over last-minute instructions and drills, then loaded back up. It was about noon on March 17.

Traffic was normal as we turned south on Highway 1, known to Coalition forces as Main Supply Route Tampa—a four-lane divided highway with a dirt median. Traffic was flowing well until we came to the bridge over the Ishaqi River. A checkpoint there caused a backup, and we had to push through the slowed and stopped cars. After several years of war, the Iraqis were used to the drill when approached by a patrol. They pulled over and got out of the way. Besides, they really didn't want to be stuck next to us if a fight started. We waved to a platoon of Strykers guarding the bridge. As we continued south, we saw other patrols and convoys heading north.

Several miles south, we reached the elevated traffic circle that was the exit for the divided highway we knew as Route Plutos. A busy highway, it held plenty of US and Iraqi traffic. It has once been a major IED danger area but had recently simmered down under increased US and Iraqi force presence. We headed east.

The first half of the stretch to the Tigris River was the most concerning to me. Wooded land came almost up to the highway. It was prime ambush country. We made it through without incident. At the halfway point, a large industrial complex stood on the right, complete with guard towers and Hesco-basket blast walls. On the left side of the highway was a stationary Iraqi Police patrol. Beyond the complex, small fields lined the road the rest of the way to the bridge. On the left was an Iraqi Police station.

First, Danny Key's Humvee passed the complex and into the open. Some fifty meters behind it, my Humvee passed the complex. Another fifty meters behind me, Mike Elledge's Humvee reached the end of the complex.

BOOM! A shock wave slapped me in the back of the head, and in the mirror, I saw a huge dust cloud at the end of the complex. Mike's C6 Humvee emerged from the dust. All four tires were flat. *Artillery-round IED*, was my first thought. I couldn't see Jay's Humvee pushing the disabled C6, nor could I see the extent of the damage on the side. I wanted some distance between the blast site and where we stopped, so Danny and I pushed forward a few hundred more meters. As we did so, we strained our eyeballs looking at the ground around us for any IEDs. It occurred to me that I had not seen the one that hit Mike's Humvee even though I passed it seconds before it detonated.

"Steel X-Ray, Blue One; contact IED mike-bravo-three-seven-zero-seven-niner-eight-five-two. Out." My Humvee had the best radios in the platoon, so I reported the IED to the company command post at Ford instead of Jay making the report. We were still slightly beyond the normal range of radios, and only the best-performing radios reliably allowed communication. On the platoon radio net, I heard Jay say he was going to check on Mike's crew. David said he had the far side secure, and his truck pulled up to the Iraqi Police across the road near the blast site.

"One, Four; we have two KIA. Elledge and Simpson are dead." Jay's voice betrayed emotion held in check by professionalism. My heart sank. An EFP had penetrated Mike's Humvee and killed him and Chris Simpson. Specialist Keith Hanson was driving at the time and was still alive.

"Steel X-Ray, Blue One; two KIA. Over."

"Copy, standing by."

In the mirror, I saw Keith get out of the driver's door and stand a few feet from his destroyed Humvee. I dismounted and headed over as Danny pointed him in my direction. Keith was a mess. He looked like he was in shock. Blood and viscera covered most of his upper body and head. I couldn't even begin to imagine what he was going through.

"Are you hurt?" I asked Keith. He shook his head no and said no. He didn't feel it and neither of us could see it, but a piece of shrapnel had hit him in the jaw. His blood was camouflaged by the blood of Mike and Chris. I didn't have anything to clean him up with. I tried to occupy Keith's mind and get him safe.

"Hanson, go sit in my seat and let me know if company wants me, okay?" Keith gave me a blank look but nodded and climbed into my Humvee as a convoy of armored Suburbans pulled up to my Humvee.

"Mate, we are heading west and need to go through. We have a tight timeline. What gives?" A thick British accent laced the question.

"We just hit an IED. There's a good chance of secondaries."

"Well, we have to keep moving."

"Okay, stay away from the south side. I can't control you." The contractors continued on their way in the far borrow ditch.

With security set and the living attended to, it was time to take care of our fallen brothers. Mike was slumped over in the commander's seat. He looked like he had died mid-sentence in a lighthearted conversation. With a massive chunk of his neck missing, it was clear he had died instantly. The door was combat locked, so that it could not be opened from the outside. The radio stack and seat made it impossible to get to him without tools.

Chris had also been killed instantly. He took hits to his head, shoulder, and side. Since the back doors had not been combat locked, Chris was easy to access. He had fallen out of the gunner's sling and into the back seats. By the time I got Keith to my Humvee, Danny and Jay were nearly done placing Chris in a body bag. Tex and RJ were helping. I knew that Danny and Chris had been very close.

With Chris safely in the shade, we tried to get Mike out of the Humvee. Efforts to remove pieces on the inside of the Humvee were frustrated. A military police patrol heading westbound arrived our location. I asked them to assume security between the bridge and us so I could pull my Humvee off security and use it to rip the door off. When in doubt, use brute force. We knew the combat lock on the door was not designed to withstand the door being pulled open by a chain. The door popped open, and we were able to reach Mike.

Gently, we pulled Mike out of the seat and placed him in the body bag. As we did so, his body twitched, and I was filled with a glimmer of irrational hope. I started to call to Mike and tried to rouse him. Jay reminded me there was no hope. With great sadness I closed Mike's eyes and we zipped the bag up. *Lord, into your hands I commend Mike's soul. Be with Carleen and the kids today.* We placed him in the shade next to Chris.

"LT! Radio!" Keith's yells to me brought me back to reality. I walked back to my Humvee.

"Steel X-Ray, Blue One. Over." I held the hand mic to my face.

"Blue One, Steel Six. Gold is en route and will bring you the flat rack so we can recover the Humvee. Confirm who is KIA by battle roster number. Over."

"Negative. The helmets are too messed up to read. By official roster position, Six Golf and Six Delta." I was so stressed and upset I forgot I had the whole patrol's roster info taped to my dashboard, right in front of me. Steel 6G was Mike's call sign, and Steel 6D was Chris. There was a long pause.

"Okay. I want you to take some pictures," CPT Looney replied. *Of Mike and Chris?!?! Are you kidding me?!?!*

"Steel Six, Blue One. NO. Negative. Absolutely not." I threw the hand mic at the radio in anger. I turned to Nick, who was ashen faced in the driver's seat. "What the HELL is wrong with him?" Wisely, Nick turned and looked out his window without replying.

After a couple minutes, First Sergeant Gonzalez got on the radio. "Blue One, Steel Seven. Six wants pictures of the Humvee. Not our guys. Do you understand? He says we will delete them off the camera once he has seen them and won't download them. Acknowledge. Over."

"Blue One; wilco." Still angry, I stomped back to the destroyed Humvee with the platoon camera and took pictures. I noticed to my horror that there were bloody footprints on the asphalt that matched the pattern on my boots. My stomach rolled.

Still, I had a job to do. Without a word, I examined the remains of C6. One projectile had hit Mike's door right on the edge of the window, slid behind it, and hit Mike. The force required to get through the door slowed the projectile enough that the slug came to a stop in the radio stack. Another had punched through the center of the rear door and smashed into the far-side door. The slug was more than an inch thick and approximately three inches long. Another penetrated the turret and hit Chris.

Spalling fragments from the inside of the armored doors had sprayed the crew compartment. The inside of the Humvee was hell on earth. A case of Rip It cans had been sliced apart, and sticky purple liquid was sprayed over the back seats, mixing with the blood pooling in the floorboards. The boxes and bags, once tidy, were now jumbled from the shock wave.

Gold Platoon and the mechanics' flat rack arrived. Their arrival was more important to our morale than our security. While we had been stationary in the road for well over an hour, we had good fields of fire. The traffic jam caused by us closing the highway to secure the blast site stretched for miles in both directions. On the other hand, we were starting to lose the focus and energy provided by adrenaline. We were nearly finished removing things from the destroyed Humvee and running out of tasks.

Lieutenant Jeff Nelson from Gold Platoon and Sergeant First Class Danny Bowden from the mechanics came up to me. Their faces were grim, and I could see the pain in their souls. Our conversation was brief. Words were wholly inadequate, and nobody dared let emotion bubble out from under the mask of professionalism. While they had been en route to our location, some seven miles from Ford, higher headquarters had coordinated a specialized team from Camp Taji to come recover both our fallen brothers and their destroyed Humvee. Additionally, the Stryker unit that owned the battlespace we were in was also responding. A pair of Apache gunships arrived overhead and began the protective circling we appreciated so much.

While we talked, the sound of a motorcycle came from the tree line to our south. A man on a black dirt bike popped out of the trees and slowly worked his way towards us on a farm path through the fields. We took cover and yelled at him to stop. I don't think he could hear our yells over the noise of the motorcycle, and he kept coming. After a few moments, he finally noticed the Humvees on the road and then saw all the gun barrels pointing at him. That message he understood, and he turned around. The man very well could have been the triggerman, but without positively identifying him as enemy, we could not shoot. The discipline of the troops invoked pride in me. Even with emotions running at their highest, they did the right thing.

The quiet hum of Strykers rose from the west as a convoy arrived. The lead Stryker pulled up to my truck and a captain got out. He was the company commander for the unit that owned the battlespace. I was glad to see him. He had brought an EOD team, and they set to work studying the blast site. In the meantime, the captain filled me in on some things we did not know.

While there was no visible change in it, the Iraqi Police station we were next to had just opened for business that morning. Iraqi Police officers had previously been posted in front to protect it and to monitor the highway, but the station itself had been vacant. The IED that killed Mike and Chris was likely a retaliation strike by the enemy to undermine the perceived competency of the police. Our patrol was just bad timing. There was no way to predict the IED, and the stretch of road hadn't seen one in months.

The EOD team quickly discovered that the IED had been expertly camouflaged in the dirt of the Hesco basket. There was no way any of us could have seen it. It was also an expertly built one, designed to destroy the forensic evidence in the blast. Most IEDs were designed with the control package on the back, and pieces often survived the blast. The best bomb builders put their control package on top so if pieces survived, they would rain down somewhere else. It was also likely one of the newer Iranian IEDs with advanced controls that allowed skilled triggermen to arm it to hit a specific vehicle long before the electronic bubble of our jammers reached the IED's location.

With Mike and Chris safely placed in a Stryker, we were released from the scene. The command post asked me to stop by Battalion headquarters at COP Callahan to pick up the chaplain. It would only take us a mile out of our way. The trip to Callahan and then on to Ford was silent. I went over the incident in my mind a dozen times as we drove. Little relief came from the knowledge that the enemy had hit us with a perfect ambush we could not have foreseen or thwarted. Part of my soul died with Mike and Chris.

At COP Ford, Keith cleaned up and got his wound checked at the aid station. The pain of losing his crew would not heal as easily. I went straight to the command post. Captain Looney pulled me into his room off the command post. He looked about as devastated as I felt. I showed him the photos on the camera. He did not say a word as he looked through them and then quietly told me to delete them.

The platoon gathered around the chaplain in our room for a mandatory post-traumatic event debrief. I'm not sure if it was by design or accident, but only experienced leaders in the platoon had actually seen and touched our fallen brothers and the carnage of the Humvee; we had all experienced death and carnage before. It didn't make the pain any less, but we at least partially shielded the junior members from the horror.

After the debriefing, I retreated to the platoon office and began writing my sworn statement and working on the paperwork associated with losing men and equipment. It gave me focus and helped me bottle up emotion. Shortly after dark, Captain Ted Perry, the battalion signal officer, arrived to conduct the required investigation. Ted was like a big brother to me, and he knew how to gently ask questions so I didn't feel like I was at fault. Ted had me walk him through the day from start to finish, listening more carefully than a priest.

Of course, the pain and guilt of losing Mike and Chris was strong anyway. I knew Chris really well because he had been the commander's driver since the previous deployment. He was a staple around the command post. Chris was generally carefree, one of Captain Looney's favorite soldiers in the company. I was sure Captain Looney would never forgive me.

I also wondered if Captain Looney was dealing with survivor's guilt. It was his truck, and Mike was in his seat, and now Mike was gone. As time went by, it was obvious the loss weighed heavily on Captain Looney.

The loss of Mike was even harder on me. Mike had been my wingman's gunner shortly after we returned from the 2005 to 2006 deployment to Baqubah. I had gotten to know him really well and became close to both him and his family. When Captain Looney selected Mike to be his gunner and took him from the platoon, I had fought hard and argued with Captain Looney to the point of borderline insubordination. In February, Captain Looney informed me that the newly promoted Mike was going to return to Blue Platoon to become a tank commander. I was ecstatic and could not wait to have him back. Mike was a steady rock of a man. I hated that I had been the patrol leader when Mike and Chris were killed. The grief stayed under my shell of professionalism for a long time. It wasn't until right after the memorial a few days later that it boiled to the surface, and I sat in a back hallway and cried rivers of tears.

Normally, a platoon is supposed to stand down for a good twenty-four hours after losing someone. We made it about fourteen hours. The neighborhood was heating up, and we were the frogs in the pot. About a mile to our north, some enemy fighters had fired RPGs near a market on the east corner of the Triangle of Death.

Rushing to the scene so fresh from a catastrophic IED hit was nerve wracking. My stomach was pitted hard as a rock, and my heart was in my throat. To say I was scared was an understatement. I was terrified, but I was sure I wasn't the only one. The only answer was to press forward and shove that fear back down with the vomit taste. It was common for skilled enemy units to place IEDs and ambush sites on the likely routes we would use to respond to another attack.

The scene was pretty well secured and stable by the time we got there. Other units had been closer, and there was little for us to do upon arrival. The enemy responsible for the attack was long gone, and our small search of the area yielded nothing. We returned to COP Ford without incident and sadly went about preparing for our next patrol.

On the twenty-second, while responding to another incident near the Triangle of Death, we had another close encounter. Just after we passed the gas station on Highway 23 and entered our ambush area, David stopped his Humvee without warning. The reason became obvious as I pulled to the right to see past him and spotted a box sitting on a Colorado barrier. There wasn't supposed to be anything on the barriers. Additionally, we had made this very clear to the locals.

Sure enough, it was a hastily placed armor-piercing IED. There ended up being a second one just a little bit farther. Perhaps the enemy was expecting us to be too rushed to notice it. Perhaps they hoped a unit not as familiar with the area would respond and not know better. Either way, we got to capture a pair of six-inch penetrator IEDs.

As the week slowly ticked by, tensions seemed to heat up in Iraq. The Iraqi Army announced it was going to conduct a major operation to seize the southern city of Basra from the control of JAM. IEDs and potshot attacks increased throughout the area with no real effect. Higher headquarters still viewed these incidents as isolated. Within our neighborhood, JAM organized a protest march near the Hawasem. It was peaceful, and we did our best to avoid it and the potential of causing an incident. We did get close enough to photograph the signs they were carrying for later translation. Every single man in the crowd wore a black uniform. *Wow, there are a lot of JAM fighters... hundreds and hundreds.*

March and April were usually active fighting months because the weather was as good as it gets in Iraq. Every spring since the invasion in March 2003 had been marked by fighting. But the looming operation in Basra some 300 kilometers away seemed insignificant, and although Sadr City was the headquarters of JAM, the cease-fire had been fairly well observed.

That naïve view was shattered on March 25. The morning started out ordinarily enough. Blue Platoon conducted a typical patrol in the Beida neighborhood. We ventured north of COP Ford, checking businesses and our supply route. The local Iraqis were abuzz about the fighting in Basra. That operation started out rocky, but a well-trained and equipped division of the Iraqi Army was making progress.

Around noon, we returned to COP Ford to rest, restock on water, and prepare for an afternoon patrol.

COP Ford's courtyard was ringed with date palms and covered with camouflage netting to provide shade. Under the shade, we had a pair of fifty-five-gallon drums converted to charcoal grills. It was our oasis and a small haven from the hell of war. I was standing next to the grill, watching my steak sizzle, when a runner from the command post found me. Captain Looney was summoning me.

Captain Looney stood next to an interpreter, who was still holding a cell phone. Colonel Allah from the Gold checkpoint had called and told Captain Looney that the checkpoint was about to get attacked. Captain Looney and I exchanged a look. We had a lot of experience with Iraqis worried about getting attacked. In 2006, sometimes the Iraqis would abandon their posts at the slightest rumor. Every single warning so far had been a false alarm. Still, we were their partners and needed to encourage them to stand their ground.

"Petey, take your platoon out to the checkpoint. Check on them, make sure they have good dispositions, and give them some encouragement." Captain Looney wanted to make sure the checkpoint wouldn't run away.

"The guys are cooking lunch; we can roll in about thirty minutes, sir." I was hungry.

"No, just go now and let the others here finish cooking your food. It will only take you fifteen minutes."

"Yes, sir." I left the command post and as soon as I got into the hallway yelled, "BLUE PLATOON, MOUNT UP! WE GOTTA ROLL"

With our meat cooking under the watch of some infantrymen, we loaded up and drove to the Gold checkpoint. Jamila Street was completely empty of cars or people. *Uh-oh.* A major artery for traffic in and out of Sadr City, normally the street was a slow-moving traffic jam and the sidewalks held a steady stream of people too impatient or smart to join the cars clogged in the jam. The current absence of locals was a major red flag. For once, every Iraqi soldier in the checkpoint had his helmet on and a rifle in his hands. Even the BMP-1 armored fighting vehicles were running and fully manned. The air was so tense only a chainsaw could cut it.

Just as my Humvee reached the heart of the checkpoint, RPGs streaked in from the apartment complex to the northeast. Machine-gun and AK fire added to the cacophony. Instantly, the radio speakers in the truck came to life. The fight was on, and this had been no mere rumor.

"Steel X-Ray, Blue Four; contact RPG and small arms, out!" Jay reported on the company radio net. In a fight, Jay would keep the company on its radio net while I directed the platoon's fight on our radio net. We would listen to both nets, though.

"Blue Two, set up facing the apartments with me! Blue Four, guard our flanks!" It wasn't exactly textbook, but I wanted our position established as quickly as possible. We deployed our Humvees rapidly to engage the enemy. Already committed through the heart of the checkpoint, David and I were forced to immediately return fire from near the apartment complex entrance.

"Blue One, Blue Four; I have the street to Sadr."

Jay pulled his Humvee into the right lane to protect our flank and rear.

"Blue One, Blue Three; set on the north side of the checkpoint, oriented north!"

Danny's Humvee stopped just short of the checkpoint and began to return fire into the apartment complex. The concrete barriers were just the right height that his machine gun could shoot over the top while the rest of the Humvee was protected. Machine-gun fire from the traffic circle area added tracers to the air in the checkpoint.

The slower-chugging fire of a large-caliber machine gun erupted past the traffic circle. A pickup truck with a 12.7 mm Soviet-built machine gun fired rounds capable of piercing our Humvees from nearly a kilometer away.

"Steel X-Ray, Blue Four; we are taking large-caliber fire from a technical beyond Grizzlies."

"Four, One; make it go away!"

Jay's Humvee mounted a machine gun that did not even have sights and was only 7.62 mm in caliber. It was a mismatch that Jay was determined to win anyway. He had his gunner pour cyclic fire on the truck's position until it went away. Fire superiority can be won by volume.

David and I positioned our trucks at the entrance to the apartment complex and engaged enemy fighters trying to move in closer to the checkpoint. Machine guns poked holes in the satellite dishes as enemy fighters ran behind them, trying to hide their movements. Within minutes the walls of the buildings were pocked with bullet holes.

"Bushell, on me!" I dismounted and ran from Humvee to Humvee, making sure that we had overlapping fields of fire and placing riflemen where we needed more coverage. Finding a gap in coverage along our immediate front, I placed Cory Bushell and his rifle behind some debris. I wanted him to make sure nobody used the buildings and numerous objects to close in against the wall and assault a Humvee from a blind spot. RPGs were still streaking into the checkpoint. As I was placing Cory, an RPG smashed into the checkpoint's concrete guard tower. Another impacted the concrete barriers between it and where Cory and I were kneeling.

The fight was at rifle range, with most of the enemy shooting from about 100 to 200 meters away. They flowed around the apartment complex with clear familiarity. Each time an enemy fighter poked around a corner to shoot, David would bound his Humvee forward to gain an angle to shoot him. David was a true tanker, aggressive at heart. But he was not in his tank. Each time, I had to remind him to move back so his flank and rear were not exposed. I still did not have enough guns in the fight to complete interlocking fields of fire on everywhere the enemy could shoot from.

David bounded forward again towards the left, and fifty-caliber fire ripped holes in a satellite dish at the corner. Movement to the right caught my eye. A head poked around the right side of the building and then stepped out to shoot. I lined up my sights and pressed the trigger once, twice, again and again. The man's rifle dropped and he fell backward around the corner. I lowered my rifle a few inches so I could look over the top of the sights, training still dominating my actions. *Whoa. Don't get sucked in. You have a platoon to fight, not just a rifle.* I blew a big breath out, then turned away to manage the fight.

Within a few minutes, Todd's Red Platoon arrived and joined us. They must have set a record for fastest load-up time to get to the checkpoint so quickly. First Sergeant and Doc Fetz added a headquarters Humvee to the fight with Red Platoon. As they arrived, I ran back into the heart of the checkpoint to coordinate their entrance to the fight.

"Red One, Blue One; I need one of our trucks up here to fill a gap." I switched to the company net and waved at the first truck from Red Platoon. The truck came forward and stopped as the truck commander got out. Staff Sergeant Josh Everett and I took cover behind his Humvee while I pointed out the enemy's positions.

"They're moving around those buildings and keep coming around that corner. I need you to slide up to the right of Rocha and watch his flank when he bounds forward to engage."

"You got it." With Everett's crew in the fight, we gained solid fire superiority at the apartment complex entrance.

First Sergeant and Doc Fetz approached on foot through the checkpoint, and I ran over to coordinate with them. That done, I went back through the apartment complex entrance to continue the fight. I never noticed the concentrated machine-gun fire that impacted all around me. Later, First Sergeant and Doc cornered me at COP Ford and told me they thought there was no way I survived it without getting hit. They watched me go around the corner and then a horde of bullets impact all around. It looked bad enough that their reaction was to get a litter, and Doc felt obligated to follow me into hell. When they peeked around the corner, I was kneeling behind some debris, unharmed.

Even without the Iraqis defending the checkpoint, we had enough firepower to overwhelm the enemy quickly. Within fifteen minutes of starting the fight, the enemy faded away into the dense neighborhood. We did not give chase; the apartment complex was littered with IEDs, and it was not worth heading into an ambush rashly.

With the shooting done, I began the process of checking on everyone. I was overjoyed that none of our guys had been hit. Furthermore, they had been disciplined in their shooting. Our ammo situation was still good. Morale was high, and previous training was shining through.

I turned to the Iraqi soldiers. The BMP driver behind my truck had popped his hatch and gave me a thumbs-up and a smile. They had stood their ground. I linked up with Todd, and we sought out Colonel Allah. He was sitting on his haunches in the center of the checkpoint. He appeared tired but happy. Amazingly, he had no casualties to report. Even the machine-gun crew in the guard tower escaped the RPG hit without injury.

Our return to COP Ford was a jubilant one. The newest members of the platoon had been baptized by fire and prevailed. For many, it was a chance to exact revenge and vent some anger over the deaths of Mike and Chris. Our interpreter announcing he refused to join us on patrols in the immediate future did not dampen our spirits the slightest bit. It was the last patrol on which I had an interpreter for the rest of my career.

While the troops refitted from the fight, I began the paperwork. Several members of the platoon earned their Combat Action Badge during the fight, and the aggressive maneuvering of David's crew needed recognition. Daniel Garcia was headed out on mid-tour leave with the evening supply run, and his critical M249 SAW needed to be reassigned while he was gone.

Reports of fighting in the Jamila and Thawra sectors were still coming in. It seemed JAM had launched a widespread series of attacks. From the sounds of it, the Strykers in Jamila were getting the worst of it. As the sun set, the fighting in Jamila continued even though the enemy had not tried us again. Shortly after dark, we received the mission to hold 83 Square so that the Strykers could drag a destroyed Stryker back. We did not know how long it would take for them to get there, or which direction they were coming and going from as they pulled back from Jamila.

Under the cover of darkness, Blue Platoon, with the first sergeant's Humvee joining, left COP Ford. I did not want to pass through the checkpoint we had just fought over. Instead, we went out to the freeway and then came up to 83 Square from the southwest. Expecting a fight, I had the platoon slowly approach in a staggered column. At the edge of the traffic circle, half the platoon covered as David and I worked our way around the west side. I expected to hit an IED at any moment, which would likely start off another firefight.

We were nearly to the far side when it happened. From an alley on the eastern side of the circle, the flash of an RPG launch lit up the night. In slow motion, I watched the glowing eclipse of the rocket coming nearly straight at my face. Little sparks floated down behind it as it flew in front of David's Humvee and then cut between the spool of wire on my hood and the windshield before smacking the concrete barrier to our left. It missed the Humvee's windshield by less than half an inch. Machine guns from both trucks rewarded the RPG gunner for his miss. As suddenly as the quiet had been shattered, it returned.

In the eerie calm, we established fields of fire from our side of the traffic circle. The island in the middle had a decorative iron fence, probably the reason the RPG gunner aimed a bit high. Now we used it to keep their aim high. The enemy did not return with more direct fire, nor did any IEDs detonate while we held 83 Square. We waited. After an eternity, the Strykers decided to take a better route home with their destroyed Stryker, and we fell back to COP Ford.

A new mission awaited us when we returned. The Strykers had lost some vehicles and taken casualties. They needed more combat power for the fight in the morning. Captain Looney gave me orders attaching me to C/1-2 Stryker. We had been sharing our outpost with a platoon of them at a time, so we at least had a general feel for the men. C/1-2's commander, Captain Northrop, was at his command post at JSS Sadr City, a joint Iraqi Police and US outpost a mile down the freeway from us. While the men worked on the trucks and equipment, I called their command post on the phone for our orders.

The enemy was using a collection of soccer fields in Jamila to launch rockets at the Green Zone. A Bongo truck with a rack of rockets on it would pull into the field, quickly fire them, and then dash back to the sanctuary of Sadr City. Captain Northrop wanted Blue Platoon to watch two fields. Unfortunately, the fields were several blocks apart, and there was no good place to watch both fields at the same time. Our orders were to maintain enough presence at the fields to deter the enemy from using them. Of critical importance, the commander stressed he did not want Blue Platoon to become decisively engaged. As such, he did not want us near Jamila Street.

In addition to the two main fields, we needed to monitor a few other open areas the enemy could use. We would begin our presence shortly after daybreak and maintain until evening. Jamila was a contested neighborhood, and the enemy was sure to fight. It promised to be a long day.

My plan was simple. Not big enough to split up, the platoon would remain mobile as much as possible and use all of the back streets in Jamila to move from field to field. Keeping our route as random as possible would keep the enemy artillery units off guard and make it harder for their infantry and IED cells to ambush us. I wanted to stay at least one block away from Jamila Street. I expected the fighting to resume around 83 Square and wanted to keep some buildings between us and the bullets flying there. In obedience to our instructions to not become decisively engaged, we would fight through any ambush and break contact from it.

A different feeling entered my chest as we rolled out the gate of COP Ford en route for Jamila. Every patrol before had come with a possibility of enemy contact. This one had a rock-solid guarantee. While we had made it through yesterday without taking casualties, a lot of that was the fortune of war. A millimeter to the left, and that RPG gunner last night would have sent the rocket into my face. Countless bullets easily could have hit one of the guys.

We exited Beida south onto the freeway on-ramp and pushed right back into Jamila. An Iraqi Army checkpoint protected the vital artery into Jamila. Once inside the neighborhood, we got onto the side streets where the risk of ambush and IEDs was less. The houses and streets looked very similar to Beida: The layout was comparable, the curbs and sidewalks were relatively clean, and the houses appeared nice. Date palms decorated nearly every front courtyard. Each gate had the white-and-blue address label next to it. I'm sure that a normal day brought the same traffic and civilian activity as Beida. Today, not a soul was in sight.

We zigzagged to the farthest field we were supposed to patrol, nearly dead center of Jamila. As I looked down streets in all directions, I could not see another friendly unit anywhere in Jamila. The feeling of being very alone was daunting. As the sun warmed the day, sounds of battle increased all around us. At the first field, we waited for a bit. A wide street ran to the northwest and southeast past the field. Unlike all the other major streets in the neighborhood, it seemed run down and poorly maintained. It screamed IED.

Only a few minutes of being stationary passed before the inevitable happened. The crack of rifle fire came from the buildings around us. "Comanche X-Ray, Blue Four; contact, small arms!" Jay's report to Comanche Six was returned with "Roger; do NOT get decisively engaged!" It was time to break contact and keep moving. Driving away with a few bursts from our machine guns, we then returned to slowly working our way through the side streets of Jamila, heading northwest to the next field.

At the next field, we had a similar experience. After a few minutes, bullets entered the air. Once again we obeyed instructions to break contact and avoid entering a large fight. It was not long before every time we turned down a street, someone greeted us with rifle fire. Nowhere near the intensity of the fight at the checkpoint yesterday, it was still constant harassment. I suspected that if we became stationary for long or ventured down a major street, we would end up in a large fight.

As the morning slowly approached noon, our maneuvering through Jamila became more difficult. Soon we were popping curbs and having to backtrack down streets. It was hard on the Humvees. Bullets can disable a Humvee. The hood is not armored, and a round through parts of the engine or radiator can ruin it. Before long, one of the Humvees was overheating. Another had transmission problems from the abuse of frequent gear changes and rough driving. The day was unraveling.

We had another trouble added to the list. One of the guys was sick and had bad diarrhea. At one point, we were working our way on the northern part of Jamila when he needed to make an emergency stop. We found a street that was quiet. While the poor soldier frantically dropped drawers, we kicked guys out to look around the corners on each end of the street. It was a short street parallel to Jamila Street. I went to the corner in front of us and looked towards Jamila. It was obvious that we had somehow lost our constant harassers. No shots rang out.

Up towards Jamila Street, I saw a group of men. While they did not have any weapons in sight, I suspected they were enemy fighters discussing their plan. As I watched them through my rifle sights, an older man approached them and pointed towards us. The group scattered. The lull in the battle was about to end, probably in a major way. As we loaded back up, the enemy began to fire. Our gunners returned fire as we broke contact yet again.

Before long, we reached a critical decision point. We had two Humvees on the verge of completely breaking down, and two others that were equally abused by the hard maneuvering. Jay and I discussed our situation and estimated that within an hour we would not be able to extract ourselves and would need someone to come help tow vehicles. Our orders to not become decisively engaged would not keep the enemy from massing on a disabled platoon. It was early afternoon at the latest, and we still had hours to go in the assigned patrol.

"Comanche Six, Steel Blue One; we are dropping to slant two and cannot continue the mission much longer." I had to tell the Stryker company commander that two of our Humvees were breaking down and I needed to extract them before I could not extract at all. I explained we had a shot-up radiator and a transmission locked up. The response I got surprised me.

"I thought your engines were also armored." Apparently, they asked for a tank platoon and received one, but nobody bothered to check if we were in tanks or Humvees. When I responded that Humvees did not have armor around the engine, the commander sounded very concerned. He ordered us to break contact and get out of Jamila. Apparently, a Humvee was not armored well enough for Jamila. Our running gun battle in Jamila was over after about six hours. By the time we made it back to COP Ford, we were assigned back to our own company.

Working through the night, the mechanics had our Humvees back in business. We didn't know it yet, but the mechanics were about to prove themselves the true heroes of Sadr City. As the fighting escalated, their job became more and more difficult. Damage increased, spare-part supplies dwindled, but their creativity blossomed.

While the guys worked to refit, I went back to the command post to build some situational awareness for tomorrow's fight. I got with Clint, who was tracking more than just our company's fight. On the map, Clint showed me how extensive the fighting around Sadr had become. While enemy attacks had pushed west into Shaab, it was obvious the main thrust was towards the southwest as the enemy tried to gain the range for their rocket attack on the Green Zone.

As Clint explained the situation to me, I noticed a new label on the map. The apartment complex next to the Gold checkpoint was now labeled *AOD*.

"Clint, what is that?" I pointed to the apartments.

Clint laughed and replied, "Apartments of Death. AOD." I smiled and laughed with him.

Jeff came and asked me to speak with him in private. We went to his room. "One of the guys from my platoon who rode with you wanted me to talk to you. The crew he was with smoked in the Humvee and the TC had his window cracked. It isn't safe, and it is not following the rules." Jeff went on to explain which crew it was and when exactly it happened.

"Okay, thank you for letting me know." I left and returned to my room. I pondered Jeff's concerns. I did not think the fighting would stop anytime soon. If anything, things were about to get way worse. I debated what to do about this situation. RPGs and EFP would go right through the armor, so the cracked window was a bit irrelevant. It was possible a bullet could make its way in the window, but I had not noticed any open windows on the trucks during the firefights. The idea of stomping out smoking in the trucks did not seem smart to me. Nobody would follow that directive, and with the level of stress, smokers needed their cigarettes. I told Jay and recommended we let things be but let him deal with it as he wanted.

With the equipment ready, we settled down for some rest. Tomorrow would be another day of hard fighting. I did not know what it would bring, or that it would turn into one of the most memorable days of my life.

Dawn on March 27, 2008, brought the eleventh day of fighting into hot sunlight. Each day had seen increasingly aggressive and longer enemy attacks. Two Iraqi Army checkpoints just northeast of our outpost came under constant attack, as they had been for the last few days. While the sun climbed higher in the sky, the enemy attacked and scattered the two closest Sons of Iraq security checkpoints—the ones I was responsible for mentoring.

It was high noon in Baghdad. As the morning matured, every checkpoint near Sadr City had come under near simultaneous attack. Checkpoints fell under enemy control at a staggering rate. To the southeast, a checkpoint equipped with Iraqi Army T-72 tanks was overrun, and at least one tank was unaccounted for, possibly captured.

Blue Platoon mounted up the Humvees and rode out to reestablish the security checkpoints. We were as loaded for bear as we could be. Two Humvees were mounted with fifty-caliber machine guns and two with 7.62 mm M240 machine guns. We had one 5.56 mm M249 machine gun and one 40 mm M203 grenade launcher. To counter the reportedly captured T-72, we had a couple AT-4 rockets. The bad news was that we were short three men.

Step one was physically seizing the intersection back. Step two was calling phones to locate and convince the security group to come back. Step three was ensuring the security group was equipped to hold their own and convincing them to stand their ground. It was an exasperating and time-consuming process.

The closest checkpoint required a brief exchange of fire to regain. It stood on the south corner of Hawasem. Just as we finally convinced our terrified Iraqi security group to stay, the sounds of battle on the eastern corner of the Hawasem grew. Once again, we mounted up and moved out. When we got to that corner where the Iraqi Army had a small checkpoint, the exchange of gunfire ceased. I dismounted and discussed the attack with the Iraqi lieutenant in charge. As we talked, the sounds of sporadic gunfire came from the main Gold checkpoint near 83 Square.

Over the last ten days, the Gold checkpoint had been reinforced to where it was the defensive position of about 100 soldiers. They were equipped with five BMP-1 infantry fighting vehicles, around ten Humvees, and a handful of Ain Jaria armored cars and Ford F-350 pickups. We called the Ain Jarias "clown cars." They were boxy, ugly, and seemed to carry an endless number of people. Along the sides of the armored car was a row of firing ports for the soldiers on the inside. The Humvees and clown cars mounted 7.62 mm PKM machine guns. The BMP-1s had the best firepower. They sported a 73 mm cannon that carried the same punch as an RPG rocket. It also had a 7.62 mm machine gun and was armored against even the 12.7 mm machine gun that had been used against us two days earlier.

At 1:56 p.m., hell unleashed on the Gold checkpoint. The sporadic gunfire stopped; then, after a pause, heavy machine-gun and steady mortar fire rained down. One RPG after another slammed into it.

Within a few minutes, thick black smoke rose from the position, obscuring my view of the fight.

Back at the east corner of the Hawasem, we readied for the fighting to reach us. Overhead a pair of AH-64 Apache helicopters circled, watching the fighting and providing us with updates from above. Within fifteen minutes, the enemy had worked its way around the north of the checkpoint to fire from halfway between the checkpoint and our location. Soon, a steady stream of Iraqi vehicles went screaming past me, carrying wounded Iraqi soldiers away. I felt the fight would reach us very soon.

At 2:28 p.m., one of the Iraqi Humvees stopped next to me, carrying a pair of badly wounded soldiers. One had been shot in the chest more than a half dozen times. His eyes already showed the look of death. The other was not as bad but still in serious condition. While our platoon aid-and-litter team worked to stabilize the men for transport, the frantic lieutenant with them explained to me that the enemy attack was overrunning the checkpoint. I listened with my hands holding a bloody bandage against a bullet hole on a soldier's waist. The lieutenant explained that his men were out of ammo, suffering heavy casualties, the BMP-1s were disabled, and now the enemy was inside the checkpoint. The lieutenant did not have a clue as to how many wounded soldiers they had already transported away.

I returned to my Humvee and grabbed my company radio net hand mic.

"Steel Six, Blue One; over." I needed Captain Looney and not just someone manning the radio at the command post.

"Steel Six."

"The IA say they are getting overrun at the Gold checkpoint. They are reporting slant zero and heavy casualties. Now the enemy inside the checkpoint. They are gonna lose it if we don't do something right now. I recommend counterattack with Blue Platoon down Route Gold. The checkpoint east end would be LOA." I told Captain Looney I wanted to counterattack and retake the entire checkpoint to the far end of it where we had fought two days ago.

"Go for it. We have Longknife in the air on our channel to aid in observation. Keep the reports coming. Out."

There was no time for second thoughts. "BLUE, MOUNT UP!" I turned and yelled at my aid-and-litter team that was still working. They gathered their aid bags and ran back to their Humvees. I gave the Iraqi Army lieutenant a thumbs-up, a "We are gonna go help them!" and climbed in my Humvee.

"Blue, Blue One; the enemy is in the checkpoint. We are going to counterattack down Gold. Staggered column left. Order of march Two, One, Four, Three. When we get to the checkpoint we will dismount and clear the enemy out of it. LOA will be the gap to the apartments. Keep your eyes peeled for IEDs between us and it. Questions? Acknowledge in sequence." Within each Humvee, every soldier in the platoon could hear the plan on the radio speakers.

"Two." David was ready.

"Three." Danny was too.

"Four." Jay's response was the one I relied on the most. If he saw a problem with the plan, he would have spoken up.

"Move out." I gave the command, and our Humvees started the long journey down to the checkpoint and the hell brewing there.

Jay let the company know we were committed. "Steel X-Ray, Blue Four; LD."

"Steel X-Ray, Longknife Two-Six. I am overhead your platoon moving towards the checkpoint. Be advised you have some seventy to one hundred—I say again, seven-zero to one-zero-zero—enemy fighters massing on the checkpoint from the north and east of it. They are currently at mike-bravo-four-six-two-niner-niner-four-eight-one." A new voice on the company radio net was accompanied by the telltale metallic flutter of helicopter rotors.

This report was a drastic change from previous fights. Never before had we fought anything larger than a platoon-sized fight. Most altercations only involved some seven to fifteen enemy fighters. I discounted the report as exaggeration, a choice I would soon regret.

As such, I did not even bother to plot them on the map. With the incoming fire, it was obvious where the enemy was.

I did know that the enemy had moved between us and the checkpoint, and we had previous reports of IEDs placed along the road. In the back of my mind, the IED that killed Mike Elledge and Chris Simpson and wounded Keith Hanson put a lump of fear in my throat. My body went into a heightened sense of awareness, focusing on the smallest details of every window, corner, rooftop, stone, and concrete-color difference. My heart rate increased to probably around 140 or more beats per minute even though I was sitting in my Humvee.

In a staggered column, our four Humvees crept down Jamila Street towards Gold checkpoint. The stream of Iraqi vehicles passing back through our advance continued. As each one passed, we saw casualties inside. It was the longest half mile of my life. By 2:40 p.m., we were in heavy contact with the enemy on our side of the checkpoint. Each enemy fire team had to be neutralized before we could pass it. The closer to the checkpoint we got, the more enemy fire shifted from the checkpoint to us. Enemy machine-gun fire and RPGs increased in volume. The mortar attack also shifted to us. It became hard to communicate through the noise.

"Steel X-Ray, Blue Four; we are at the edge of the objective," Jay updated the command post. We had reached the checkpoint's tactical obstacles—strings of concertina wire, metal pieces, and concrete blocks. We were still about 200 meters from the checkpoint itself. An Iraqi Humvee burned fiercely on the other side of the wire. During our careful advance, a trio of clown cars raced up and down the street, firing in all directions. The clown cars darted between our vehicles and went as far away as the Hawasem before turning around. They were more dangerous to us than the enemy, and they created an air of panic.

"Blue, Blue One; establish an SBF here, orient on the apartments. Watch your left flank." As we positioned the trucks to suppress the enemy both in the checkpoint and the area north of it, I realized the depth of disaster that had befallen the checkpoint. Four out of five of the BMP-1s were clearly out of commission. The fifth was now in hiding. There was no sign of Iraqi Army resistance to the roar of JAM fire. The taller concrete barriers in the heart of the checkpoint prevented us from seeing towards 83 Square. A small group of men in black clothing darted from the concrete wall around the center of the checkpoint and ducked through a gap in the wall on the south side of the street. The enemy had penetrated all the way through the checkpoint.

"Blue, Blue One; dismounts on me!" I commanded on the radio. I jumped out of my Humvee and stood in the cover behind it with Cory. Danny climbed out of his and ran towards us, stopping for a moment behind Jay's Humvee. To my right, Tex prepped himself to sprint to me. I figured we were dealing with around thirty enemy fighters based on what I had seen. At this time, I thought well-placed shots and a high volume of fire from a platoon-sized enemy force had been enough to collapse the checkpoint.

With strong support-by-fire from the Humvees, the platoon's four dismounts could overcome the enemy in the checkpoint. My plan was for us to attack down the south-side frontage street and sidewalk so we could use the barriers to protect us from enemy to our north. This would also give a clear visual limit to the Humvee's machine guns, preventing them from accidentally shooting us in the haze of the battle. We would clear the enemy from the checkpoint and then hold it while the Iraqi soldiers regrouped and returned or another platoon from our company came to relieve us. As soon as all of the platoon's dismounts arrived at my truck and took cover behind it, I explained my plan and we began our assault.

"Steel X-Ray, Blue Four; assaulting." Jay updated the command post with our latest move. It was 2:47 p.m.

The din of gunfire increased as we dashed through the gap in the wall. On the other side, destroyed vehicles and other large objects lay scattered. We took turns dashing forward from cover to cover. "I'm up, they see me, I'm down" was the cadence trained in boot camp. Under fire, this guideline gained near religious importance. Dash forward, get behind a good piece of cover, shoot while the others moved up, repeat. With more than seventy pounds of combat gear, this was exhausting and time consuming. Heart rates rocketed.

About fifty meters into the assault, I saw a group of thirty Iraqi soldiers lying down between the curb and the barriers, trying to mold into the pavement. They were wild with terror. I did not see any weapons with them, and they showed no desire to move from their hiding spot. It looked like some were already casualties anyway. *Pay no mind to the bodies in the gutter.* One hundred fifty meters to go.

A little bit further down the street, a clown car was parked on the frontage road with the engine running. When we got to it, Tex convinced the driver to creep forward with us as we crossed a thirty-meter opening in the wall. Unfortunately, the driver panicked halfway across, and the four of us were forced to dash the remaining fifteen meters totally exposed to fire from three directions. One hundred meters to go.

As we moved closer to the checkpoint, the angles of view opened up towards 83 Square. Soon I could see the four-story buildings on the east side of the square. And they could see us. Machine-gun positions in those buildings shifted their fire onto us as we moved directly towards them. *This is getting ugly. Hail Mary, full of grace...*

Cover grew more and more scarce. We passed the building where the company's infantry platoon had fought from hours earlier. We were almost to the checkpoint, and nobody had been hit yet. I mentally counted the number of places I wanted to use a fragmentation grenade on and calculated which ones we actually had a grenade for. A few more rushes would put us at the heart of the checkpoint.

Without warning, the enemy in black suddenly darted back through the checkpoint, away from us. Initial glee was replaced with dread when a few seconds later I heard the loud, hollow thud of mortars firing. *I need a plan B right now—actually about five minutes ago.* It was time to get off the street, and within the next fifteen seconds.

A two-story building happened to be the last structure on the street before the checkpoint itself. It would do.

"Blue, Blue One; taking the last two-story now!" I radioed our new plan. The four of us burst through the front door at a sprint. Once inside, we divided into teams of two and rapidly cleared the rooms. Nobody was home, friend or foe. Outside, large explosions rocked the platoon as mortar rounds rained down with disturbing accuracy.

"HOLY SHIT!" One of the barriers next to a Humvee took a hit on the top and vanished into a shower of concrete chunks. Words of warning from an instructor at West Point popped into my head: *Taking indirect fire is a significant emotional event.*

Rounds impacted along the frontage street at the edge of the checkpoint. It takes talent and training to drop an accurate time-on-target barrage that is synchronized with the retreat of the front line. This enemy unit was a legitimate contender.

"Steel X-Ray, Blue Four; we are taking heavy mortar fire also now. Dismounts stopped the assault just short of the mosque. Slant four, negative casualties," Jay informed the command post. Our assault had fizzled out, but at least we still hadn't taken any damage or casualties.

We now owned a lot of building for four people with prior engagements. On the second floor, a couple rooms with windows overlooked Jamila Street, the checkpoint, and the sprawling neighborhood to the north. I placed Tex in one window with his M4 and Cory in the other with his M249. The house had a front and back door. To ensure our protection from visitors, we gave up the first floor, and Danny Key watched the stairs from a position where he could also see both Cory and Tex. The only worry remaining was our right flank.

I went up to the roof to keep an eye on that blind spot and see better in all directions. The roof was the standard Iraqi flat roof with a parapet. The north parapet was only about twelve inches tall, but the others were about forty inches. In order to see our flank, I had to expose myself fully to enemy fire from the north. I found an answer in a pigeon coop on the backside of the roof. While it would never stop a bullet, it might prevent me from being seen and thus shot at. I dragged the coop to the front corner and settled in to come up with a new plan.

While positioning everyone, I took stock of everyone's condition. Nobody was hurt. I noticed Danny Key had brought along an AT-4 rocket. Cory had brought the "oh-shit" extra ammo bag from our Humvee. Nobody told them to bring them. Later they told me they had a feeling I was signing us up for a rough day and figured it might help. Morale and focus was high.

The enemy fire was amazing. Never had I experienced or even dreamed of this level of incoming fire. My pigeon coop was not doing much to hide me. I realized after a few minutes that it was in fact getting shredded at an alarming rate. The enemy had several machine-gun positions in the apartments across the street and a few more in a tall building on 83 Square, east of the checkpoint. *Jesus, into your hands I commend my soul.*

I spotted around a dozen men darting through the neighborhood to the north in ones and two, circling in towards our Humvees. As a pair broke from cover behind the apartments, I lined up my sights and started squeezing rounds off. They both made it across the alley. *Shit. How did I miss? Or did I? Five-five-six won't knock them over. Focus. Let it go. Breathe. Look around. Check our immediate right. Clear. Where did that group at the traffic circle go?*

My biggest worry was a much bigger force moving towards our right flank from 83 Square. If they got around the flank and behind us, our position would not be tenable. To our southeast, an Iraqi soldier hid in the back courtyard of the mosque, hugging his knees and crying. *When he gets shot, I'll know we just got flanked.* I suspected there might be a few more soldiers hiding in the mosque, but they were out of the fight. As it was, we were outnumbered and receiving huge amounts of fire. We were effectively pinned down and getting maneuvered on. *This really got ugly.* We needed help.

It was a bad time to ask for help. The whole city seemed to be spilling over. Every other platoon was either engaged in a fight of their own or busy refitting from a fight and not ready to come to our aid. Red Platoon promised to come as quickly as they could. Gold was already involved in something else. A new pair of Apaches started to orbit overhead like vultures. The pilots informed me they did not have permission to fire at anything yet, but they were working on that. In the meantime they would help me keep track of the enemy maneuvering on us. Thank God for that; my pigeon coop took a round in a joint, lost its structural integrity, and collapsed. I dropped to my belly to stay behind the short front parapet. With rounds cracking overhead, I had zero motivation to get high enough to look over the side parapet.

I directed the Humvees to move in closer where we could protect them from close-in threats. With the Humvees closer, their lines of sight and fire were similar to mine. Capitalizing on this, I called out targets for them to mass fires on.

"Rightmost apartment building, second floor, third window." The M240s would aim at the window itself to suppress the enemy machine-gun team and force them to stop shooting and duck. The fifty calibers would aim just below the window and to the right. This sent the wall-penetrating bullets where the enemy would likely duck to. A few bursts later, and the window was quiet.

"New target. Third floor, left window." The process resumed. Each time we silenced a machine gun, another would take its place in a new window. Before long, we were running low on ammo and still receiving a huge amount of fire. The plan was not working towards ending the fight. On the radio, Captain Looney's concern was evident, even if I could barely hear it over the racket of rounds cracking overhead or smacking into the parapet. We needed to change the tone of the fight.

"Blue One, Steel Six; I need you to do something to improve your situation. I have a fast mover, but it can't drop ordnance. The Apaches are working on getting permissions for Hellfires, but I don't have an ETA. Feel free to use AT-4 and 203."

"Bring the AT-4 up here!" It was time to up the ante, demonstrate we also had some firepower, and at the same time eliminate my personal menace. I was afraid that if I just had Danny throw up the AT-4 and I got up alone to fire it, I would get hit, and then the guys would have to perform the difficult task of extracting me. This was going to be a two-man job.

Danny's head poked out of the bottom of the door and looked at me. "LT, you're gonna get me killed!" He tossed the AT-4 onto the roof and then crawled out to join me in the right corner.

"You see that window? Leftmost, second floor?" I pointed out a machine-gun position that would not go away in the leftmost building.

"Roger, sir!"

"That is your target! I have to draw fire to the other side of the building for you, though, so wait for my command!" I then crawled over to the left corner of our roof and prepared to draw fire. My pulse jumped into overdrive, and my vision narrowed to a tunnel focused on the machine-gun nest. "On three, okay?!"

Danny nodded and prepped the AT-4 rocket for firing, popping open the folding sights and arming the rocket. As Danny did a quick scan of the rooftop, his eyes lingered on the pile of debris that had been the pigeon coop. Satisfied the roof was safe enough to fire the rocket, Danny gave me a thumbs-up. I inserted a fresh magazine of ammo into my rifle and gave him a thumbs-up back.

I got up on a knee and started firing my rifle at the machine gun, slowly yelling, "One, two—three!" At "three" Danny rose up to a knee and fired the AT-4. The backblast from the launch threw the remains of my pigeon coop into the air to rain down on us. One splinter went through my right ear. As the dust settled, I saw a hole in the wall next to the machine-gun-nest window. It was a great shot. An eerie calm settled as everyone in the fight seemed to pause and ponder the new development. Danny seized the moment to safely return to his post in the stairwell. It was 3:20 p.m.

Just as the enemy machine-gun fire started up again from 83 Square, a loud *BOOM* and the shriek of jet engines stopped my heart. I looked up at an F-18 disappearing back into the haze above us, a pair of torches roaring from its exhaust pipes as the pilot poured on full afterburners. *He didn't drop a bomb, but man, you could have fooled me.* Once again, the entire battlefield stilled as everyone sucked in their breath, restarted their pounding hearts, and shook heads to clear the ringing in their ears.

The growl of a diesel engine and squeak of tracks broke the calm. To my astonishment, a BMP-1 backed out of a concrete enclosure in the checkpoint. It backed out some ten meters and started firing its 73 mm cannon into the apartment complex. It was awesome, a highlight of my career. More importantly, the tide of the battle was shifting in our favor.

A moment later, the Apaches stated they had permission to engage and were going to fire Hellfire missiles at the enemy on my right flank. A pair of missiles streaked down towards 83 Square. To my horror, one detonated much farther to the right than I thought the enemy had gotten. It was 3:26 p.m.

Enemy fire slackened significantly. Only random bursts from machine guns and sporadic sniper fire peppered us. Over behind the mosque, the Iraqi soldier was still hugging his knees. As I left my rooftop position to check on everyone, I looked around the roof. There was nothing left of the pigeon coop. Inside, everyone remained unharmed. The back walls of the rooms were pocked with bullet holes. I'm sure the exterior looked even worse. I fully expected someone to be hit and did a pat-down check for blood on the other three. Thousands of rounds had come so close to us, yet we escaped without being hit. We had broken the enemy attack and regained the checkpoint, and it had been a cheap victory for us.

We were thirsty. We each started the counterattack with more than two liters of water each, but without even realizing, we had drained our CamelBaks. Ammo was a concern also. I had Jay move a case of water out of the back of a Humvee, then ran down and brought the water up. The relative calm allowed our bodies to stop pumping adrenaline. Suddenly we were exhausted.

Red Platoon arrived and took up positions with us at 3:40 p.m. Todd came to the door of our building with an ammo can in each hand, his rifle slung. With our position strengthened, Todd and I began to reorganize the Iraqis. Frankly, I was exhausted and glad to have Todd lead in his energetic fashion. Secretly, I thought he was better at working the Iraqis than I was anyway.

Colonel Allah reported four BMP-1s were destroyed, two Iraqi soldiers were killed, and seven wounded at the checkpoint. He did not mention the destroyed Humvees or the casualties that had left the checkpoint. Todd's platoon also brought some ammo for the Iraqis and the thirty or so Iraqi soldiers who had hidden and now returned to the checkpoint.

Colonel Allah regained control of the checkpoint. He started the day with a hundred soldiers, five BMP-1s, and a large collection of Humvees and clown cars. Now his checkpoint was about forty soldiers, one BMP-1, and one clown car. During the night, more of the Humvees and clown cars returned to the checkpoint. We never got an accurate report on their casualties.

Enemy mortars started firing on the checkpoint again. With the Iraqi soldiers reestablished with a new air of confidence, it was time to go refit. We loaded back into the Humvees and broke contact, bounding one pair of Humvees back at a time. It was 4:07 p.m.

Blue Platoon's counterattack, from start to finish, lasted ninety-nine minutes. During that time, we drank all of our water and expended three-quarters of our ammo. The Apaches were able to confirm eleven enemy dead lying in the street during the fight. Like nearly all of our fights, we never really knew the true damage we inflicted on the enemy. We did know that we had stopped a major attack and retained a key checkpoint. The enemy never again mounted a concerted attack against the Gold checkpoint.

Back at COP Ford, an exhausted group of men set out to refit and ready for the next battle. We managed to escape the day without mechanical damage to the trucks, a minor miracle. My kit weighed like the world on my shoulders as I trudged into the building. Inside, I found the headquarters section's soldiers and mechanics loading magazines for us to exchange.

"Thank you, guys. You rock." I traded our empties from the "oh-shit" bags for fresh magazines. I grabbed an ammo can to load our personal magazines and went into the platoon room. A couple of the guys brought in our platoon medical bags to restock them. Jay brought in a case of water for the guys to refill CamelBaks. Each task was done in relative quiet as everyone sorted through the day in their minds. *The mood of the platoon is different tonight.*

Once the weapons and Humvees were ready, it was time to tend to our bodies. We grilled dinner in the courtyard, our personal sanctuary from war. Tomorrow would bring renewed fighting; everyone knew it. The platoon settled down into guard rotation, and I began paperwork.

After dinner, Danny came in and talked with me. We didn't say a lot, but the message was clear. That rooftop had been absolutely nuts. We had both overcome personal fear, crossing the river Styx and returning with our hides. His AT-4 shot had made the difference, and I was incredibly proud of him. I was immensely proud of the entire platoon. Their courage, skill, and tenacity had covered for my failings. I screwed up, bit off more than I could chew, and they rescued me. It was only Lady Luck and God's mercy that nobody in the platoon was killed or wounded.

The fight marked a turning point in how we fought the 2008 battle for Sadr City. It marked the first day of using larger weapons like AT-4s and Hellfire missiles. That night, plans to bring the tanks and Bradleys down from Camp Taji were made, and we began to receive our tanks the next night. Additionally, all mid-tour leaves were canceled until further notice. We were going to need all the soldiers and equipment we could get.

The dragon had awakened.

THE DRAGON EMERGES

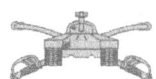

THE US ARMY WAS NOT prepared to suddenly conduct mechanized operations in Sadr City on the morning of March 29. While efforts had begun thirty-six hours prior, the logistical requirements were no small hurdle. Each piece of the puzzle needed to be in place, or at least found, or the operation would be crippled quickly without any input from the enemy.

Our tanks and Bradleys had been sitting in storage at Camp Taji for three whole months. During this time, they got very little love. A tracked vehicle is a jealous beast. When it feels neglected, it breaks down without even moving or turning on. A dusty, hot environment makes it even worse. Since we were not around to care for the tanks or monitor them, each platoon left the specialized tools and equipment for the tanks in locked containers that the battalion's small supply staff could monitor for tampering. The vehicles were left with a nearly full tank of fuel and a full load of ammo. They were not, however, stocked with the various lubricants and oil cans to replenish what the tanks burn through.

On the night of March 27, while we readied for another day of battle on the corner of Sadr City, a small group of underappreciated supply and maintenance staff scrambled to get tanks shipped to us. The plan was for heavy tank-transport trucks to drive the tanks down the freeway in darkness on the evening of the twenty-eighth. Since the trucks were too ungainly to get into the neighborhood, we would go out to the freeway and drive the tanks off the trucks and bring them into COP Ford.

There was one major problem. The specialized trucks were few and far between at the time. The convoy on the twenty-eighth could only bring down two tanks, two Bradleys, and the M88 recovery vehicle.

While Blue Platoon spent March 28 playing whack-a-mole with small enemy teams in the neighborhood and protecting the right flank of the Gold checkpoint, we had received little enemy fire and fired little ammunition. Most of our fights were small, probing attacks, indicating the enemy was trying to either pin down our resources or find a weak spot to get their artillery through and in range of the Green Zone. Most fights were very brief and forgettable. Only one burned into my memory.

About halfway between Palestine Street and the Gold checkpoint, we encountered a small band of JAM fighters on the south side of Jamila Street. During the fight, I took our dismount team into a four-story apartment building overlooking the enemy path back to Sadr in order to engage them as they broke contact. On the roof, enemy fire caused me to dive for cover. I got up to return fire, emptying my ammo magazine. I reloaded another into my rifle, but it kept falling out. After the second time it fell out, I selected a new magazine and inserted it, but it too just fell out. I discarded both, inserted a third magazine, and finally was able to return fire. When we got back to COP Ford, I discovered I had smashed the magazines when I dove for cover. To this day, nightmares take me back to the roof, and I find myself in desperate need to fire, but my rifle won't.

Red Platoon spent the day recovering from helping a route-clearance patrol battle its way into Jamila. They had endured a brutal fight up Kumeil Elashteri Road and needed time to refit. While we held the line in Beida, it was obvious the fight had shifted to Jamila. As a result we were able to refit quickly and prepare to receive our tanks.

Reinforcements began to flow in from the west and the north. In the morning, Bradleys from a cavalry troop out of the 3rd Infantry Division stopped by on their way into the fight. I was happy to see armor. Another Stryker company arrived. I recognized the company commander from West Point as he had been the first captain for the class of 2001, Captain David Uthlaut, and one of the platoon leaders who came with his company was a classmate of mine, Ben Raphael. The reunion was brief as they moved out into the fight. Over the next month, COP Ford went from being home to about 120 soldiers to being the temporary hotel for some 400. Before long, there were cots in every empty space in the hallways, and the gym was packed.

While our outpost population boomed, logistics did not, initially. We started getting a logistic package every evening to help with food, fuel, and ammo. Eating chow shipped down in insulated containers every day was bittersweet. While we had more variety, it also meant the days of grilling all of our meals were over.

An unwelcome logistical change was our porta potties. We now needed the contractor who came and pumped them out more than ever before. The problem was that he lived in Sadr. With all traffic in or out of Sadr stopped, we could no longer get the porta potties pumped. It wasn't long before they were nearly overflowing. First Sergeant worked a miracle somehow, and we never had a flood.

The same night, White Platoon moved from being attached to our sister infantry company in Hussainiyah to being attached to the Stryker company fighting in the Jamila neighborhood to the southeast. Comanche C/1-2 Stryker would finally get the tanks they wanted. Part of their company shared COP Ford with us, so White Platoon moved in with us. Since White Platoon drove their tanks down from Camp Taji, they were ready for operations on the twenty-ninth.

Dawn on the twenty-ninth brought another hot day to Baghdad. Blue Platoon spent the morning working on the two tanks that we received during the night. Red Platoon flew to Camp Taji in UH-60 Black Hawks so they could bring down their tanks. Another convoy would bring the rest of ours. White Platoon departed for operations in Jamila and Thawra I neighborhoods with C/1-2 Stryker.

As we began work on the two tanks we received, we found a major problem. None of the tools and equipment for the tanks were loaded into them prior to departing Taji. While we had a few tools for the Humvees, certain track-specific tools were not on hand. Fortunately, the mechanics had a great collection. Furthermore, we had a great relationship with our mechanics.

By noon, we had the machine guns installed and readied. The radios and their associated equipment were up and running. Track was tensioned and moving parts lubed. Oils and fuel were topped off. Inside the ammo compartment, each tank had a total of thirty-six rounds of 120 mm "big bullets." About thirty were HEAT rounds. It was actually an obsolete round being phased out of service. Ours had been sitting in storage in Kuwait for around a decade before we loaded them into our tanks. We didn't know it yet, but age had not been generous to them.

While obsolete, the HEAT round was a great general-purpose round, powerful enough to kill an Iraqi T-72 and anything less armored. It was useful against bunkers and troops hiding in buildings. The remaining rounds were "CAN," or canister rounds. These were a 120 mm shell filled with about a thousand tungsten ball bearings. It was a fairly new round and a very potent infantry killer.

In the afternoon, I was quickly summoned to the command post. White Platoon was in trouble. They had gotten into a firefight at the traffic circle at Thawra and Umal Streets. While they had been dominant in the fight, mechanical breakdowns had crippled the platoon. They had taken three tanks into the fight; now one was broken down and in need of a tow, and a second had run out of fuel. The platoon was unable to extract itself with only one operational tank and was stuck at the Thawra Street on-ramp to the freeway.

We would use our two tanks to escort the company's M88 to recover the stranded platoon. Danny Bowden, Jay, and I made our plan. The two tanks we had were Jay and Danny Key's. I would ride in the loader's spot on Jay's tank. This would give us a chance to discuss tactical considerations together as we saw them in Sadr City. Danny Bowden would use the M88 to transfer fuel into the empty tank. Then the M88 would hook up to the disabled tank and tow it back.

We quickly mounted up and rolled out the gate. It was a short drive to Thawra Street. Being combat conditions, there was no civilian traffic, so we drove the wrong way on the freeway to shorten the drive. It felt great to be back in the beloved chariot. A tank exudes a feeling of might. It is the most powerful thing on the battlefield. The vibration in the feet and the wind in the face are addictive. The blast of the cannon is exhilarating.

The M1A2 Abrams tank is not an invincible dragon. I already knew this firsthand from being wounded in one back in Baqubah. The memory of that hard-earned lesson was never far from the front of my mind. The rescue mission to Thawra Street was actually the first time I'd taken a tank into combat since that fateful day. Surprisingly, I did not feel fear or hesitation. Perhaps the previous two weeks had given me resiliency.

As we neared Thawra Street, Jay and I discussed the challenges we faced in Sadr City. The buildings near Thawra Street were tall. Many were several or even a dozen stories. With only a thirty-degree angle of elevation possible with the main gun, we would need to back up to engage enemy fighters on the upper floors. Windows that still had glass in them prevented our thermal sights from seeing into the rooms. The places where the enemy could engage us were endless. Rooftops, windows, alleys, streets, junk—too much to watch at once. The streets themselves presented obstacles. Much of the curb was tall and thick enough to damage track if hit just wrong. Most of the medians had some level of fencing. Some was decorative, and some was tall, woven wire with concrete posts. While the tank is the supreme all-terrain vehicle, getting wire or metal tangled in the tracks could disable it. In addition, throughout the neighborhood, small markets on the sidewalk provided concealment for enemy fighters to get close and hide armor-penetrating IEDs. Urban environments are called complex terrain by the military. It is a gross understatement.

White Platoon was in a stressful position. They had broken down in a precarious place, next to buildings where the enemy could get in close to them. I couldn't imagine the frustration and fear at being completely stuck in place. As soon as we got there, we positioned our two tanks to provide more security, and White Platoon and the mechanics scrambled to rapidly prepare the disabled tanks for movement. The mechanics transferred fuel into one tank, and White Platoon took advantage of our extra security. They pulled in their remaining functional tank and hooked it up to tow the other disabled tank. It was good thinking, but I expected nothing less from Sergeant First Class Sean Rinder. He was a tanker's tanker, and when he had been my platoon sergeant, he showed that level of forward thinking consistently.

In just a few minutes, we were all ready to return. With a huge sigh of relief, we rolled back up the freeway and home to COP Ford. On the way back, I thought about how neglected our tanks had been. I vowed to always do my best to recover our own breakdowns and prevent the need to bring the company's M88 out into danger. The M88 was the company's only recovery vehicle capable of dragging back heavy-armored vehicles. It was also our only crane capable of lifting the tank engine and our only armored fuel can. Without it, critical vehicle maintenance at COP Ford would be difficult if not impossible.

That night, Red Platoon returned to COP Ford in their tanks, and my other two tanks arrived. With White Platoon still attached to another company, Team Steel now had eight tanks and four Bradleys. There was a problem, though. Between manpower shortages and mechanical breakdowns, only four tanks and three Bradleys were ready to fight.

Captain Looney summoned all of the platoon leaders for orders. Todd, Jeff, and I brought our platoon sergeants with us. On the morning of the thirtieth, we were going to conduct a reconnaissance in force. Battalion wanted to know how far into Jamila we could push before hitting enemy resistance. Captain Looney explained he was borrowing a page from the Battle of Aachen in regards to task-organizing the teams. We would organize into platoon teams with two tanks and one Bradley. The tanks, with better armor, would lead, and the Bradley, capable of angling its cannon up forty-five degrees, would protect us from the close-in buildings.

Jeff would command the Bradley assigned to my platoon team, though I would be the patrol leader. Our biggest concern was IEDs, so we were not going to bring the infantry squads, keeping the number of people in the Bradleys down to a minimum. Having two tanks together was a requirement to be able to extract a disabled tank. A tank could always tow a Bradley, but not the other way around.

The plan was to depart together and then travel southeast on Kumeil Elashteri Road. From there, each platoon would turn off onto the major streets in the Jamila section of Sadr City. We would try to get to Jamila Street and then return on another of the major streets. While I had been assigned to this neighborhood on the twenty-sixth and a Stryker company was trying to secure it, the enemy completely controlled the vast majority of Jamila. We knew we would get hit. The question was where and how bad.

My crew and David Rocha's crews would take our two operational tanks. My crew would use the C33 tank. That night, we went over the tanks again, double and triple-checking everything. The plight of White Platoon was fresh on our minds.

The sight of the company rolling out and turning through the neighborhood as we departed COP Ford was majestic. There is just something stirring about a column of heavy armor, turrets slewing back and forth. The column split and separated in Jamila. An armored unit needs a lot of room to maneuver. David was the lead tank, my tank was second, and Jeff's Bradley brought up the rear.

Our advance took a slow, deliberate pace. I wanted to tempt RPG gunners to step out of hiding in order to get their shot off earlier. I knew there were going to be IEDs and nearly 100 percent would be armor-piercing ones. My heart was in my throat in nervous anticipation of the impending ambush. We turned up into the industrial section of Jamila on Husseineya Street. Towering buildings stood on both sides. The place was filthy. Trash and refuse liberally coated the ground. The street was so abused that the pavement had broken up and become a bumpy dirt road.

Our limit of advance was to be a couple hundred meters prior to reaching Jamila Street. We reached our limit without the expected ambush. Carefully, we turned and pushed down to a cross street so we could move over to the next major street.

"Steel X-Ray, Red One. Contact, IED, mike-bravo-four-six-four-five-niner-three-four-niner, out!" To our northwest, a series of explosions split the air: the inevitable came. We had found the front-line JAM's IED belt. But there was no RPG or machine-gun fire. It was time to return.

An IED takes only about thirty seconds to place and were often disguised as a concrete block or dropped inside a vendor tent. The route we took to enter Jamila was probably loaded with fresh IEDs. Instead of going back on the main routes, we used the technique we had used previously with Humvees and wove through the maze of smaller residential side streets. We still needed to cross some of the main routes, though. As we worked our way out, the rest of the company returned to COP Ford and were soon out of Jamila.

Our trouble started with a touch of bad luck and some rusty tank-driving skills. As David's tank crossed a major street median and then turned left onto the far-side lane, the outside edge of the left track stayed on top of the curb just a little too long. A loud pop and series of crunching crackles announced the track had come off its correct alignment. The crew stopped the tank immediately, rear facing the known enemy positions.

A thrown track is not necessarily the end of the world. It depends on how far off it is and in which direction. A good tanker can often "walk" the track back into alignment by moving the tank back and forth and changing the tension on the track by steering back and forth. It is called walking the track on because you need to be off the tank to see your track and know what adjustments to make. The alternative is to "break track" by disconnecting a block of track and then driving the tank off the track and then back onto it. In the best of conditions, this is a half-hour task that requires multiple people off the tank and working.

"One, how bad is my track?" David asked over the radio.

"Left track is off the sprocket to the outside, center guides not showing."

"Okay, I need to hop down and see exactly."

"Give us a minute to set some security first."

We were still deep in enemy-controlled territory. My biggest concern was the enemy would take the opportunity to shoot at a tanker on the ground and create an even bigger problem for us. Snipers, machine guns, and other sporadic weapons had been the norm for the last couple weeks. In a few minutes, the enemy would know what was going on and start to get into position.

Jeff took his Bradley down the left on the near side of the median and set up security in front of the tank. I moved my tank to the right so I could see down the street just behind David's tank. It was just a few meters. To increase our weapons' coverage, I popped up out of the turret and charged the fifty-caliber machine gun. Cory, my loader, saw this and came up to man the loader's M240. I tapped Cory on the shoulder and pointed him at a side street to cover.

"Two, One; we are set." With my message, David quickly popped out of the turret and slid over the side to look at his track. A couple seconds later, he scrambled back up the tank and dropped out of sight.

BOOM! A blinding flash of light and a sledgehammer kick to the chest hit me.

"Move, move, move!" I yelled at Nick.

BOOM! A second blast followed nearly the instant we started moving. As the dust and smoke cleared from the turret, I was tangled up with Cory in a heap on the floor. We struggled to get to our feet, and the tank continued to lurch forward.

"Back, back, back up!" I yelled, intent on getting us away from the IED belt instead of further into it. As Nick complied, Cory, Edwin, and I checked each other for wounds and called up our status. Quickly I gave a contact update over the radio. I didn't realize my helmet's cable had come unplugged in the blast, so nobody but Edwin and Cory heard it.

The tank engine screamed like it was straining harder than it should. The sound of ice in a blender came from the left track. We had been hit, and the tank was damaged, but it was still moving at the moment. We backed up 100 meters before stopping. We got ourselves plugged back in and completed an internal assessment of our tank.

"Two, how bad is it?" I needed to know what the damage was, but there was no way anyone was going to dismount again now.

David told me I was missing three of my seven left-side road wheels. Another was missing a chunk. The track was still connected, but in a fragile state. David then told me he thought we got hit from the right side also. The good news was that David thought his tank could make it back to COP Ford, but it would not be able to make any left turns. Making a left would put slack into the left side track and risk it popping off. *Convenient; we won't be able to make any left turns either.*

We moved the platoon back onto Kumeil Elashteri Road. Jeff took his Bradley out to the left of the intersection to view my right side. The right side was okay. The company command post wanted to know if we need the M88 to recover our tank. No, we could make it back. We were southpaw-only tanks, but the only left turn we couldn't make by making a right was the last turn into COP Ford, and it was gentle.

Our pace back was a labored, noisy limp. The popping, grinding, and groaning of metal was awful. After just a couple blocks, I was worried the tank would not hold together all the way back. Finally we got to the end of the street and began the 270-degree right turn to head out of Jamila and to the freeway on-ramp. David's tank made the turn pretty well—a bit wider than normal, but it was smooth.

Our turn was terrible. We had to make a couple back-and-forth passes because the track sounded like the center guides were going to pop out of the remaining road wheels, and the tank was stubborn in turning. I'm sure the Iraqi soldiers guarding the intersection were both amused and terrified as we wallowed around the turn.

Finally, we pulled safely into COP Ford and stopped in front of the maintenance area. The rest of the platoon and the mechanics were all waiting for us. The C33 tank looked terrible. The limp home had nearly destroyed the damaged road wheel. While the tank had taken a massive hit, we were all able to hop down on our own. Cory and I both had an eardrum blown out by the hit and were slightly bleeding. I didn't think I was too bad, but that night, Captain Looney made me go to the aid station because I was struggling to understand things in our orders briefing. The problem with concussions is that once you get one, the next is easier and easier to get. Next thing I knew, I was on a medevac helicopter, heading to the combat support hospital in the Green Zone. Once there, I did my best to convince the docs that I was just fine and to let me return. I think I came off as an ass, but at least I was allowed to return to my company instead of getting flown to Landstuhl. I did not want to repeat that experience. Still, I was out of the fight, and it would be a week before I returned via hitchhiking on convoys.

We had confirmed what we really already knew. The enemy had planted a bunch of IEDs in Jamila, and if you went in on the main roads, you were pretty much guaranteed to hit one. Miraculously, we only suffered two casualties in the process. The mechanics had their work cut out for them, something that would become the daily norm. Despite having all fourteen tanks on hand at COP Ford, we were never able to roll more than half at any given time because of damage.

On April 4, while I was still out of the fight, Blue Platoon rolled out on another patrol into Jamila. AJ Boyes stepped up to fill my role as temporary platoon leader and commander of C31. When they got to Husseineya Street, disaster struck. An IED blasted the tank hard. It immediately came to a stop. Flames flickered out of the back deck, then crescendoed to a full-on fire. At first, there were no signs of life from the tank, but finally the turret swung to the left and the crew bailed out. Vulnerable, they ran for the safety of the Bradley. C31 quickly became a raging inferno. When it got hot enough, the ammo blew up. With some thirty rounds of high-explosive HEAT rounds, the blast obliterated the rear half of the turret. After more than seventeen hours of burning, the tank cooled down enough to get loaded up on a heavy transport truck and hauled off to the scrapyard.

My hitchhiking journey took me through Taji, where I examined my old tank and inspected the remains of a burned-out Humvee from White Platoon. A few weeks earlier, they had one catch fire on accident, and while the crew got out okay, the equipment inside was ruined. I put my arms-room hat on and inspected the scraps to verify serial numbers. In disgust, I discovered the serial numbers, clearly legible on the rusted and scorched weapons, did not match what White Platoon's leader had emailed me. I got with Sergeant O'Rorke to get the paperwork fixed and turned to my old tank.

The remains of C31 were sobering. The IED that hit it was clearly specifically built and aimed to kill a tank and its crew. It was a multi-penetrator array IED. One penetrator went through the combustion chamber of the turbine engine. This instantly crippled the tank and unleashed a fire inside. Another penetrator went through the rear fuel tank up high and through the battery box, also doing the same. Another penetrator went through the rear fuel tank down low, allowing fuel to spill and spread fire on the ground. One penetrator went through the drive sprocket of the right track, instantly destroying the transmission and the tank's ability to move. Another went through the hull ammo compartment. Fortunately, the compartment happened to be empty; otherwise, the rounds surely would have exploded.

C31 had caught fire instantly and was rapidly engulfed. The crew had been dazed by the blast, and their escape was barely in the nick of time. The M1A2 is equipped with a fire-suppression system that automatically senses a fire and works to put it out with halon. While it is effective at nipping a flash fire in the bud before it really takes root and becomes too large and hot to put out, C31's fire started too large and powerful for the system to work.

The main ammo compartment is in the rear of the turret. A blast door separates it from the crew compartment. When the loader pulls a round out, he hits a switch, and hydraulics open the door for a couple seconds and then close it. The door is nearly an inch thick. The tank has two large blowout panels on the roof of the ammo compartment. When the ammo explodes, these panels are supposed to be the path of least resistance and channel the explosive blast upward. These panels had worked very effectively on tank fires both during training mishaps and during the invasion.

C31's ammo detonation completely obliterated the turret. Everything from the blast doors to the rear was gone. The turret sides were even peeled away forward of the blast doors. The loader's blast door ended up on the floor of the turret. Of course, the fire had totally gutted the crew compartment anyway.

I had some major concerns about the demise of C31. The first was that it caught fire so quickly. With the crew buttoned up, another tank crew would be totally unable to save a crew in a burning tank, and the time window for getting them out was tight. There wasn't really anything we could do about it other than to practice tank-evacuation drills repeatedly. My second major concern was the fact that the enemy hit an ammo compartment with a penetrator perfectly. We immediately pulled all ammo out of the hull ammo compartments and agreed to never place anything there. It was not worth the risk for six hard-to-access rounds.

My biggest concern was the main ammo compartment. If the enemy was capable of hitting the hull ammo, a much smaller and hidden target, it would be easy to hit the main ammo compartment in the turret. We had an intense debate about the sequence of the blast door's failure and how it ended up inside the crew compartment.

Did it get overwhelmed by the force of the explosion and cave in, or did it later melt out of its track?

The tank's manual prescribes a specific pattern for loading ammo into the compartment with a certain mix of high-explosive rounds and nonexplosive sabot, or canister, rounds. The manual warned a failure to adhere to the correct mix and placement could result in catastrophic results. Since we were nearly exclusively using HEAT rounds in the urban fight against guerrilla infantry, we were carrying a lot more HEAT in the ammo compartment than recommended. Was it possible that the overload of HEAT caused the ammo compartment to fail? If the explosion was powerful enough to send multi-ton chunks of tank flying thousands of feet, would it also be enough to knock out or kill the crew?

The loss of C31 would be felt again a month later. C31 had been in the second push of tanks down from Camp Taji. After our first two came without tools and equipment, we made some phone calls to ensure the second two had everything they needed. The hardworking soldiers at Taji did just that, and C31 and C32 came stocked. When C31 burned, it took half of our platoon's tools and equipment with it. Jay and I decided to keep the remaining set at COP Ford instead of risking it to combat loss. Even if we did send it out with a tank, we would have to guess which of the three remaining tanks would need it.

DRAGON'S FIRE

WE REFER TO THE NIGHT of April 11, 2008, as the night of the thermo-nuclear bomb. Words fail to really portray that night. The newest phase in the fight was spectacular.

After two weeks of increasingly hard fighting to hold the line on Jamila Street and to control the neighborhoods of Jamila and Thawra I, we did not have much to show for our efforts. We had held the western corner at the Gold checkpoint. The loss of vehicles and soldiers continued to tick upward daily, but the front line in Jamila was closer to the freeway than it was to Jamila Street.

So far, the fight in Sadr City had been broken into two phases. The first was the initial defense. JAM units viciously attacked every US and Iraqi Army unit they could find in an attempt to break out of Sadr City and get their artillery within range of the Green Zone. JAM's artillery units had been busy launching rockets at the Green Zone at unprecedented rates. Their most common weapon was the 107 mm rocket. While JAM had a seemingly endless supply of them, the rockets' range was just short enough that they needed to move from Sadr City into Jamila and Thawra I in order to reach the Green Zone. To stem the rain of rockets, US units scrambled to control the soccer fields and open spaces that made good launch sites.

The second phase was controlling Jamila and Thawra I. Our reinforcements from north of Baghdad joined the fight and established strongpoint patrol bases inside the neighborhood. In Jamila, one of the patrol bases was across the street from a frequently used launch site. It was named Patrol Base Texas, a site in the heart of Jamila and slightly tenuous. Patrol Base Florida was established closer to the freeway to try and protect the supply line. Patrols from these bases worked to find and engage the enemy infantry hiding in the dense neighborhood.

Team Steel's armor daily patrolled the major streets, the "lines of communication," to the patrol bases in order to keep them open. It was brutal work. The enemy IED teams were incredibly prolific at their sowing. We got better at looking for them but still hit many. One day, Red Platoon's C13 came back looking like the USS *Cole*. The IED caused a massive sympathetic detonation of reactive armor tiles. The entire right side was blackened, and a large area was blasted inward. The entire crew miraculously walked away from it intact.

One afternoon I led a patrol that included an EOD team to find a reported IED. Upon entering Jamila, the normally busy Kumeil Elashteri Road was devoid of people—a sign that we were about to find trouble. At the first major intersection, we found a suspicious-looking block in a chicken-wire cage. We set up security around the block so EOD could investigate.

Compared to the tanks providing security, the little tracked bomb robot looked even more toy-like. It scrambled up next to the cage and started to poke around. After a minute or so, the EOD team called over the radio that it was a definite IED and they were going to blow it up in place. The little robot went back to the EOD truck. A couple minutes later, it crawled back carrying an explosive charge in its claw. The robot got to the cage and conducted a series of thwarted attempts to get the explosive over or through the wire.

"Blue One, Blaster. I'm going to have to hand-place it."

My stomach rose to my throat. The idea of a person walking out to a known IED did not sit well with me, but when it comes to reducing

IEDs, EOD was the boss. The whole platoon scanned for the triggerman with extra vigilance. I turned to keep an eye on the EOD team. A soldier got out of their truck and walked towards the IED.

BOOM! When the soldier got about ten feet away, the IED went off. Dust filled the air. In my thermal viewer, I saw the soldier running back to the truck.

"Sitrep!!!" I demanded a report from the platoon.

"Blaster okay, just need some new pants!" The most vulnerable soldier in the patrol was okay. Whew.

"Blue One, Gold Two; I have the triggerman and camera!"

"Engage!" I directed the Bradley to shoot the triggerman. By this point in the campaign, I trusted the soldiers to positively identify enemy combatants and relied on their well-honed judgement. A burst of 25 mm high-explosive rounds rocked a window on the building next to me, with several bursts inside the room. It was very unlikely that anyone inside the room survived. Yet we did not have the manpower to go inside the building, clear it, and find out.

One IED down, thousands still to go.

Another patrol I led made it to Patrol Base Texas without incident. It seemed that the enemy was a bit wary of engaging the tanks in an ambush. As we headed back up Kumeil Elashteri Road, I noticed something out of place. A new concrete block was sitting on the side of the road. David's tank had already passed it. It must have been meant for me or Staff Sergeant Mark Peck's Bradley.

"Driver, stop!" We came to a stop about 200 meters short of the block. I stopped David and Peck, and they set up security where they were. I looked around the area. The small groups of civilians on the street earlier had vanished. That was a bad sign.

Listening to the radio, I knew that EOD's bomb squad was busy. I could not see any telltale wires coming out of the concrete block. Perhaps it was harmless. I wasn't willing to take a chance, though.

"Gunner, coax, concrete block!"

"Identified."

"Engage from backside, top down, and then forward. Fire."

I gave Edwin the fire command to shoot the block with the coaxial mounted M240 machine gun. Tied in to the fire-control system, the tank's coax was as precise as a sniper rifle. I wanted to chip the block apart to remove the possible threat. By working the backside first, we might be able to break up an IED's explosive enough to prevent a large, coherent blast.

"On the way." Edwin operated the trigger like a surgeon, working the edge of the block and taking advantage of the tracer rounds' flatter trajectory to keep them out of the block. After putting about ten rounds through the block, it was breaking up in chunks instead of concrete fragments. Edwin then hit the block with a tracer. Instead of a blast, the tracer started a fire on the block. Hot, blue-green flames came from the chunks as the explosive burned in a nice, controlled manner. After a few minutes, the explosive finished burning away, leaving the copper plate and control package of a cell phone, motherboard, and battery.

As we returned to COP Ford, I was doubly relieved that David hadn't gotten hit when he passed the IED; it was his last patrol with the platoon. Blue Platoon still had a pending leadership change, put on hold when Mike had been killed. David Rocha transferred to the headquarters section, and newly promoted Staff Sergeant Christopher Bryant took his place. I knew Chris from when I was with White Platoon in Baqubah. He was steady, a solid man, a man I knew I could count on. As the newest staff sergeant to the platoon, Chris and his new crew became Jay's wingman, and Danny and his crew became my wingman.

Chris had a rough welcome to Blue Platoon. On one of his first patrols, we were to take a three-tank platoon patrol up Thawra Street to Jamila Street and then return. My plan was to enter the neighborhood from the freeway at Thawra Street, then return down Kumeil Elashteri Street.

As soon as we turned off the freeway, I pulled my hatch down into the partially closed position we called "open protected." I was worried about snipers in the tall buildings. Steadily, we drove around the traffic circle and then turned up the right lane of Thawra Street. It was a nice path, with the park on the right and the lane to the left giving us space.

BOOM! About a third of the way up the street, an explosion even with Chris's tank but on the other side of the park sent a cloud of smoke and dust into the park. As the edge of the cloud receded from the tank, I saw the bright light of flames licking out of the right-side armor blocks.

"Blue Three, Blue One; fire in your reactive armor!" I called to Chris on the platoon radio as I opened my hatch with my other hand. Without waiting to hear the report to company, I disconnected my helmet cable and jumped out. As I opened my sponson box and grabbed the fire extinguisher, I realized our turret was slewing.

"Edwin, give me a second to dismount!" I yelled down the hatch and then scrambled over to the left side of the turret to avoid the coax machine gun, expecting Edwin to shoot as soon as he found a target. I slid off the front slope of the tank and sprinted to Chris's. He too was grabbing his extinguisher.

"I don't think they will blow, but we gotta get it out!" I yelled to Chris as we were both wearing our vehicle helmets. Together, we blasted the nascent flames with powder.

"LT, I'm gonna pull the block!" From the top of the tank hull, Chris pointed at the block that had been burning, the bottom block. The top block had detonated. I set my extinguisher down and starting pushing up on the hot block so Christopher could grab it. Quickly, he set the block in the empty bustle rack like a hot potato. There were some flames in the next block forward, so I blasted it again.

"Sergeant, are you guys okay?"

Chris gave me a thumbs-up.

"Can your tank still roll?" I heard the engine still running normally. Again, Chris flashed a thumbs-up. I responded by pointing my finger up and making a circle motion. *Mount up; let's get out of here before a sniper gets one of us.* I grabbed my extinguisher and ran back to my tank as Chris disappeared into his hatch.

We aborted the patrol and returned to COP Ford down the freeway. There we examined the tank. We had put out the fire quickly, but the tank turret was penetrated and the tank thus destroyed. It was amazing: the IED had been at least fifty feet away, yet the slug had penetrated into the gunner's sights. Copper was melted into the turret and hull. Some ten other blocks had been mangled by shrapnel. At least we didn't lose anyone or any of the tools and equipment inside it. Still, the tank was ruined.

This patrol was the calm before the storm. While we were out, a new plan had been formed. It was time to change tactics. The newest phase of the fight was simple on paper. US forces would build a concrete obstacle down Jamila and Al Qouds streets to prevent the JAM artillery forces from being able to move within range of the Green Zone. Team Steel would be responsible for the Jamila obstacle. We would begin during darkness on April 11.

The reality of the operation was not going to be simple. For the mission, Team Steel had the battalion's route-clearance platoon. A National Guard engineer unit was providing the crane and a few Humvees of engineers. Kellogg Brown & Root provided the trucks and drivers to deliver the prefabricated concrete barriers. The brigade military police company would provide security for the convoy as it came down from Camp Taji and then returned.

I had been part of large-concrete-barrier missions a few months earlier in the Beida neighborhood, but this would be vastly different. Those missions had been undertaken during the cease-fire and were never contested by the enemy, while if you came within even a block or two of Jamila Street, the fight was on. As the front line of JAM's territory, they would defend it with vigor. The street was also heavily mined with IEDs.

In the company's homemade command post, Team Steel's leaders gathered in the hot morning to plan the operation. The size of the operation dictated the approach we would take. The company would link up with the other elements on the freeway and then drive to

Thawra Street. There, the route-clearance platoon would clear the street up to Jamila Street. Blue Platoon would follow and support them. At the intersection of Jamila Street, the platoon would secure it while the route-clearance platoon cleared Jamila Street to Husseineya Street. While they cleared Husseineya Street back towards the freeway, the engineers would move up and start placing the barriers.

Thawra Street was wide with a long park running along its entire length. It would allow good maneuver space for our tanks. The street was also the estimated boundary between two JAM battalions. Exploiting the seam could allow us to fight a less coherent defense. The complex intersection of Thawra and Jamila was dominated by tall buildings. On the west corner was an Iraqi Police station that had exchanged hands back and forth during the fighting. It was currently in friendly control but was not likely to provide support.

Over the course of three weeks of fighting, the civilians in the contested area had left home. Both the Iraqi government and JAM had issued evacuation notices to the entire neighborhoods of Jamila and Thawra, as well as the neighborhoods immediately inside Sadr City. A darkness-to-dawn curfew was in place. The intensity of fighting was enough to convince anyone with common sense to leave. By April 11, only combatants remained on the battlefield.

Jamila Street was a mess where we were planning to breach the obstacles. Both sides of the street were lined with a large maze of market-vendor shacks and tents. The center median had a tall wire-and-concrete-post fence.

The street was no man's land, and this would be the first major attempt to breach down it since the establishment of JAM's relative sanctuary over a year ago. Sadr City was the realm of JAM, with only the occasional Special Forces raid entering it—always a spectacular firefight with AC-130 gunships orbiting and pounding the enemy to allow the Special Forces to fight out.

For the mission, Blue Platoon would use all three of our tanks and a Bradley from Gold Platoon. Without a tank, Christopher's tank crew sat out the mission on April 11. We needed to leave someone behind to man our guard post anyway.

Jay and Danny, still used to operating together as a section, would secure the intersection, and I would protect the column's right flank on Thawra Street. We were just as concerned about an attack on our flank from Jamila and Thawra. We would roll into the fight fully buttoned up. With a three-tank platoon and a complex operation, we decided to remain flexible in case the standard roles did not meet the situation.

As darkness descended on the city, we completed our final crew briefing and inspections. It was time to roll. The happy whine of turbine engines filled the air as we assembled at Ford's gate and then rumbled out to the freeway. Inside our neighborhood, a few Iraqi citizens gave us a thumbs-up or a wave as we passed.

At the neighborhood exit onto the freeway, I saw the engineers and concrete convoy idling on the far side. Our battalion's sappers were waiting next to our exit. So far, so good. The sappers led the way down the freeway. As we neared Thawra Street, I sat down out of the commander's hatch and pulled it shut behind me.

My display screens gave the inside of the tank a yellowish hue. Over in the loader's seat, Cory shot me his standard grin. My night-vision goggles dangled on a string from my body armor so I could find them quickly. My thermal viewer gave me great detail, but it was like looking at the world through a paper-towel roll. In order to see anything out of my 360 degree of periscope blocks, I needed to carefully hold the night-vision goggles to my eye and gently move my head around inside the cupola. It was less than perfect, but it had to do.

Thawra Street looked like something out of a movie in the starlight. The night was clear and dark. Despite the tall buildings and dense urban feel, not a soul was in sight. There were no cars on the road or parked in the spaces next to the long park running along the street. Not even stray dogs ventured out. There were no lights on in any of the buildings, and the streetlamps were extinguished. The city had a postapocalyptic feel. My skin crawled and my hair stood on end.

Halfway up Thawra Street, I stopped the truck convoy. I had them in the left lane of the street so I could use the right lane for maneuvering. Jay and Danny followed the sappers up to the Jamila Street intersection. They moved slowly and carefully, led by Specialist Defino of the sapper platoon. I had known him since 2006. Now he was driving the road grader–like Husky, a one-man vehicle designed to provide maximum protection from explosive blasts while allowing the best chance of detecting IEDs first.

Edwin's voice broke the silence. "LT, I've got someone for you to look at." I looked into my sight to see a head with a cell phone up to it poking around a corner approximately halfway back down the convoy. This was the same spot where an expertly laid and detonated IED destroyed Christopher's tank earlier. This was not good. I had Nick accelerate the tank towards the middle of the convoy. There was enough moonlight that we were not completely invisible to the enemy lookout. As we got closer, the head disappeared. Once even with the alley, I had the tank stop, and we waited with the gun aimed and ready. Our patience was not in vain. A few minutes later, the face peeked around the corner, and then a man darted towards some cover on the other side of the street. As he peered over an object, I gave the order to fire. A short burst of machine-gun fire tore into the enemy lookout, and he fell over into the street. Another pair of hands pulled the man out of view. I glanced at my mapping to see where the laser range finder had plotted the lookout.

"Steel X-Ray, Blue One; engaged and destroyed OP, mike-bravo-four-seven-five-six-niner-two-three-four. Out."

As we moved our tank to a new position, the truck drivers watched us nervously. The military police escort asked me over the radio what was going on. I explained I engaged and destroyed a lookout. The truck drivers responded by asking for assurance I wouldn't leave them. *Wimps.* Contractors bothered me. They were getting paid nearly double what I was getting paid, but they were totally unwilling to place themselves in harm's way.

Up ahead, Jay and Danny took up positions in the intersection as the sappers made their turn onto Jamila Street. *Any minute now...* The question was where we would start taking fire from. We knew it would be intense. The engineers' Humvees moved closer to the traffic circle so they could start looking for where they would place the barriers.

BOOM! Down Jamila Street, Defino's Husky was hit by an IED. It stopped for a moment and then pressed forward some more. *BOOM!* A few meters farther, Defino hit another IED. Once again, he paused and then slowly moved forward. *BOOM!* A third IED went off on Defino. This time, when the dust cleared, a small red light came from the cab of the Husky. Defino was hurt.

This was the moment the enemy was waiting for. In an instant, the entire east side of Jamila Street erupted in gunfire. RPGs flew in from alleys and over walls. The radio burst to life with urgent voices giving commands and reports.

Without hesitation or orders, Jay immediately dashed his tank up Jamila Street to put it between Defino and the enemy. Jay knew that getting Defino out was going to be difficult, and many soldiers would be vulnerable as they extracted him. The enemy's fire concentrated on Jay's tank. His gunner, Will, returned fire with the cannon. The sharp crack of the cannon fire added to the symphony of violence from RPGs, machine guns, and 25 mm. Acting as a shield for the sappers, Jay was unable to move around as tanks do in a fight.

From the intersection, Danny's tank and the Bradley returned fire while receiving a high volume. Tracers crisscrossed the darkness, and explosions lit the night like a summer thunderstorm.

"Blue One, Easy One Seven; I need you to help me run one litter urgent back to Ford!" the sapper platoon sergeant called over the radio. He had Defino in his Bradley and needed an escort to get him back to the aid station quickly.

"Roger, meet at the intersection and I will lead." I was already moving towards Jamila Street in support of the rest of the platoon. As I got there, Sergeant First Class Dennis Mitchell's Bradley came racing around the corner. I pivoted our tank around, and we began a forty-mile-per-hour sprint back to Ford.

Without warning, night turned to day as a massive explosion ripped the air. A huge fireball rose thousands of feet above Jay's tank. The light and heat was overpowering. It seemed like the whole neighborhood was on fire. Jay and Will were still shooting, so I knew they were okay. Quickly Jay came over the radio with an update, and I continued the casualty evacuation run, knowing the platoon was still in good shape.

As we pulled into Ford, I stopped our tank on the side of the landing zone and jumped down to help Dennis get Defino into the aid station. Dennis's Bradley came to a halt and backed up to the building and dropped the ramp. Defino was lying on the bench in the back, his backside bloody. We were quickly joined by more soldiers, and we slid Defino on a litter and rushed him to Doc Anderson.

With Defino in good hands, it was time to rejoin the fight. We rapidly mounted back up and sped out of Ford and down the freeway. We had only been at Ford for maybe three minutes total. As we got back to Jamila Street, things were quieting down. The sappers were just about done hooking the damaged Husky up to be towed home. The rest of the platoon was in closer to the Sadr City side of the street, turrets twisting back and forth as the gunners sought out targets.

Jay and Danny filled me in on the situation. Both tanks and the Bradley were okay. The enemy had engaged them from both sides of Thawra Street with small arms and RPGs. The massive fireball had been a secondary explosion from a building next to Jay's tank. The fires had been so intense that thermals were not effective, and the gunners switched to daylight sights. Everyone was okay. The sappers had extracted themselves without further damage or casualties, but now they were not equipped to continue to the breach.

Near the intersection, a heavy tow truck was hooking up to a mangled Humvee with its engine was crushed down. During the fight, an engineer Humvee had moved up to apparently hide behind Danny's tank. I'm sure that tucking behind a seventy-ton chunk of metal seemed like a good idea at the time. The problem is that in a fight, tanks move around—a lot. Tankers will take full advantage of the mobility to adjust their firing positions, getting better angles and thwarting anyone trying to pinpoint the tank's location. To keep the frontal armor towards the enemy, the first movement from a firing position is generally backward.

After firing his first round, Danny had the tank back up so they could move to a new position, unable to see the Humvee that had snuck up behind him in the darkness. Suddenly the tank's rear was in the air, so he stopped the tank and had it pull forward, but the damage was already done; the tank had climbed the hood of the Humvee all the way to the turret. Danny shrugged it off and continued the fight. Once things calmed down, the engineers had the convoy's recovery vehicle tow the destroyed Humvee away. To the engineers, it was a harrowing close call. To us, it was simply hilarious.

In the meantime, the KBR truck drivers realized the tank guarding near them had disappeared in the chaos. That sent their worry into overdrive, and the sight of tanks firing cannons and RPGs flying in all directions was enough to push them to the verge of panic. The military police escort pestered me to move closer to the middle of the convoy. None of my reassurances to their relative safety seemed to register.

With the sappers unable to continue the breach and not enough of Jamila Street cleared to begin to emplace barriers, the mission was aborted and we all headed back to base. The withdrawal from Jamila Street was uneventful.

Back at Ford, we learned that Defino was going to be okay. He had a long recovery ahead of him, but he would live. Jay's C34 tank was blackened in the massive fireball. Other than cosmetic damage, all of the tanks and the Bradley were unscathed. The soldiers who had been at Ford during the fight were flush with awe and excitement. Even from four miles away, they had witnessed much of the explosions and fire lighting up the sky. We would later learn that units some sixteen miles away heard the sounds of battle and saw the massive fireball.

Frustrated by the defeat, we were determined to try again. We did the next night. Our next attempt at breaching the enemy minefield so we could place our own concrete obstacles started on the other end of Jamila Street. This time we were only going to place obstacles across the intersection on the Jamila side of the street from the buildings on the left to the buildings on the right, closing the street at the curb instead of trying to breach down the length of the enemy minefield. The plan was less ambitious, but it was going to be a little more complex. At some point, we would have to pull our tanks back through a small gap in our obstacle and then finish closing it off. The last couple concrete blocks would be emplaced with weakened security.

Intelligence indicated the enemy had expanded their IED minefield down the major routes into Jamila. We had already hit plenty of IEDs throughout the neighborhood, but a line about halfway up seemed to mark the beginning of a consistent minefield. The main line of the enemy's defenses was Jamila Street. Reaching that meant a guaranteed firefight. The enemy also had ambushes, patrols, and lookouts to the south and west of the minefield, and sniper activity had increased significantly.

To make things harder on the enemy, we attacked at night once again. Our technology allowed us to own the night, and as tankers, we were extremely comfortable fighting in the dark. Coming into Jamila on the end closest to Ford, once again the sappers would lead the way with our tanks in support. This time, Blue Platoon would provide two tanks and get one Bradley. We would follow the sappers until they got to Jamila Street. There we would establish a support-by-fire position in the middle of the minefield and secure the intersection as the brigade's transportation company brought up the concrete barriers and emplaced them. Red Platoon would provide another section of tanks to protect our rear and flanks inside Jamila.

Danny Key would be my wingman. Staff Sergeant Mark Peck's Bradley would join us. We would not have much room to maneuver in the small intersection. I would take the right side, looking down towards where the previous fight had been. Danny would take the left side. It was only 200 meters to 83 Square. There was only one alleyway between his position and the 83 Square traffic circle. Directly across Jamila Street from his position was another small street that led up towards a hospital. Danny's efforts would be concentrated on that street. We would keep the Bradley in the middle and back a little where its higher angle of gun elevation could engage the buildings right next to the intersection. When it came time to pull back through the wall, the Bradley would cover our move. Once behind the wall, only the Bradley was tall enough to shoot over the barriers. If needed, the tank commanders and loaders could pop the hatches and come up to man the exposed machine guns, which were also high enough to fire over the barriers.

In the early darkness, engines came to life, and the company's two small platoons went out to link up with the sappers and the transportation company at our exit. I was glad to see that all of the trucks were crewed by soldiers and not contractors. There would be no repeat of the panicky trucks. The transportation company had its own armored cars to help provide security along the length of the convoy. The sappers began our procession into Jamila, their last remaining Husky scouting the path.

My tank crew was quiet and tense as we turned off Kumeil Elashteri Road towards Jamila Street. This was the site of our platoon's mishap during the reconnaissance in force on March 30. At least this time we had the sappers to help find the IEDs instead of us just getting hit by them.

The sappers inched forward. As space became available, we bounded the tanks from one side-street intersection to the next to ward off any enemy patrols. Back at Kumeil Elashteri Road, Red Platoon held the intersection with the convoy behind them. Hours went by. Finally the sappers completed the breach up the street to the intersection at Jamila Street. As they pulled back, Danny and I moved our tanks into the breach. Jamila Street was incredibly devoid of signs of life. There were no cars parked on the street, no people. It was a ghost town. The enemy was not tipping his hand.

After a few minutes of adjusting our positions to ensure the best coverage, we were ready for the convoy to come up and begin the emplacement of the concrete barriers. It arrived in a few minutes, and the crane started lifting the heavy blocks off the trucks and placing them. They started on my side of the intersection and worked towards Danny.

SSSPPFT-BOOM! BOOM! BOOM! A series of RPGs streaked across Jamila Street at us. A head popped over a courtyard wall directly across from my tank and fired another RPG. It missed high. The head ducked back down just as fast as it had appeared.

"Gunner, CAN, wall!" I used my override joystick to point the gun tube at the spot where the head appeared.

"Identified!" Edwin replied. From the other side of the turret, Cory sprang into action, arming the cannon. "Up!" he yelled.

"Fire!" I barely finished the short command before Edwin hollered, "On the way!" The cannon barked, and the breech snapped back about eighteen inches and spat out the spent casing. To our front, the courtyard wall and the whole front of the building behind it vanished. Before the dust settled, Cory had already pulled another round from the ammo compartment and fed it into the cannon breech. "HEAT up!" he called out. The turret slewed to the right as Edwin returned it to our primary sector of responsibility. I continued to watch the buildings for more trouble.

To our left, Danny was slinging rounds up the street. The crack of his cannon was followed by a long burst of machine-gun fire. There was a pause; then his cannon fired once more. After a few minutes, the street was silent again.

"One, Three. Engaged and destroyed an RPG team. We are okay." Danny's report over the radio attracted my attention in his direction. As I looked to my left, I noticed something different about his tank: the loader's M240 machine gun and its mount had been hit and destroyed. It was a good thing we all had been buttoned up.

I backed the tank up close to the new concrete barriers to check on the soldiers on the ground who had been placing them, popping open my hatch to glance around. Nobody shot at me. Yay! I grabbed my rifle, scrambled off the back of the tank, and trotted over to the captain in charge of the ground team. I instantly recognized her from the class ahead of me at West Point. It was a small world, though I couldn't remember her name. All of her soldiers were okay, and all of the RPGs missed their marks. As she finished updating me, the soldiers quickly got back to work. I returned to my tank and climbed in.

We crept down the street to our right. Now I could see a few meters of side street a bit better. We settled in for the long wait until the new wall was ready.

Down the street about 400 meters, a man started crawling on his belly from the Sadr side to the center median, dragging a bag. *You've got to be kidding me.* Surely he didn't think he was actually hiding from us. When he got to the median, he dug a hole in the soft dirt and then pulled a blocky item from the bag and set it in the hole. As he fiddled with the object, we slowly aimed the gun at him.

A quick fire command, and Edwin unleashed a burst of machine-gun fire at him. The man seemed to have a sixth sense and flinched to the side right before the first burst pelted the dirt he had just been lying on. Edwin quickly adjusted, and the man twitched involuntarily from the impact of rounds as he tried to retreat to a side street. With some ten meters to go, he fell. It was clear he would die, but he hadn't given up yet and started to crawl towards a parked car on the side street. There was the roar of a diesel engine to my right and the staccato bark of a 25 mm as the Bradley came up to engage. High-explosive rounds are the equivalent of a hand-grenade burst when they hit. The man instantly stopped moving, lying prone in front of the car. Another burst of 25 mm churned up the dirt around the hole where the new IED was located, breaking it into pieces.

Silence again returned to the neighborhood. Behind us, one concrete block after another slowly closed off the intersection. We were going to be successful. The enemy did not try us again for the rest of the night. Two hours later, we were ready to withdraw through the wall. Nobody had tried to reach the dead sapper. As we backed through the wall, I noticed in the thermal viewer that the enemy sapper's body temperature was the same as the street he was lying on. *Jesus have mercy on my soul.*

With just two concrete blocks left to place after we pulled our tanks back, the wall was quickly finished. The transportation company swiftly loaded back up and pulled out towards the freeway. We followed shortly behind them. The successful mission felt really good. Not only did we complete the wall across the intersection, but we had done so without casualties.

When we got back to COP Ford, we found yet another difficulty to work around. The old HEAT rounds we were using had become very fragile. All 120 mm rounds have a cellulose casing. When the round is fired, only the aft cap remains. The aft cap is an aluminum base that the cellulose attaches to. In the center is a long primer stick that allows the primer to introduce the spark to a larger area of the powder. The age, combined with the extreme heat of the rounds when placed in a hot cannon breech, would cause the cellulose to separate from the aft cap with the slightest of tugging. When we returned from the fight, we needed to pull the round out of the cannon so we could clean the cannon and ensure nobody accidentally fired a round inside our compound. As we did so, the cellulose separated, spilling gunpowder on the turret floor and ruining a precious round. The only thing left to do was carefully place the round in our growing dud-pit collection.

During this time, the media and higher-up commanders started to come to COP Ford to check out the fighting. The media was an interesting dynamic I had never thought much about before. We'd had a combat photographer or a newspaper reporter stop by a few times, but never anything mainstream.

During the Sadr fight, all of the major new networks sent reporter teams, including Lara Logan and Richard Engel. The CNN crew got to experience an ambush firsthand with Red Platoon. They did not enjoy it. Richard Engel offered up a satellite phone to call home with when he came by and even spent a few hours in the platoon room talking with soldiers. He then honored Mike Elledge and Chris Simpson on Memorial Day on his segment of what the day meant to soldiers in combat.

Over the next week, Team Steel attacked nightly up to Jamila Street on the major streets of Jamila. Red Platoon drew the lead for Husseineya Street. They got into a large fight near the truck depot and never even made it to Jamila Street. The enemy closed within range to throw hand grenades onto the vehicles but were ineffective with them. By April 17, we still had not completed all five major streets in Jamila, much less the eight side streets that intersected Jamila Street. As soon as the enemy discovered our operation's intent and methods, they pushed their minefields deeper and increased their patrols and ambushes. Some nights we were not able to emplace a single barrier. It was time to change things up.

THE DRAGON ON THE MARCH

THE TEAM TOOK A BIT of a holiday on April 17. That night, we did not attack. Instead, we spent the day at COP Callahan for an awards ceremony. The division commander, Major General Hammond, came down to present Bronze Stars for Valor to Jay Weatherly, Danny Key, and RJ Williams. I had the honor of joining them on the stage. Jay and RJ earned theirs while protecting Defino's extraction on April 11. Danny earned it during the counterattack on March 27. I was proud to be leading such a great platoon. The men were lions. By this point of the fighting, nearly every single man in the platoon had an award-for-valor recommendation submitted. The ceremony was not long, and we got to spend the rest of the day resting and working on the tanks.

The supply chain started to catch up with the pace of combat, providing plenty of machine-gun ammunition and fuel. However, we were still firing 120 mm ammo faster than it could be resupplied, and parts remained extremely difficult to come by. The explosive armor blocks in particular were a challenge, and we burned through them quickly. As a result of the shortages, finding a working part required a lot of effort, and we shared what we could. If a tank could roll and fight, we would fight it, regardless of being in degraded mode.

The team's leaders gathered in the company command post to prepare for the next phase of the fight. Brigade decided to change the operation. Instead of us slogging forward every night to seize one intersection, placing some barriers and then withdrawing by dawn, we were going to tag-team with another unit to keep an uninterrupted advance.

To the southeast, 1-2 Stryker Cavalry had been rotating companies through the breach on Al Qouds Street. Like us, they were only building at night, but they would occupy the buildings near the wall and defend it during the day. While daytime brought a much harder fight, they did not have to re-breach the approach streets to Al Qouds over and over. Brigade's new plan was to have 1-68 Armor join the rotation and concentrate all efforts on one continuous breach. This would allow 1-2 Stryker to pull some of their combat power away from the attack and use it to secure the Thawra I neighborhood on the left flank. It would be a four-mile-long, deliberate breach in complex terrain. While it would be slow and concentrated, we would be able to keep unrelenting pressure on the enemy defending the dense minefield of IEDs.

The battalions would relieve each other about every sixteen hours, with the brigade support battalion keeping the supply of "T-wall" concrete barriers steady by establishing a large cache of them on the southeast end of Al Qouds Street in an open field. From there, their trucks would bring the walls up to the slowly advancing construction site. A construction engineer battalion would emplace the T-walls. We still needed to provide a squad of infantry on the ground to help. The engineer's horizontal construction company was on standby with dozers in case we needed to remove rubble from the path of the wall.

Multiple route-clearance sapper platoons were dedicated to the operation. Periodically, they would move up and breach farther through the minefield. Both 1-2 Stryker and 1-68 Armor would provide the firepower to cover the breach and the construction of the wall. In support, Apaches and armed drones would keep a nearly constant presence overhead.

The plan was for 1-68 Armor to stick with what was already a cohesive and experienced team. Team Steel would continue its role as the company at the point of attack. We had already figured out how to work well with both the sappers breaching the minefield and the engineers building the wall. The battalion's other tank company would provide security at the barrier cache site and along the routes we used. In a pinch we could ask for them to come up in support. It was fun to be part of the team undertaking the main effort of the battalion, the main effort of the brigade, the main effort of the division, and the main effort of the corps. We were the very pointy tip of the American spear.

Team Steel had been augmented with a tank platoon from another division. One should never look a gift horse in the mouth, but as a platoon, they were not useful. They did not perform well, and the team broke it up and gave a tank section to each platoon to tuck the inexperienced crews in with the well-seasoned ones. I was not particularly excited for the help.

There was no finesse in the plan. It was going to be a blunt and brutal effort. Never before in history had anyone undertaken this sort of operation. When breaching, attacking forces aim to pierce the thinnest portion of an obstacle possible and then penetrate rapidly beyond the defenses behind it. We were instead breaching down the length of the minefield, down the face of the enemy defenses. To make the effort more unusual, we were building our own obstacle as we went. The point of construction was going to be in the very middle of our breaching effort.

To complicate the effort, we had restrictions on our firing. Units from 1-2 Stryker were trying to secure Thawra I with the help of an Iraqi Army brigade. Because they were scattered all over the neighborhood, they did not want us shooting towards Thawra I. We were to keep our fires oriented up Al Qouds Street and deeper into Sadr City. In addition to this limitation, 1-2 Stryker had already placed barriers across most of the intersections in the same way we had dealt with Jamila. These barriers now restricted our maneuver room. Fortunately, Al Qouds Street was wide.

As with previous weeks, we organized the company into tailored platoons. The first change was that the company headquarters would roll out to the breach site in its two MRAP armored cars. The commander, first sergeant, executive officer, and fire-support officer would pair up and take turns controlling the fight on the ground while the other pair ran assistance from COP Ford. The pair at the wall would provide command and control to the elements there and feed an accurate assessment of the fight to Battalion. The pair at COP Ford would monitor drone feeds and relay that information rapidly on the company radio net instead of waiting for higher-ups to decide if something needed to be shared. Additionally, they would tend to the logistical needs of the company. Some members of the headquarters section, such as Sergeant Doc Fetsurka, would spend nearly every minute of the company's shifts on the wall.

The plan was to breach about 200 to 400 meters of minefield at a time, secure it, and build the wall forward. When there was less than 50 meters of maneuver space left, we would breach some more. Any time an intersection fell within the 200 to 400 meters, we would always breach just past the far side. This is not very much space for an armored force to work in. As such, we would not be able to fit the whole company into the fight. In fact, fitting our whole platoon team of seven tanks wasn't possible.

The other problem was that sixteen hours was too long to fight on one tank of fuel. In heavy fighting, six hours was as long as you could comfortably expect a tank to last and have enough reserves for a bad day. Six hours was also a long time for a squad of infantry to perform under fire, but sixteen hours was definitely too long. The men would be performing at nearly maximum exertion in 100-degree heat with maximum stress.

Red Platoon and Blue Platoon would take turns securing the breach site with reinforced sections. Out of fairness we would alternate which platoon took the first and third shifts and which took the second and fourth shifts. Neither platoon had enough tanks or soldiers to take consecutive shifts. Since we were going to be crossing multiple intersections in addition to needing to secure both directions of the street, we would need three tanks and a Bradley. We also agreed to plan thirty minutes of overlap for battle handover in addition to travel time to and from the breach. A four-hour shift would mean nearly six hours of patrol.

Unlike the previous attacks, we were bringing a squad in the back of the Bradley. The tanks would be allowed some freedom of maneuver but would also need to position to shield the men on the ground. As the T-walls went into place, we would adjust our tanks and the Bradley to maximize the cover available to the squad. The Bradley would remain behind the tanks, concentrating its scanning and fires on the buildings next to us. It would also be at the squad's demand for close-in cover.

The headquarters' MRAPs would stay tucked behind the wall where their height would allow the gunners to see the rooftops across from the wall. They would be the designated casualty-collection point. The MRAPs would also carry extra ammunition for the infantrymen, allowing them to restock on magazines in a sheltered area during the fight without needing to make the Bradley pause its maneuvering. While we rotated the platoons during the company's shift, the headquarters section would remain at the breach without break. They did not need to break off for fuel and ammo like the tanks needed to. The crane and forklift operators would be under the control of the engineers. Their leadership would take care of their rotations.

Jay and I decided we would split the section reinforcing our platoon in half, adding one Black Platoon tank to each of our sections. We were confident in our plan. We were proven in our abilities. We were ready for the coming fight.As we rolled down the freeway to the far end of Sadr City where the wall had been started, there was a sense of adventure in the air. This would be our first time venturing beyond Thawra Street. We had traveled extensively in the areas to the north, all the way to the Hamrin Mountains on the edge of Kurdistan. Never had we been further to the south than Jamila.

The sun was high and hot. With the fighting in its fifth week, there was no traffic on the normally busy freeway. Off to the south, we saw the famous split-onion dome—the Shaheed monument—and a cluster of ministry buildings. Being on the pointy end of the American stick, we never got to go exploring historical sites. For now we settled for seeing the blue onion dome from a half mile away.

To counter the hotter daytime temps, we rolled with our hatches open as we made the four-mile trek down the freeway. US and Iraqi Army vehicles were everywhere you looked: every entrance to the freeway, every overpass, every few miles of traffic—there was no doubt a major operation was underway.

Overhead, we saw Apaches and, higher up, drones. The drones both cracked us up and made us mad. We called the drones the "flying lawn mower." The operators and some of the higher-up commanders swore that nobody could hear them at observation altitude. In truth, the drones were ridiculously loud. If you were never out on the battlefield, though, you would never experience it and understand.

The frustrating part about drones was that often higher-up commanders would rely more on them than reports to understand what was going on. The drones did not really show enemy positions under cover, or enemy fire, or convey the sound, smell, and taste of the battle. Some commanders were bad about having the drone look at us instead of the enemy. Those officers would tend to give micromanaging orders about "moving your vehicle just a little to the left." Sometimes they would ask questions about what we were doing because from above, they were unable to understand the ground dimension of the fight. There is nothing more annoying than answering armchair quarterbacks who don't even bother to listen to the reports or trust their subordinates.

While the Apaches operated on a radio frequency to talk with us, the drones never did. The drones reported what they saw directly to higher-headquarters video screens, and instant text chat would convey orders and such between the operator and the commander.

When an Apache fired a Hellfire missile, we always knew about it first. When a drone fired a Hellfire missile, our first indication was usually the impact of the missile. Every now and then, they lost track of where the target was relative to us and would fire a missile dangerously close without ever bothering to warn us first.

As we pulled off the freeway and turned northeast, pulses picked up. On the off-ramp, tank commanders and loaders reached up and pulled their hatches closed and locked them down. It was time for battle. Ahead, a platoon of Iraqi T-72 tanks sat in the middle of a traffic circle, guarding it. While the crews were actually in their tanks for once, they did not appear the least bit concerned. I had to smile. Those crews were clearly not born-and-bred tankers. True tankers are aggressive at heart. They itch to be where the action is, and if given the slightest bit of slack, they will push their boundaries so they can engage.

As we drew closer to Al Qouds Street, I saw the sprawling cache site on the right. Destroyer Company's tanks were in positions around it and at the Al Qouds Street traffic circle. A heavy forklift loaded T-walls onto the big supply trucks for the run up the street to the construction area. Just short of the slowly expanding end of the wall was the crane. They were trying to keep it tucked behind the wall some so it would be protected. Another forklift worked near it, unloading the T-walls from the trucks and then bringing them closer to the crane. A ladder was propped against the end T-wall. Each time a new barrier was put down, a soldier would run to the ladder, move it over to the new T-wall, and scramble up it. With urgency, he would unhook the crane hooks and then scramble back down and disappear to cover. Each time this happened, the volume of gunfire increased.

When Blue Platoon's little task force turned onto Al Qouds Street for the first time, the wall was not very long. It might have been a bit over a quarter mile. In fact, it was so short I had no reservations about driving a pair of the tanks down the Sadr side of the wall.

Red Platoon was on shift and ready to switch out with us. For a short period, the radio was busier than normal as they explained the position to us and what the enemy had been doing. For the most part, the enemy was using machine-gun and rifle fire against the soldiers trying to build the wall. Some RPGs had been used, but the enemy seemed to be holding back.

On the Sadr side of the street was a massive apartment complex. It may have been some sort of university. The buildings were large and all nearly identical. It reminded us a lot of the apartment complex next to the Gold checkpoint. And just like that complex, the enemy was using the large buildings to mass fighters and move out of sight. The complex was a lot easier to deal with from the tank than the Gold checkpoint had been on foot.

Our formation worked pretty well. The enemy seemed to have trouble adjusting to our methods of fighting and building. I reminded myself this was a different enemy battalion than the one we had fought the last few weeks, who were used to fighting 1-2's Strykers and infantry. The Stryker is not meant to go toe to toe with an enemy of any kind, and so the soldiers used buildings and smaller weapons to fight. We were the armored dragon capable of owning the street. But it was only a matter of time before the enemy changed tactics to adjust to our presence.

One block later, the enemy tried a new trick. While a tank was looking down the major street into Sadr City, a pushcart suddenly got shoved out from a side street a few hundred meters down. On the cart was a 107 mm rocket aimed to shoot flat and straight down the street at the tank. It did not work. The rocket was never aimed properly, and then the tank destroyed the cart. While it did not achieve any results, the attempt showed the enemy was starting to change its tactics. It was now directly targeting the tanks, understanding they were the infantry squad's bodyguards.

During this effort, 1-2 Stryker was reinforced with its own tank company team: Dealer Company, from the 3rd Infantry Division. After a couple days, it became clear they had a different style of fighting. One day during the change of units at the breach, their commander called us a bunch of cowboys on the radio. We did not mind. Everyone does things differently, and as long as we kept the wall moving forward, we were all winning the fight. We did chuckle about it, though. We thought they were a bit timid.

As dawn on April 27 broke, a thick sandstorm moved into Iraq. The only way you could tell the sun had risen was that the sky went from black to a weird, yellowish-tan hue of pale light. A shamal sandstorm is very different than the dust storms in America. American dust storms are full of windblown air that blasts the sand and dirt at you. A shamal dust storm is caused by high wind aloft that sucks the sand into the air. It just hangs there and then slowly covers everything in a fine powder. The dust burns the lungs, gums up mechanical things, and is even thick enough that thermal sights don't see far or well.

Before we rolled out, we cleaned our air filters well for both the engine and the crew air-filtration system. Unlike previous approach marches, we stayed buttoned up to keep our tank from filling with sand. The drones would not be in the air. While we didn't feel like the drones helped us directly, the enemy tended to be more active when the drones were not out. The Green Zone took more rocket fire during the storm, and the enemy artillery units were not the only ones getting busy.

The wall was about one block short of the intersection with Dakhal Street. That block was occupied by a nonfunctioning, walled gas station. A pair of large, four-story buildings dominated the intersection, one on the west side with a massive billboard sign on top, and the other about three buildings into Sadr. The buildings between that one and Al Qouds Street were two and three stories. On the Thawra side of the street next to the wall was a series of two-story residential buildings. A few had ramps down into their garages. The Sadr side had more of the typical two and three-story commercial-and-residential-mix buildings.

While US and Iraqi Army units were in Thawra, they were not very close to Al Qouds Street. As we approached Dakhal Street, the enemy filled the void to allow a stronger defense of the intersection. Dakhal was going to be the enemy battalion's main effort, but we did not know it yet.

The enemy allowed the breach across Dakhal Street without significant resistance. They offered the typical amount of machine-gun fire and RPGs to disrupt the sappers' efforts at finding and neutralizing IEDs. Our sappers completed the breach across the street and then pulled back out of the way. The enemy continued to wait.

As the wall crossed the small side street next to the gas station, the enemy opened fire, throwing everything at us, including the kitchen sink. A new addition to the enemy's effort quickly made his presence known when a sniper hit one of the engineers who was with the crane. The engineers were not in the mood to risk it any longer. While the crane operator and forklift driver were more than willing to continue, the engineers' leader decided they would no longer be on the ground to hook up and unhook the T-walls. Our infantry squad would have to take on that task. I couldn't judge the engineer officer since I was fighting from a cocoon of the best armor the Army had to offer, but I did not envy the infantry squad. I knew what it was like to be a foot soldier in a massive firefight where nearly everyone had a bigger weapon than you.

Shortly after the first sniper hit the engineer, the enemy attacked the cache site with mortars and snipers. One of the snipers was firing a large-caliber rifle that punched holes in armored trucks, nearly killing two soldiers. This disruption to our rear was cause for concern, but we soon had troubles of our own.

During Red Platoon's shift, the enemy steadily increased their fire from the two tallest buildings. Then the enemy moved into the buildings south of the wall, an area we were not allowed to fire cannons at. The infantry had to deal with those enemy squads. As the fight increased, an enemy RPG team managed to hit the forklift in the boom. Fortunately the driver was okay and the machine still worked. Then they hit the infantry squad leader, Staff Sergeant Anthony Farina, in the neck with RPG shrapnel. He was a tough guy, and it barely slowed him down. Then a bullet struck Private First Class Bagwell in the spine, dropping him to the ground. Tank cannon fire, 25 mm from the Bradleys, AT-4 rockets, Hellfire missiles, and copious machine-gun and rifle fire were not having much effect on suppressing the enemy defending Dakhal Street.

The reports of the fighting on the company radio net prepared us for the coming brawl as we approached the wall to relieve Red Platoon's mini task force. Things were not going well. I hoped our fresh fuel, ammo, and energy would make a difference. The sandstorm was thick enough that I could not see the massive smoke columns rising from the battlefield until I was already moving up Al Qouds Street. Even with the hatched buttoned up, I could hear the roar of gunfire. Flashes in the distant haze oriented me towards the two tallest buildings.

The intensity of enemy fire made the battle handover from Todd easy. There was no mistaking the enemy positions. Unfortunately, they were still very active from the same positions they'd been using all morning; we were not making much progress. As Todd's tanks moved back, I had room to work again. I had my tank at the tip of the platoon, in the front left position. Our attached tank was next to me, slightly back. Further back was my wingman, Danny. Playing free safety was Mark's Bradley. Mark dropped the new squad off at the crane, and we went to work.

A few minutes later, the squad asked me to get creative to drive the enemy to our south away. The rifle fire from those houses had been sporadic, but it needed to stop. We could not conduct a 360-degree fight and make progress as well. I backed my tank down the street to where the squad was hunkered down by the crane. They pointed out a building with a ramp down to the door, and I looked into the second-story windows through my periscopes. *I can't shoot a cannon round into it... but do they know that?* An idea flashed into my mind.

"Driver, pivot left to the ramp." Nick obeyed, and we spun until pointed at the house. "Driver, forward, slowly." I could hear the unspoken question in Nick's mind as we slowly crept the tank up against the building. I had Nick continue until our cannon was poking through a window, and then I watched a group of men scramble out the back windows and disappear. None of them had weapons with them as they ran.

With a laugh, I had Nick back up. Without firing a shot or even damaging the house, we had driven them off. I'm sure those men thought the only reason I didn't fire the cannon was because we had seen them run away already. In fact, the muzzle blast would have killed anyone in the house, but God only knew who was located at the distance the round itself would have armed and then detonated at.

Fire from the buildings at the intersection increased. It was time to go on the attack. "Driver, forward to the intersection. Kick it up!" We all lurched back in our seats as the tank rapidly accelerated towards the intersection. Just at the near side of it, I had us stop.

"Identified RPG team!" Edwin called out. I hit a button to have my sight see the same thing. I spotted a group of men trying to poke around a corner some 200 meters down Al Qouds Street. "Fire and adjust!" I gave Edwin the permission to fire at will as the targets came and went. The metallic rattle of the coax machine gun firing filled the turret. Out of the corner of my left eye, I saw Cory perched over the ammo belt, watching it for trouble.

BOOM! Dust filled the tank, and the tank shook. I looked to our right in time to see an RPG gunner duck back into an alley up Dakhal Street. I hit the override button on my joystick and slammed it to the right. Hydraulics screamed as the turret rapidly spun right. I let go as it approached the direction of the alley.

"Gunner, HEAT, RPG in the alley."

"Identified!" Edwin called out. The head had popped out of view, but I knew he was probably about three feet back in the alley, readying another rocket. Edwin placed the crosshairs a couple feet to the left of the corner.

"UP!!!!!" Cory's yell caught my attention. I glanced over and saw him plastering himself against the left wall of the turret, clear of the cannon's recoil.

"Fire!"

"On the way!" The cannon barked. The HEAT round slammed into the building and detonated, throwing concrete rubble into the alley beyond. The shot had been right on the money, just like I had trained our crews. Edwin had already switched to the coax, ready to send a stream of bullets into anyone who staggered out of the alley, the crosshairs right on the edge of the corner at chest level.

"Target, cease fire! Is everyone okay? Is our tank okay?" I looked around the turret.

"I'm good!" Nick called out from the hull.

"We are good, sir." Edwin's gravelly voice betrayed no concerns. *And this is why you are my gunner. Thank you.*

Cory flashed me a thumbs-up. He had already fed another HEAT round into the cannon, and his hand was on the arming lever.

"Steel X-Ray, Blue One engaged and destroyed RPG team mike-bravo-four-eight-eight-eight-niner-two-two-one, negative casualties, negative damage."

"HEAT up!" Cory finished reloading the cannon with another HEAT round. At this point in the fight, we were out of CAN rounds. We had a mix of HEAT and a few OR (obstacle reducing). The OR round was a great new round. It was a variation on the newest HEAT round, which was called an MPAT. The MPAT round had sabot pedals on it. It shot straighter, farther, and faster than the old HEAT round. It was also better for piercing armor. The OR round had a slight modification: the tip was a steel penetrator tip, and the fuse was slightly delayed. This allowed the round to penetrate something big and solid before detonating. It was great for concrete objects that needed to be made into small rocks.

With no further fire command, Cory disarmed the cannon and rechecked the coax's ammo belt. Again I gave Edwin permission to engage any targets that came out of the alley and focused my attention up Al Qouds Street. I traversed my R2D2-like commander's thermal sight to look down it just in time to see an RPG gunner step into the street and fire.

BOOM! Again the tank filled with dust. I was already slinging the turret to the left, matching Edwin's sights with mine. Another quick fire command, and Edwin placed a HEAT round into the corner where the RPG team was hiding. This time he followed up with a stream of machine-gun bullets.

BOOM! An intensely bright flash blinded me. *Ouch! Where did that come from?* The RPG hit about eighteen inches from my face. I never saw it coming. I tried to turn my thermal view to the right to see where the RPG had come from, but it was not responding.

"Sir, GPS thermals are out!" Edwin called out at my feet.

"Black, Blue One; GET UP HERE NOW!" I called for our attached tank to get up to the intersection and protect my right flank. I saw him move forward, stopping about a tank length behind me and off to the right. "Watch that alley and stop them from putting RPGs into my side!"

Reaching down with my right hand to switch to the company net, I called out an update. "Steel X-Ray, Blue One; contact RPG. Taking hits and some damage but we can still fight." At this point, we were only calling contact reports up if we actually took a hit or very near miss.

With a little help, I could focus on what was in front of us. My thermals were stuck, but they happened to still be aligned with the cannon. Edwin's sights were damaged, and he was not able to see very far in the dusty haze without thermals. We still had a long time before Dealer Company was scheduled to show up, so we had to fight in a degraded status. Oh well; this was war.

BOOM! An RPG slammed into the ground about three feet to our left. It was a clean miss, but there was only one place they could shoot from to achieve that trajectory. I was taking fire from the building on the left corner.

"Blue One, Gold Two; back up! I'm engaging that building."

Before I even ordered Nick to move, 25 mm rounds blasted away at the top of the building. Glowing red fragments whizzed all around the tank, bouncing off the top. It was mesmerizing; in my heightened adrenaline, I watched it in slow motion. I trusted Mark's aim, so we stayed buttoned up. In tanker terms, he was scratching our back. He continued to place rounds in the building while Edwin and I engaged in a game of whack-a-mole with enemy infantry down Al Qouds Street.

"Blue One, Gold Two; can you put a round in this building? Third floor, center." I backed up enough so Edwin could get the cannon aimed at the enemy position on the third floor. As we did, the Black tank also backed up to avoid receiving muzzle blast. Edwin placed a couple HEAT rounds into the building, and then we darted back up to the intersection. An Apache placed a few Hellfire missiles for good measure. Black smoke poured off the top of the building as something flammable ignited. The billboard was in shambles and hanging at a limp angle.

The infantry squad called out they were taking a lot of fire from the other tall building, the one north of the intersection. I had the Black tank start working on it. Mark also engaged it, with 25 mm. More Hellfires dropped from the sky and hit the building, sending large clouds of smoke and debris out the growing holes on the upper floors. Still, machine-gun fire poured down. The enemy was persistent.

"Guidons, Steel One-Four; I've got a rocket inbound. Everyone needs to button up, and we need to back up four hundred meters from that building." Lieutenant Clint Rush, the company fire-support officer, had just pulled off what I thought was impossible. He got an artillery strike for us in a city. As I backed up, I thought about how big of a warhead a GMLRS rocket was. These rockets were fired from multiple rocket-launch systems from very long distances. A single launcher could practically destroy everything in a square kilometer with the right warheads. Now one was going to impact less than half a kilometer from me. I trusted Clint's instructions but said a Hail Mary anyway.

Even though the rocket was huge, I never saw it coming in from the left. There was no sound preceding its arrival. As the bright orange ball flashed in front of the building, the thunderous explosion rocked the tank and took my breath away. A huge fountain of dirt burst into the air. While very impressive, the blast did not seem to affect the building. Clint called out for everyone to stay put. A second rocket was inbound. Higher headquarters had used a drone feed to get the grid location of the building, and somehow they ended up some ten meters off. The second rocket arrived just a few moments later. It exploded in the middle of the upper floors of the building. Walls came apart, and when the dust settled, the support columns were naked, and the interior was a pile of rubble.

As soon as the dust cleared enough to know the rocket had been a hit, we all assaulted back up to the breach site. Our return was not contested. Feeling confident, we resumed our assigned roles for security, and the infantry resumed working on the wall.

Soon the volume of fire increased and the RPGs started flying in again. The enemy attacked the tanks with a renewed confidence and fearlessness. A man jumped into the side street just a couple hundred feet away from Danny's tank and fired an AK-47, seemingly oblivious to the futility of his efforts and his exposed stance. Danny's gunner, Juan Perez, had just fired a cannon round, and the controls were still set for the cannon instead of the coax machine gun. The crack of the cannon ended the enemy fighter's brazen and foolish stand. The only thing left was a sandal.

Up at Dakhal Street, I was trying to address enemy fighters on two different streets. The Black tank was not helping me much with the RPG teams on Dakhal Street, so we had to pull his weight also. Up Al Qouds Street, the enemy was placing fire on us, but not from the alley corners. I was really struggling to locate their position and getting frustrated. The dust storm's haze was thick enough that my thermal sight was not providing sharp detail. Edwin's sights still had not recovered from the earlier RPG hit.

As we scanned up the street, something caught my eye. A couple buildings up was a store with an awning over the sidewalk. Under that overhang were what appeared to be large stacks of grain bags. The stacks were almost five or six feet tall. What caught my eye was that there seemed to be a gap where a bag was missing from each stack. *Bunkers.* In the dust storm, the bunkers were perfectly camouflaged and completely hidden from the drones by the overhang.

"Steel Six, Blue One. I have a cluster of bunkers up the street at mike-bravo-four-eight-seven-seven-niner-two-one-seven, over." I reported my findings to Captain Looney.

"Destroy them!" was his reply.

"Gunner, HEAT, bunker!" I commanded over the tank's intercom.

"Cannot identify! My thermal is broken. Daylight only." Edwin's reply reminded me he was shooting blind. I bent over to look through my gunner's sight extension, which showed me exactly what he could see. I only saw the tan hue of dust at first. Using the building columns for reference, I matched the hazy picture to what I saw in my thermal sight.

"You see the stack of bags? That is the first bunker."

"Identified!" He recognized it now.

"Up!"

"Fire! Fire OR." With a poor sight picture, Edwin was not in a position to fire independently of my direction.

"On the way!"

The HEAT round slammed into the bunker. The dust in the air got infinitely worse, but I could see the bunker. The occupants might be dead, but the bunker was still in business.

"OR up!" Cory yelled out, ready for the next shot.

"Reengage!"

"Identified!"

"Fire!"

"On the way!" This time, Edwin's round obliterated the bunker. A loose pile of debris remained.

"New bunker!" I aligned the sights on a bunker just a bit farther down the street. Cory finished feeding the gun, his hand ready to slap up the arming lever.

"Identified!"

"Up!"

"Fire!"

"On the way!" The OR round once again did the trick. The bunker was gone. As the dust cleared, I spotted an RPG launcher in the middle of Al Qouds Street, and rockets scattered between the launcher and the remains of the bunker. I felt a bit smug about being right.

Another round later, the bunker cluster was fully destroyed. The enemy was back to fighting from buildings and alleys. Unfortunately, they were still adept at that, and the enemy was fighting hard.

Time slowly crept by, and our ammo supply steadily decreased. Enemy fire was not nearly as effective as it has been earlier in the battle, but it continued raining down with a vengeance. Being at the tip of the breach did not leave me much room to maneuver. The infantry had made progress with the wall. As each new T-wall went into place, it took up a little more of the room we had to work with in our quest to keep the enemy from stopping us. Behind me, the Bradley used the sidewalk as he constantly sought better firing positions. The Black tank had returned to nearly even with me, hanging back about a full tank's length. As far as I could tell, it had not yet fired a main-gun round.

Up in the dusty haze, I spotted a man trying to low-crawl out into Al Qouds Street, possibly trying to recover the RPG launcher that we had blown into the street. Incredibly paranoid about our cannon, the man was very quick to run back to cover whenever our gun tube started traversing his way. Each time, I had Edwin put a few rounds from the coax into the corner he used for cover to reinforce his fear.

The enemy seemed to be coordinating their efforts to hit my tank. When we traversed one way, a team would engage us from the other street. When we traversed back, the enemy teams would keep the pressure up by switching roles as bait and shooters. We stuck mostly to using the coax. A large pile of aft caps ejected by the cannon grew on the turret floor. We were dangerously low on cannon rounds, and we still had a while to go before Dealer Company showed up.

Once again, the man crawled out into the street. Trying to hit him was getting frustrating. Again, I had Edwin traverse left to engage the man. He quickly scampered back to safety before the turret was even halfway there. I toyed with the idea of putting a cannon round into the corner anyway.

BOOM! Once again the tank rocked from an RPG explosion. This one seemed to have hit down low, possibly in the tracks.

"Steel Six, Blue One. Contact, RPG!" I called out on the radio. Switching to the intercom, I had Edwin and Cory check the turret for damage and had Nick back the tank up and pivot some to make sure the track was not damaged. Everyone said they were okay. The latest RPG did not seem to have damaged the functionality of the tank any further. "Negative casualties, unknown damage, still fighting," I updated Captain Looney.

BOOM! Another RPG skipped in low and in front of our tank. I figured out they were coming from the left alley on Dakhal Street— the alley I had instructed the Black tank to watch. Black had just let two RPGs fire into my side and did nothing about it. *Fine, if that's the way it's going to be . . .*

"Gunner, HEAT, RPG team!" I traversed our turret to face the alley on Dakhal Street. Our cannon muzzle was only feet away from the Black tank's front. Firing would mess them up hard. I did not care now.

"Identified!"

"Up!"

"Fire!"

"On the way!" Edwin fired a round into the corner of the alley. The muzzle blast from our cannon rocked the Black tank. A small pile of rubble indicated our shot had blasted debris into the alley where the RPG team was hiding.

Looking back to Al Qouds Street, I saw the man finish scampering back to the corner with the RPG launcher in hand. He probably had the rest of the team there to watch for him and a small collection of RPGs to fire.

"Gunner, HEAT, RPG team!" I called out before Cory even finished pulling a round out of the ammo compartment.

Before Edwin could reply, Cory yelled out, "Last round! OR!" I was suddenly filled with a mix of anger and frustration. Somehow either he forgot to tell me our round count as we passed certain points, or I missed them. I quickly realized that even though the Black tank had not fired any main-gun rounds, Danny had. As a platoon we were probably sitting at about 50 percent ammo. This was a crucial point for a unit in a fight. Actions at higher levels were required to prevent a disaster when units reached 50 percent ammo.

"Okay! Correction, Gunner; OR, RPG team!" I changed the order to reflect what we had. With the OR round, Edwin slid his point of aim further over. The round would penetrate better, so it needed more building to go through than the HEAT rounds. A bit of sadness entered my heart as the cannon barked and our last round's aft cap spat out onto the floor of the turret. At the alley, body parts mixed with rubble at the edge of Al Qouds Street.

"Steel Six, Blue One; black on ammo. My tank is Winchester one-twenty." I winced for the verbal lashing, but none came. Over the radio, I heard Captain Looney instead telling the command post to tell Battalion that we needed Dealer Company to hurry up, stressing that we were fighting with damaged tanks, dangerously low on ammo, and might not be able to keep up this level of fighting for much longer.

Dealer Company was late even by the original timeline. Before they even got there, the sappers arrived and started to breach farther up Al Qouds Street. Surprisingly, the breach actually went well. I secretly hoped it was because we had inflicted enough damage to the enemy that they were not able to resist. But we all knew that the enemy was probably just regrouping and we would see hard fighting again when we returned in about twelve hours.

Exhausted and frustrated, we finally backed away from Dakhal Street, leaving the fight to Dealer Company. On the radio, everyone was short with each other, drained from the stress of what was easily the most intense fighting any of us had ever endured. As we made the eight-mile drive back to COP Ford, I started to assess the platoon's condition and plan for the next morning's fight. It would be a long night for the crews. In addition to the routine daily maintenance, we were going to have to cross-level ammo and repair all of the damage we could.

At COP Ford, I got out and viewed the damage to our tank. Most visible was the results of the RPG that hit the cupola. The periscope blocks were cracked, the metal bracket ripped up, and the mount for the fifty was holed and twisted. My R2D2-like thermal viewer's armor was blackened and pitted.

I had a raging headache that would not go away, and I was puking even though my stomach felt fine. I did my best to hide it from everyone because I did not want to get pulled from the line again. While the men got to work, I went to the platoon office to start the paperwork and planning for tomorrow.

I was still beyond pissed at the Black tank. I could not recall it firing its cannon or even coax. After asking Jay to deal with the lack of performance with Black's platoon sergeant, I quietly, selfishly decided I wouldn't bother to get to know the men from that platoon. I would be leading them into battle, but my bond with them would not progress beyond them being fellow US soldiers.

A bit later, I was trying to catch up on paperwork in my platoon office. At least my rage had subsided. Some of the paperwork was rewarding, like typing award recommendations for valorous soldiers. Some of it was just painful, like sworn statements and forms for damaged equipment. A knock on the door interrupted my work. It was one of the guys from White Platoon. His eyes were moist and his face red. Something was wrong.

"Can we talk in private?" His request did not bode well. Jay shared the office with me, but he was out working on the tanks. The soldier came in and shut the door behind him. I asked him what was wrong. Struggling to hold back tears, the soldier asked for advice and then told me what happened on Al Qouds Street.

White Platoon had been at the tip of the breach for 1-2 Stryker's turn to fight up the street. An RPG team fired at Sean Rinder's tank, hitting right at the turret ring and penetrating into the turret. Private First Class Colt Webb had been filleted open from his armpit to his wrist, and the RPG penetrated his body armor and into his torso. At the time, Colt had been slouched to the right in his loader's seat with his arm resting on top of the seat back. Had Colt been sitting correctly in the seat, the RPG would have hit him square in the back and killed him. The hot spalling from the RPG then flew across the turret and hit Sean in the butt.

The tank went into protective mode, where the engine revs up but little power is transferred to the transmission or anything else, just like a human body pulling blood to the vital organs in a crisis. The RPG had also destroyed the turret's ability to traverse, keeping it locked in place with the gun tube just to the right of front center. Sean and his battered crew fought like lions, though. Even with a crippled tank, they pivoted the whole thing and fired the cannon back like a World War Two assault gun.

With Colt in bad shape and Sean also injured, the crippled tank was in no condition to continue the fight at the lead end of the breach. Sean asked for the platoon leader to move his tank forward and take over so he could pull back and start dealing with his problems. The platoon leader did not speak up on the radio net and take charge. The platoon leader refused to act or give orders. Fear or indecision had completely frozen him. With no signs of the platoon leader snapping out of it, the platoon leader's crew had to take action into their own hands, and essentially led a crew mutiny against their tank commander. They moved their tank in front of Sean's crippled one and continued the fight with the platoon leader just sitting in the commander's seat like a bump on a log.

The mutiny allowed Sean to inch his tank back to the cover of the wall. There, the Stryker soldiers helped pull Colt from the tank and put him on a stretcher. They loaded him up in a Stryker so they could whisk him to an aid station. Before the Stryker could leave, an RPG slammed into it, catching it on fire and destroying it. Poor

Colt had to be pulled out, along with a freshly wounded Stryker crew member. Another Stryker finally got him away from the battlefield, and before long, he was on a Black Hawk to the Green Zone. In the meantime, Sean got his tank to come out of protective mode. He could not fix the turret jam, but at least he could get the tank home on its own power.

Once White Platoon returned, the whispering started. The tale broke my heart. I hated seeing my old platoon hurting. I knew the soldier was tormented. He was loyal to the platoon as a whole and knew they deserved better from their leader. At the same time, he was loyal to his platoon leader.

I thought about the time back in Kuwait when the platoon leader refused to train with his men. Was it because he was afraid of revealing he did not know how to fight or how to be decisive? It wasn't just his performance under fire I worried about. The platoon leader had been sloppy with paperwork when one of their Humvees had burned up. He was not performing well enough in my book. Sure, we all made mistakes and confronted our own fears, but leading a platoon through intense combat is not the time for crippling fear. Right now, White Platoon needed a lion.

Unfortunately, I knew that there were no lieutenants on the bench. Everyone was already placed with a platoon. The fighting was taking a toll on leaders across the battalion. Blackhawk Company's first sergeant had already been severely injured and sent home. Two other platoon sergeants had been injured badly enough to require evacuation. I had already been evacuated and returned once already. Another platoon leader had been hit in the face by shrapnel and evacuated back to the US. I told the soldier I was always available to talk and that I would see what I could do for them.

I went in search of Sean and found him in the aid station. Doc Anderson had just finished looking after his wounds. Sean was amused. While taking a solid dose of metal in his butt cheek, his Nomex coveralls did not have a single hole in them. Magic.

We had a long talk. It was a bitter and sobering one. After chatting with him, I decided to go to AJ first instead of straight to Captain Looney. There was no point in confronting the platoon leader as it had no effect in the past. By going to AJ, if I was out of line, he would filter it. If I had a solid case, AJ would share it with the commander. In the end, Colt ended up okay, healing up enough to return to duty. The platoon leader did not get fired.

While talking with AJ, he informed me that division was going to come collect Sean's destroyed C24 tank. They wanted us to tarp over it and not let anyone see it or know that it had been destroyed by an RPG. We both thought this was stupid. The enemy knew what they had done. They watched it happen. We all knew what had happened. We needed to study C24 first to see what we could learn. We also needed parts. The supply lines were failing miserably at keeping up with the pace of battle damage. C24 was suddenly a jackpot of parts, with the exception of armor and turret ring and a few wires.

As dusk settled in over Baghdad the following day, I climbed into C24 with Danny Bowden. We measured the penetration from the RPG, studying how it pierced the armor. We looked at what the spalling destroyed and the pattern of its spread. The penetration was only about half an inch wide, yet it had destroyed the tank and wounded two crewmen. I could not help but notice the large bloodstains in the loader's area of the turret. The fins of the RPG and the rocket tube were stuck in the penetration, plugging the hole. Danny and I discussed how the damage compared to another tank that was hit by a suspected RPG-29 a mile north.

The enemy was rumored to have a small supply of these more advanced RPGs, although the term *advanced* was relative. The RPG-29 was actually three decades old. The difference was that the Russians had not shared the weapon with other countries like they had proliferated the fifty-year-old RPG-7 that was a dime a dozen. Iran recently made copies of the RPG-29, and those were starting to turn up in Sadr's arsenal.

With the damage inspected and minds sobered, it was time to get what we could out of C24 before it was hauled away. With gratitude, we emptied the well-stocked ammo compartments and split the ammo between the company's remaining tanks. Danny Bowden's mechanics quickly pulled needed parts off and switched them with the damaged parts on other tanks. Within about forty-eight hours, they had pulled some seven million dollars of parts off C24. Division was less than impressed. The tank costs about four million dollars if you buy it whole. But like all machines, individual parts cost more when purchased separately. It made the bean counters furious, but those parts made a huge difference for us. Instead of rolling few tanks into battle, all of which had some level of damage, we were able to roll more tanks into battle, some of which were nearly completely functional again.

April 28 also saw the enemy artillery change up their game. That afternoon, they drove a Bongo truck to a firing spot just a few blocks from the Stryker's JSS in Jamila. Several lob-bomb rockets with more than 300 pounds of explosives each slammed into the building, causing extreme damage and many casualties. The attack hit close to home; we had gotten to know the Strykers as they rotated through COP Ford. Additionally, it showed the enemy was willing to target small bases with this dangerous weapon.

Block by block, day by day, we continued up Al Qouds Street. The intensity of the firefights died down. The enemy would start small-scale fights throughout the day. At times, there would be quiet in between. Even their effective sniper seemed to have disappeared. It seemed like we had smashed through the heart of their defensive position. Perhaps we had bled them so much only weaker resistance was possible. We were still breaching up the heart of their obstacle, though. IEDs were so dense we averaged one every ten feet—denser than a textbook Soviet minefield. When the sappers missed one, the enemy would command-detonate it on a tank.

On May 4, we were on the verge of reaching the end of Al Qouds Street at Thawra Street, a major milestone. Thawra Street now hosted an Iraqi Army compound in the old police station on the west corner. Once we had the wall past Thawra Street, we would be able use it to approach instead of having to go all the way to the south and come back up the freeway.

Red Platoon saw the sappers breach all the way to the intersection, but the wall was still well short of it. With the intersection exposed, everything moved up to the breach site. While Red Platoon defended the infantry building the wall, the enemy had moved into the buildings on the "friendly" side of the street again. The fighting caught palm trees and buildings on fire. With the sun down and darkness reigning, burning fires lit up the battlefield, taking away our advantage as the intense light washed out our night-vision goggles used by tank commanders and the infantry on the ground.

The remains of the market at the intersection made an eerie scene. The tents and shacks that once sold various items were destroyed and in piles at the curb where the engineers had pushed the debris to clear the street for the wall. The piles were as high as twelve feet of twisted steel and rubbish. A meandering path just wide enough for a tank wove through them. One burning building happened to be the last one on the block that had a walled-in front yard. Between it and Thawra Street was a small alley about six feet wide and a four-story building that had been blasted and gutted over the last month and a half, its rubble heaped at the base of the outside wall.

Approaching the breach site, we knew we were likely to see an increase in enemy activity. This was the same intersection where we had the huge fight on April 11. We were tense. Danny Key led the platoon column as we approached the breach. The plan was for him hook around the end of the wall; I would then pass him and replace the Red Platoon tank looking into Sadr up Thawra Street, and the Black tank would look up Jamila Street.

The crane and its outriggers completely blocked the street as it placed T-walls. We would have to find our way through the piles on the sidewalk. Danny announced he found a path, and his tank disappeared into the debris. Some fifty meters behind him, I followed. The path was clear, but required some tight turning. Then disaster struck.

Nick gingerly nosed our tank onto the sidewalk, and we approached the first turn in the collection of piles. About halfway through our turn into the lane, there was a loud pop, and the tank suddenly stopped turning. We had broken a track. Now the crane blocked the street, and our tank was blocking the bypass. To our front, a large pile of debris stood less than ten feet away. To our right was another large pile, too close for another tank to squeeze by. Some six feet from our back corner was the wall to the burning building's compound. We were in the way, and half the platoon was still behind us.

We still needed to replace Red Platoon, so I had Nick inch the tank up against the junk pile so others could get behind us, even though they would have to drive over the top of our broken track. We still had a mission to complete, so I had the Black tank take the Thawra sector of fire and the Bradley take the Jamila sector as soon as it dropped off the squad. Without fanfare, they passed behind us, finding a new path along the edge of the gutted building and through the debris. Fortunately, both made it without incident. Now only my tank was stuck. I was unable to see where they went because the piles blocked my view. I could not see the crane either.

I reported our problem to the company commander, who was currently running the fight from back at COP Ford. I asked for some additional security since we were exposed and unable to see any friendly forces. The request was denied. I overheard a comment on the radio about how we were "screwing around" and because we got ourselves into the debris and broke track, we could fix it ourselves. Furious, I hopped off the tank to start the repairs.

I had worked on track a lot before. Back home, we would race to see who could break track and then reconnect it the fastest. My crew's best time was thirty minutes, but that had been in the motor pool with perfect conditions and all the correct tools. To fix the track, we needed to roll the tank forward to lay out the track. The only way you could really pull it back together and reconnect the blocks was if the ends were right under the front of the tank. As you moved forward, you would use a rope to pull the back end of the track up onto the rear sprocket. It would then feed the track forward over the support rollers to the front idler wheel. From there it was a matter of using giant clamps to squeeze the ends together so you could put the connectors on.

Our current situation was a mess. The rear end of the track was about six feet from the wall of the burning compound, bathed in bright light from the fire. The debris pile in front of us blocked us from the twenty or so feet more that we needed to lay the track out. As much as it would anger the commanders, I needed to stop the wall construction long enough to borrow the forklift and move the debris out of the way. A dozer would have been better, but a forklift was all we had. I set Edwin and Cory to work readying the tools and parts we would need while I got the forklift.

While the forklift moved the debris out of the way as best he could, I reviewed what we had. We were still short a rope. Without it, we would never get the track onto the sprocket. Nobody in the platoon had one at this point. Even getting the tools we did have required every tank chipping in. Then I had an idea. I sprinted across the breach to the Bradley and got a stretcher strap out of the back. It was a canvas strap about eight feet long. It would have to do. As I got it out of the Bradley, I looked towards the debris piles and noticed none of the other vehicles in the platoon could see the first or second-floor windows of the buildings next to us. It was unnerving that nobody would be able to help us if we started taking fire from there. The enemy had used those very positions earlier in the day.

In the mix of dark shadows and bright light, we laid out the tools and parts we needed in order on the front slope of the tank. Nick remained in the driver's seat, listening to the radio and keeping an eye on the engine. He would be completely unable to see us working on the track behind the tank, though.

Edwin and I grabbed the breaker bar and a pipe extension to remove the broken track shoe. Cory took up his rifle and tucked into the shadows to provide some security for us. Despite the fact the track was weakened and brittle enough to snap on clean concrete, the bolts did not want to budge. Edwin and I sat side by side at the end of the pipe and worked together to row the bolts apart, bracing our feet against the track itself. It was extremely hard work.

Without warning, a stream of tracers flew between our faces, impacting into the debris beyond us. Instinctively, I pulled my pistol and turned towards the sound of the machine gun firing at us. In the darkness of a first-floor window, a muzzle flash betrayed its location, just fifty meters away. I fired my pistol at it, and Cory ran towards me, moving between the machine gun and me. He took a knee and started firing. The machine gun stopped shooting, but muzzle flashes from other windows caught my eye. The enemy was trying to take advantage of our exposed crew. The sound of the fifty caliber firing from the top of the turret announced Edwin, who didn't carry a sidearm, had joined the fight by scrambling onto the turret and firing the machine gun from the exposed top of the tank. His tracers streamed into another pile where the enemy was trying to get closer to us.

The firefight caught the attention of everyone else in the breach. The dark interior of the upper floors erupted with bright flashes as the Bradley poured 25 mm rounds into the third and fourth floors. Some of the hot fragments rained down on us. Out of pistol ammo, I holstered it, ran to the tank, and picked up my rifle from where I had stashed it on the back deck. As suddenly as the fight had started, it ended.

Mark Peck came to check on the crew. Miraculously, we were all okay. He relayed a message from the commander to hurry up and fix the track because I was in the way. Higher commanders were still under the impression I broke our track by trying to drive over the piles of debris. I asked Mark if he would lend some help to provide security so my crew could concentrate on fixing the track. He agreed. With an infantryman in place to trade fire with the enemy, we set to finishing our repairs. Still, we periodically needed to stop work and return fire with our rifles. By the time we finally got the broken pieces off, I was exhausted.

Just as we were bolting the new track block on, the battalion commander showed up with his entourage. With an additional ten or so people standing around in a lighted area, I knew we were about to get another dose of enemy fire. Right on schedule, the enemy noticed and opened fire from the dark corners of the building. The commander's group scattered in search of cover.

When the shooting stopped, I checked on everyone again. A few of the commander's security squad had taken firing positions at the front of the tank. In the processes of doing so, they managed to knock my crew's carefully laid out tools and parts into the junk pile. Things were going from terrible to worse. I lost my temper and yelled at them. With obvious embarrassment, they sulked away to different positions. Still angry, I got on my hands and knees to search for the missing items.

The sound of another tank coming up the street caught my attention. Apparently, the colonel had realized how exposed we were and called for more help. Sergeant First Class Jason Ferrari from Destroyer Company arrived and placed his tank between us and the enemy positions in the building. With better cover to work from, we continued our repairs. Over someone's radio, I heard the company's M88 staging on the freeway to come tow the tank. I was determined to prevent that since more people would have to be exposed to pick up the track and get it on top of the tank for towing.

The stretcher strap was just barely long enough. After tying it on and routing it through the sprocket, I had about six inches left to hang on to. With my hands actually inside the sprocket, holding the strap, I worried I would lose my arms. Gently, Nick bumped the tank forward block by block, trying to go slow enough I would not get tangled. Finally, we had the track on the sprocket and passed it over the rollers.

With the track over the top, we ran into our next problem. The bottom end of the track was positioned just right for the curb to cause the weight of the tank to twist the track. The twist made getting the connectors on extremely difficult. The battalion sergeant major, John Kurak, lost his patience and started barking orders. Jason dismounted his tank and came over to lend fresh muscles and years of experience. Another problem came up. The additional armor bolted to the belly of the tank made it impossible to slide under the tank while wearing body armor. A crewman had to take it off in order to put the inside connector on the track. Under fire, this was not a popular move. Finally, we had the track reconnected.

It was already time for Dealer Company to take over the fighting, and they were on scene, waiting for us to get out of the way. Embarrassed, exhausted, bitter, and full of rage, I got everyone and our tools loaded up. The track was still too loose for maneuvering, but we could make it back to safety without going through the process of tightening the track tension. I just wanted out of there. A thirty-minute repair job had taken several hours. Adding insult to injury, the route back traveled through fresh sewage floodwaters as major sewer pipes had been damaged in the fighting along the wall. Tightening the track tension would be a nasty proposition.

Tomorrow would be a better day. It would be hard for it to be worse.

TIPPING THE SCALES

OUR NEXT SHIFT WAS A bizarre one. It was midday when Blue Platoon returned to the wall and moved into the breach, which went all the way across the Thawra Street intersection and partly along the length of the Iraqi Army outpost on the west corner. For the first time in more than two weeks, we approached the breach up Thawra Street instead of going to the far end of Sadr City. A whole company of Iraqi Army T-72 tanks was parked in the median, the crews resting on the tops of their vehicles. Clearly they did not feel like a fight was upon them.

As we positioned ourselves and made sure our sectors of fire were overlapping and thorough, I was struck by how quiet it was. Thawra Street was the boundary between the JAM units we had been fighting. Our relentless attack up Al Qouds Street had been hard fought and the enemy severely mauled in the process, but I did not expect them to be as weakened at this point. After all, they had enjoyed nearly a month to rest and reorganize since we attacked Al Qouds.

The infantry squad quickly went to work, and soon the wall was nearly all the way across the intersection. For once, I was without targets. It felt like the eye of a hurricane. With our progress steady, the sappers moved up Thawra Street to prepare for another couple hundred meters of breaching. Behind them, engineer dozers readied to clean up the remains of the market that was in the way.

Clunk. Clunk. Something hard hit the tank, echoing inside the turret. It sounded like someone was dropping big rocks on us. With fresh concern, Edwin started scanning, and Cory stared at me with a funny expression. Urgently looking around, I spotted nothing. While the objects were not doing any damage, they were concerning.

"Blue One, Blaster. Your tank facing up the street has a collection of mortar rounds around it," the EOD team called over the radio, and the mystery was solved. I had Nick move the tank a few meters, and I looked back. On the ground were some two dozen 60 mm mortar rounds that had clearly been fired at us. Not a single one had exploded. With the noise of the engine, I never heard the baseplate of the mortar ringing with each round. After a bit, the mortar rounds stopped falling. A soldier from the EOD vehicle came over, picked them up, and, after examining them, reported that none of the rounds were armed with a fuse. It was unbelievable. An enemy mortar crew was accurate enough to get consistent "steel on steel" hits on my tank, but was inexperienced enough to miss this critical step. For the first time in weeks, I smiled while in the breach.

Time passed, the wall progressed, and no RPGs or machine-gun fire interrupted us. The enemy was either regrouping, too defeated to fight, or changing tactics. There were still no civilians on the street within more than a mile, so I knew the fight was not yet over. The quiet was becoming uncomfortable.

A head popped out of an alley in Sadr City, some 300 meters or so back down the wall. It looked towards us and then disappeared. Several minutes later, the head popped out of another side street a bit closer. He was an older man with white hair on his head and in his beard. After ducking back into Sadr City, the man then came out, striding towards my tank with purposeful steps, holding a large bag to his chest. He had my attention fully. The infantry squad was working on preparing T-walls about ten meters down the wall on the "friendly side." They would not see the man coming at them. Something about him made my skin crawl.

"Edwin, put a warning shot to the front and right of that man." The man was now probably 100 meters away. Edwin fired a short burst from the coax, sending puffs of dust up between the man and the wall. The old man looked at the impacting rounds, looked at us, and then moved forward with a sense of urgency.

"Edwin, again." Edwin put the rounds a bit closer this time, kicking up dust about three feet to the right of the man. Instead of the expected flinch and dash away from the impacting rounds, the man continued to stare at us. He moved the bag under his right arm, holding it like a running back would hold a football, and then darted right towards us. He was now maybe seventy-five meters away. *Suicide bomber!* My heart jumped into my throat.

"Gunner, coax! Fire!" I gave a hasty order. Edwin adjusted the sights onto the man's chest and fired longer busts, sending eight to ten rounds at a time. In the magnified sights, I saw the rounds impacting the center of the man's torso, yet he continued running with seemingly superhuman strength. The man was now less than fifty meters away and coming strong. He changed his grip on the bag and swung it back and forth like he was generating momentum to get it over the wall.

Just as the man seemed ready to fling the bag, he suddenly lost his ability to keep moving forward. He staggered and then slumped over to the base of the T-walls, sitting directly across from where the infantry were working. He was still fiddling with the bag. He was so close that the gunner's sights had too much angle for the ballistic computer to precisely aim. I grew concerned about hitting the bag on accident with our machine-gun fire and setting off a bomb.

One of the infantrymen poked around the end of the wall and fired his rifle. The man's head came apart, and he fell to the side, on top of the bag.

I was shaking like a leaf on a brisk fall day. I had nearly failed in keeping the enemy away from the infantrymen. I could not believe how far the old man had run while taking 7.62 mm bullets to the chest. He must have been high on some powerful drugs.

EOD sent their robot out to investigate the bag, but the robot was not strong enough to move the man's body. The sappers moved up with the Buffalo, which had a long hydraulic arm. To shield the Buffalo, I had Nick move our tank farther out into the enemy side of the wall. The Buffalo pulled the body away and removed the bag.

"Steel X-Ray, Blaster; looks like just cigarette cartons."

Unbelievable. No way. What is really in those cartons? The EOD team disposed of the bag, and the infantrymen resumed work. As high headquarters debated having us remove the body for intelligence and caring for the dead, the wall progressed rapidly. Soon the body was a long way down the wall, too far for any sane person to retrieve. We let the old man's body lie, and the rest of our day went without incident.

The wall reached the end of the Iraqi Army compound during Dealer Company's shift. Our return was to start with breaching farther. Blue Platoon would provide the support-by-fire position for their breach, and then we would attack forward into it. We hoped to make it more than halfway to Husseineya Street.

With our tanks set in positions at the end of the wall, the sappers slowly breached forward along the destroyed market. Somehow the tall wire-and-concrete fence in the median was still intact. We relied on thermal sights in the darkness, enjoying the technological advantage. In the distance, I saw a couple people watching us from a balcony on the Jamila side of the street. While they were clearly combatants, I did not want to engage them. We knew Navy SEALs had set up positions somewhere nearby, and it was not worth taking the risk of killing friendly forces.

BOOM! An IED went off next to one of the sappers' Huskies. The vehicle was destroyed, but the sappers still had one more. The remaining Husky continued forward in the left lane. It did not make it far. *BOOM!* Another IED pierced one of the sappers' other vehicles, wounding a soldier. Once again, we needed to extract a wounded soldier from a destroyed vehicle in the middle of the enemy's kill zone.

"Driver, move out!" I had Nick take our tank forward to put it between the destroyed vehicle and the enemy. A feeling of déjà vu came over me as we smashed through the fence in the median and zigzagged through the sappers' vehicles. We were on the same block where the fight on April 11 had been fiercest. Unlike the previous fight, our wounded soldier was in the left lane, and I had more room to work with than Jay had.

Once my seventy-ton piece of mobile cover was in place, the sappers quickly pulled their wounded soldier out and ran him to another vehicle. At the same time, another vehicle moved up behind the destroyed vehicle; a soldier quickly attached a one-inch-thick tow cable, and with the soldiers out of the way, the new vehicle hastily dragged the destroyed one back to Thawra Street. They were like a well-oiled machine. Sadly, it was because this was probably at least the tenth time they had executed a recovery operation within the last few weeks.

Surprisingly, the enemy did not fire a single shot during the recovery. Perhaps they had learned their lesson, or maybe they were weakened enough that they did not want to start a firefight with our tanks. Either way, I was happy.

An awkward silence descended on the battlefield as our sapper team backed off, unable to continue. Another sapper team was called and prepared to take over the breach effort. We did not want to lose the area we had just breached, though; if we backed the tanks out of it, enemy sappers would sneak in and plant more IEDs to replace the ones that we found or detonated. On my right, the destroyed market still had small pathways through the carnage that allowed enemy fighters to close within a few feet of the street unobserved. We needed to move to the front of the breach to prevent enemy tampering from those paths.

I had noted a small rock cairn near where the farthest Husky had reached and used that as a reference for our advance. We inched forward, track pad by track pad, towards the end of the breach. We did not want to go beyond the end, and we did not want to blunder into an ambush. Finally, we neared the rock cairn and stopped about twenty feet short of it. I had a creepy feeling something was about to happen.

BOOM! A flash of light and a shock wave of energy erupted next to the rock cairn. *And that is why you never stop right next to a rock cairn or anything that looks like a marker.* The IED's penetrator sailed harmlessly into Sadr City, and the blast of the explosion only rocked the tank without damaging anything.

As we slowly breached up Jamila Street, it was clear the tide was turned completely. The enemy had been fighting hard for over a month and a half. We were tired, and our equipment was battered, but we had a steady flow of reinforcements. In addition to the forces that had already joined us, a fresh new battalion was moving in: 1-6 Infantry had just arrived in Iraq and was going to take the Jamila neighborhood. Additionally, they would take shifts on the wall operation.

Until they were fully ready, 1-6 Infantry attached tanks and Bradleys to our platoons. Initially, they provided leaders to ride with us to learn how we were conducting the breach, attack, and construction. Once their leaders were shown the ropes, those leaders joined our efforts with their own crews and vehicles. Before a single 1-6 Infantry platoon fought on its own, every one of their crews and squads got a taste of the operation under our tutoring.

I was jealous of 1-6 Infantry's older M1A1 tanks. They did not have the R2D2-looking commander's thermal viewers that our M1A2 tanks had, but the urban fighting upgrade for the M1A1 put a thermal camera on the commander's fifty-caliber machine gun. That machine gun could be fired from the safety of inside the turret, whereas ours required us to come out of the hatch to fire.

To replace battle-lost equipment, I was using AJ's C65 tank, and Sergeant Chris Bryant had the colonel's HQ66. The colonel's tank had the names of his crew stenciled on, while none of ours ever did. The platoon put a pool on how long the tank would last on the wall before getting hit since *LTC Pappal* was stenciled on the side. It was hit by an RPG within hours of attacking into the breach.

We no longer had M240 machine guns for all of the tank loaders' mount. The couple extra machine guns we had stayed in the safety of the turret. The C33 mount was still too mangled to mount the machine gun anyway. As tanks were hit, many of the sponson boxes that we used to store tools and weapons had been destroyed, taking the contents with them. By the time we returned to Jamila Street, numerous soldiers in the platoon had newly issued rifles or were missing pistols or weapon optics for their rifles.

The enemy defending Jamila Street had been thoroughly mauled during the fighting over the previous month and a half. Never again did we fight large-scale firefights. The enemy still provided sporadic shooting, though, and the occasional lone RPG punctuated each day's breach and wall construction. The enemy's extensive minefield of IEDs remained.

The Jamila Street minefield was denser and more elaborate than Al Qouds Street had been. While our sappers were excellent, more and more IEDs slipped past their prying eyes. For every ten or so the sappers found, they missed one or two. It was not their fault; the enemy was very creative in their placement and camouflaging efforts.

As we approached Jamila Market, we had some very close calls with IEDs. An enemy rifleman fired at the infantrymen building the wall from near the market. To provide some concealment, one of the infantrymen tossed a smoke grenade towards the enemy. The hot flame from the grenade caught a market stand on fire, and soon the fire transformed to hot blue and green flames as explosives burned. When the fire smoldered down, a collection of copper plates and melted batteries smoldered. The infantrymen had been working right in the kill zone of a massive IED that either the enemy forgot about or was waiting for a better opportunity to use.

Just past Jamila Market, the sappers missed a whole cluster of IEDs. Nearly every tank in the platoon hit one on that block. To aid their ability to sort through the old market stands and large chunks of debris, the sappers asked us to fire a canister round down the street before they started the breach. On the first canister round, Jay's tank caused an IED to go off and exposed a few more. This really encouraged the sappers. When we ran out of canister rounds a day later, the sappers were disappointed.

The days became a blur with no major fights to mark the operations. It did not help that in addition to fatigue, concussions were taking their toll. More days than not, my journal at the end of the day had the entry, "I can't remember what we did today."

A few days still stood out. One night we were almost in front of a Navy SEAL team position. They had taken to coordinating with us on the radio. It was nice to have extra sets of eyes on the battlefield. This particular SEAL-team position was on the upper floors of a tall building looking up a major street into Sadr City.

The enemy had been relatively quiet. As we steadily made progress on the street, the SEALs announced their sniper was going to engage an enemy team. A single shot rang out in the darkness, then another. The second shot was followed by a steady staccato of fire from the same rifle. After a few seconds, the rifle stopped shooting. While we wondered if the multiple shots signaled terrible shooting or just a lot of targets, the SEALs asked for a Hellfire strike on the building they had been shooting at. After the Hellfire streaked in, the battlefield returned to quiet.

A few blocks later, we were defending the breach lane while the infantrymen built the wall in hot sunlight. Danny's tank was positioned looking up a side street into Sadr City. The quiet was broken by an RPG slamming into the front slope of his tank. It had no effect, and he fired a cannon round back. Just as the dust cleared, another enemy gunner stepped up on a roof some 400 meters up Jamila Street and fired an RPG at him. It was the longest RPG shot I ever witnessed the enemy make. It was so long, the RPG's smoke trail was actually visible as it streaked in and missed to the rear of Danny's tank. It was the only time in Iraq that I ever saw a smoke trail from an RPG. The enemy gunner received a cannon round for his efforts. Edwin did not miss.

On another night, the SEALs decided to move their position to a large four-story apartment building that was right next to my tank. Several minutes after they entered, the SEALs called out over the radio that they were going to blow up a pile of weapons they found. We did not mind, or even think much about it—until the dark quiet was shattered by a huge explosion and debris rained down on my tank from the top of the building. The movie line from *Butch Cassidy and the Sundance Kid* instantly came to mind: *Think you used enough dynamite there, Butch?*

By the time we were halfway up Jamila Street, some normalcy had returned to the population. In the distance, large crowds of people went about their days. They never came within 1,000 meters of us, but they were no longer afraid of bullets straying past our targets. Seeing the civilians was encouraging. The locals always knew of a coming fight long before we did. Closer to the freeway, we had to push through traffic again as we made our approach march to the battlefield. The end was literally in sight, and we all felt a sense of relief.

Soldiers from 1-6 Infantry took their own turn in the rotation, allowing us time to resume patrolling Beida as well as tending to the COP. AJ and I were flown to Taji on a mission to secure more supplies, and among other things, I signed for a backpack full of cash we could use to improve our COP. AJ managed to coordinate a new generator to replace our worn-out one. While we were there, we stopped by the airfield to thank the Apache pilots. They had been great to us. One happened to be Ryan Plowey, a West Point classmate, my battle buddy from Air Assault School back in 2003.

There was no celebration when we finished the wall. We expected to be told to turn the corner and wall off the north side of Sadr City. That order did not come. Instead, we stood back and let the Iraqi Army's 11th Division breach holes into our new wall and pass into the heart of Sadr City. The operation went without a hitch. JAM was so thoroughly beaten that they did not resist the Iraqi Army. The amount of weaponry and ammunition found in Sadr City was astonishing.

The army piled all the confiscated ordnance in a school in Jamila, filling it up. A Marine advisor team at the school worked with the Iraqi headquarters. Outside the school compound walls, our tanks stood watch.

Blue Platoon was attached to E Company for the effort. To say their commander did not understand any aspect of tanks was an understatement. We called him "Boom Boom" and had no respect at all for him. His plan called for our platoon to sit at the school and guard it until further notice, keeping at least a section there at all times. Boom Boom did not even plan any refueling for us. Boom Boom did not understand when I explained we would have to break from the school for a short period of time for fuel and crew changes. It was a tragic waste of combat power and extremely frustrating.

After eight hours of sitting stationary around the school, we needed fuel and would switch sections out. The Black tanks had returned to their original unit. Between the resumed mid-tour-leave rotation and the guard-post and work-detail requirements at Ford, we could not man more than two tanks. We could not even rotate the sections without returning to Ford and having two guys go right back out with the other section. As soon as we rolled in the gate, one guy had to run to the guard post and replace that soldier, who then had to run straight to his tank so they could roll out. The plan only allowed two hours of rest for the guys, and burnout was going to come quickly.

Boom Boom was unavailable to talk to in person about the problem. Blue Platoon took turns at the school. Both Jay and I went to Captain Looney, explaining how bad the plan was and asking for some intervention. Captain Looney had me put together a troop-to-task list to show how unsustainable the plan was and a detailed account of what we were doing at the school. After twenty-seven hours of being in the tanks, we finally were released from E Company and returned to COP Ford.

Back in Beida, we returned to using our Humvees so we would not tear up the streets and could get out and interact with the populace more. We continued using tanks for patrols on the fringes of what was still the enemy's territory.

As it was, the tracked vehicles had already done a lot of damage to the road into COP Ford. The turn just inside the gate had become a deep hole. Some silly ideas had been implemented to try to keep the hole from becoming so deep that MRAPs would get stuck or flip in it. The most harebrained idea was to use the Air Force pallets designed to lock into cargo aircraft. Of course, they were never designed to be driven on, so they were destroyed instantly. Outside the gate, where the tanks made the gentle left turn on the south corner, the tracks had dug a hole that eventually broke a sewer pipe. The result was a ditch of sewage to cross every time the tanks came and went. Fortunately, we were not taking tanks down the main approach, and the wheeled vehicles were able to avoid the nasty ditch by continuing to use the main approach.

We finally got a new C31 tank to replace the one that burned up in early April. While I was happy I didn't need to borrow a tank anymore, I was not happy with the new tank. It was equipped with the latest armor idea. Outside of each reactive armor tile was a piece of Spanish tile. The turret was also lined with the tiles, giving the tank a lizard scale–like impression. It was pretty cool looking; the problem was it added more weight and yet another foot of width to the tank. I could not think of a single instance where penetration of a tank had hit a reactive armor block first. Our armor weaknesses were all the areas not covered with blocks, not the blocks themselves. Furthermore, if we had the only tank that looked like this, it would be a target for sure. The enemy would want to test it out.

One afternoon I was asked to take a section of tanks and respond to the brigade headquarters where the freeway reached the Tigris River. The traffic jam on the freeway was insane, and getting there was frustrating. Whether the people had just gotten tired of yielding the right-of-way or their wait in the jam had eroded their patience in general, nobody would move out of the way. Pointing the gun tube of the tank at them had no effect. Pointing the fifty-caliber machine gun had no effect. Finally, in desperation, I pulled my pistol and held it above my head. Only then did people start moving out of the way. The pistol was reserved as an execution weapon in Saddam's time and was feared more than anything.

On June 7, my war came to an end. I led a section of tanks on a patrol on the east edge of our area. A battered street ran between the nicer houses of the Beida neighborhood and the slum of Ur. A wall of the shorter and thicker Colorado barriers lined the Ur side of the street.

I was already suffering from too many blasts. I had a near-permanent migraine-strength headache. Entries in my journal indicated I was suffering from memory loss and inability to concentrate on mental tasks. Somehow, I was still patrolling, leading the platoon in combat.

At some point along the edge of Ur, we got hit by a massive IED. The blast was powerful enough that it destroyed some ten feet of the two-foot-thick concrete wall and then ripped through the tank, cracking two-inch-thick metal in half. I was knocked unconscious. The tank was still capable of moving, so the crew rushed me back to COP Ford. With a sandstorm preventing helicopters from flying, the company quickly put together a convoy to drive me to the combat support hospital in the Green Zone.

Apparently I came to for a few short moments before getting to the Green Zone. Our company medic, Doc Fetsurka, asked me about the last thing I remembered. Apparently I told him my last memory was of it snowing—at Christmastime. I next came to at the hospital, but it would be months before I reliably retained any memories. The blast did other damage to my body, cracking a rib, tearing up a shoulder, and damaging internal organs, and it was nearly eighteen months before I was able to "fully" return to duty. Without the support and patience of my chain of command, I would have been discharged long before then.

By June 9, I was back in America. Between March 25 and June 7, I had taken seven direct hits from IEDs, more than twenty near misses from IEDs, and four RPG hits. I never deployed again. Four years later, my career succumbed to the residual effects of the injury, my neurologist confidently but softly telling me that one more big blast would kill me even if the shrapnel didn't.

EPILOGUE

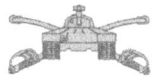

I SLEPT HARD LAST NIGHT for once, but woke exhausted once again. It's Memorial Day 2018, and I am getting ready for work. In two hours, I will leave the house and clock in to my job. As I sip coffee to try to shake the cobwebs from my mind, I'm worried about whether I will be focused and energetic enough to meet the demands of the day. At least the nasty headache that has plagued me the last month has finally subsided to a level I won't even bother with Motrin and Tylenol for.

With time, you become used to pain and it bothers you less. Just as a body can build up tolerance to drugs, the mind can build up tolerance to pain. I cannot let the pain stop me from functioning. I just buy medicine at Costco so I can afford it and self-medicate. After a decade of learning to cope with my injuries, I have reached the point where I don't feel the need for further medical interventions.

I can tolerate the pain, and only a few times has it forced me to call off work so I can curl up in the fetal position and ride it out. I have learned to avoid things that I know will cause my shoulder or guts more pain. I have learned to not exercise too intensely, which causes a nasty headache to brew from the normal one. I have finally gained back the forty pounds I lost in the months following June 7, though the former strength isn't there. With very few visible physical scars, I can hide my injuries pretty well, and most people would never know. Only those who knew me well before Iraq can tell the difference. As my loving wife, Sarah, constantly reminds me, I cannot let my injuries define me. Better men than me are living with even more devastating wounds and carrying on well. So too must I.

I still struggle to communicate. I often use the wrong word or write or say things completely backwards. Sometimes I forget what I was saying mid-sentence. At times, I'll say something in my mind that my mouth never conveys. Often I forget what I was supposed to be working on.

It takes a lot of mental effort to come off as normal as possible, which is exhausting. Most of the time I can pull it off well enough that those around me don't notice. In groups, I often find myself being overenergetic and a bit of a clown to mask my issues. Over the years, my coworkers have learned and some can tell when I'm really struggling. They are great people and do their best to help me through the shift when that happens. The hard part for me is knowing I possess a mere shadow of my former ability.

One of the more challenging adaptations has been learning to live with a dysfunctional sense of balance. That first year, I fell down a lot, usually down the stairs. With time I learned to trust my eyes more than my inner ear, and as long as I have a fixed point of reference, I'm generally able to stay upright. Still, there are times when all I can do is lie down and hang on for dear life as the world seems to spin and twist out of control. A concentrated mental effort can fight through the associated nausea. Often these episodes come with catastrophic suddenness, faster than I can get a third point of contact before I crash to the ground. It is still extremely embarrassing when I fall in front of my kids or strangers.

While I have learned to adapt to where everyday life is not affected too much, my unreliable balance keeps me from many of the things I could do before. I avoid heights with exposure now, and my skiing and biking is very subdued and less ambitious. Amusement parks often find me watching the family enjoy the rollercoasters. I no longer have my sea legs for fishing in rough waters, and any fish over a couple pounds requires me to get a third point of contact for the fight.

I have a profoundly different view of life and its sanctity. Before Iraq, I hunted and I fished for food. Now, I cannot find it in me to hunt anymore, and I only catch and release fish. When one doesn't survive the struggle, I find myself quite saddened.

This appreciation for the value of life is good for my work, though. To really serve, you must love your fellow humanity. Other changes in me affect my work. I have been so thoroughly inoculated to danger that I stay very calm in lethal-force situations and use tactical advantages to protect the priorities of life. At the same time, I'm very aware of my limitations and take great care to avoid a blow to the head. I intentionally do not pick up overtime to mitigate exhaustion.

The hardest thing has been the cost to my family. Sarah and the girls put up with a lot. After working five days, it takes nearly three whole days to recover back to a normal level of energy. Projects around the house progress at a slow rate, and just as likely as not, I will forget what I was working on in the very middle of it. Being exhausted nearly all the time makes me a bit of a dud and seemingly withdrawn.

The effort it takes means there isn't much in the tank to try to maintain friendships. Over time I have drifted farther and farther away from the friends I once had. As I forget passwords and forget where they were written down, I lose contact information. The prospect of battling to figure it out is too daunting.

The burden of memories is a heavy cross to bear, but it is mine. I'm blessed to have escaped PTSD, meaning the memories do not negatively affect my daily life to the point of dysfunction and disorder. Still, I rarely fall asleep quickly, my mind still grasping for peace. There are days when I wake up in sweat to Danny's "LT, you're gonna get me killed!" I can still, in exquisite detail, see the face of the enemy lookout as rounds ripped into him and the stupid sapper crawling towards the car and growing cold. My heart still thumps heavily when the old man with his satchel charges to the front of my memory. The hollow anguish I felt as I closed Mike's eyes still won't release me. This written memoir was suggested to me as a means for trying to release some of the pain.

Not a day goes by when I don't think about Iraq and the men I served with. Throughout my career, I was surrounded by lions of men. I was very fortunate to always have many around me who were more talented, more passionate, and more courageous. I relied on them to accomplish our missions and to grow professionally. When I came up short, they picked up the slack. Looking back, there were so many things I could have done much better, so they did a lot of picking up for me.

Even now, I cannot shake the worry that today might be the day my luck runs out. But fear not; I am ready. I do not want to waste time with sadness or boredom. Every day should be worth its sunrise. The challenge is to not let things outside my control bother me and to try to pack in as much fun as I can.

Shortly after I came back from my first deployment, my uncle Joe, who was a Vietnam veteran, counseled me that the hardest thing I would ever have to do is reconcile with the fact that the American government placed me in a war that really meant nothing. At first I didn't believe him. Vietnam was different. Yet something nagged at me. We gave the best years of our lives and, for some, our last full measure of devotion in waging the war on terror. But what did we actually accomplish for our country?

At the end of the day, we fought for each other. We all joined the Army to defend our nation. We all had a sense of duty to serve others. The men of Blue Platoon fought honorably and courageously. While we don't have much to show for our efforts, we carry the pride of a job well done, even if the job was too nebulous to fit into the grand scheme of things.

For us, there is no VE or VJ Day to mark victory like the Greatest

Generation. Instead, we privately mark anniversaries of hard days in Iraq and see our country less secure and more full of hate. However futile it may have been, it does not take away at all from the heroism of the men and women who fought on behalf of the people of the United States. We lived up to our motto to strike hard . . . and we expected no mercy.

CPSIA information can be obtained
at www.ICGtesting.com
Printed in the USA
LVHW051940161022
730833LV00002B/325